Personal Income During Business Cycles

By Daniel Creamer

Foreword by Geoffrey H. Moore

Studying business cycles as far back as 1879, Daniel Creamer shows for the first time how the different kinds of personal income—wages and salaries, property income, dividends, farm income, etc.—respond to ups and downs in business activity. Property income, as it is here defined, is the most resistant to cyclical hazards.

Dr. Creamer's work also provides a statistical analysis of how far farm price supports, unemployment insurance, and federal income tax reductions have offset losses in personal income during recessions.

The study shows that total personal income has grown at fairly uniform rates in different business expansions. During contractions, on the other hand, personal income drops at strikingly various rates. This is one piece of evidence supporting the hypothesis that the American economy may have an inherent tendency to expand at a definite rate.

The author prepared this study as a member of the staff of the National Bureau of Economic Research. He is now Director of the Falk Project for Economic Research in Israel.

Personal Income
during
Business Cycles

NATIONAL BUREAU OF ECONOMIC RESEARCH

Studies in Business Cycles

1. *Business Cycles: The Problem and Its Setting*
   (originally published as No. 10 in the General Series)
   WESLEY C. MITCHELL
2. *Measuring Business Cycles*
   ARTHUR F. BURNS AND WESLEY C. MITCHELL
3. *American Transportation in Prosperity and Depression*
   THOR HULTGREN
4. *Inventories and Business Cycles, with Special Reference
   to Manufacturers' Inventories*
   MOSES ABRAMOVITZ
5. *What Happens during Business Cycles: A Progress
   Report*
   WESLEY C. MITCHELL
6. *Personal Income during Business Cycles*
   DANIEL CREAMER with the assistance of
   MARTIN BERNSTEIN

Personal Income during Business Cycles

BY DANIEL CREAMER

WITH THE ASSISTANCE OF
MARTIN BERNSTEIN

A STUDY BY THE

NATIONAL BUREAU OF ECONOMIC RESEARCH, NEW YORK

PUBLISHED BY

PRINCETON UNIVERSITY PRESS, PRINCETON

1956

RELATION OF THE DIRECTORS TO THE WORK AND PUBLICATIONS
OF THE NATIONAL BUREAU OF ECONOMIC RESEARCH

1. The object of the National Bureau of Economic Research is to ascertain and to present to the public important economic facts and their interpretation in a scientific and impartial manner. The Board of Directors is charged with the responsibility of ensuring that the work of the National Bureau is carried on in strict conformity with this object.

2. To this end the Board of Directors shall appoint one or more Directors of Research.

3. The Director or Directors of Research shall submit to the members of the Board, or to its Executive Committee, for their formal adoption, all specific proposals concerning researches to be instituted.

4. No report shall be published until the Director or Directors of Research shall have submitted to the Board a summary drawing attention to the character of the data and their utilization in the report, the nature and treatment of the problems involved, the main conclusions and such other information as in their opinion would serve to determine the suitability of the report for publication in accordance with the principles of the National Bureau.

5. A copy of any manuscript proposed for publication shall also be submitted to each member of the Board. For each manuscript to be so submitted a special committee shall be appointed by the President, or at his designation by the Executive Director, consisting of three Directors selected as nearly as may be one from each general division of the Board. The names of the special manuscript committee shall be stated to each Director when the summary and report described in paragraph (4) are sent to him. It shall be the duty of each member of the committee to read the manuscript. If each member of the special committee signifies his approval within thirty days, the manuscript may be published. If each member of the special committee has not signified his approval within thirty days of the transmittal of the report and manuscript, the Director of Research shall then notify each member of the Board, requesting approval or disapproval of publication, and thirty additional days shall be granted for this purpose. The manuscript shall then not be published unless at least a majority of the entire Board and a two-thirds majority of those members of the Board who shall have voted on the proposal within the time fixed for the receipt of votes on the publication proposed shall have approved.

6. No manuscript may be published, though approved by each member of the special committee, until forty-five days have elapsed from the transmittal of the summary and report. The interval is allowed for the receipt of any memorandum of dissent or reservation, together with a brief statement of his reasons, that any member may wish to express; and such memorandum of dissent or reservation shall be published with the manuscript if he so desires. Publication does not, however, imply that each member of the Board has read the manuscript, or that either members of the Board in general, or of the special committee, have passed upon its validity in every detail.

7. A copy of this resolution shall, unless otherwise determined by the Board, be printed in each copy of every National Bureau book.

(Resolution adopted October 25, 1926 and revised February 6, 1933 and February 24, 1941)

TO THE MEMORY OF
MY PARENTS

FOREWORD

BY GEOFFREY H. MOORE

IN THE experience of the 70 million wage earners, farmers, business-men, landlords, and other recipients of income in this country, "business cycles" count as but one of the factors that cause their incomes to rise or fall. The ability or good fortune to hold a job, get a raise, avoid illness and accidents, pick a good spot for one's store, enlarge one's capital, and so forth, also is significant in the minds of many people. Indeed, the incomes of many individuals do not move in recognizable cycles; earnings are often fairly steady for long intervals but jump up or dip down every now and then as the vicissitudes of life unfold. Nevertheless, when the incomes of large numbers of individuals are added together these erratic variations largely disappear from sight, and instead we find that business cycles are a dominant factor, if not *the* dominant factor, causing fluctuations in aggregate income.

The layman, again from his individual point of view, has still less reason to reflect on the influence that changes in his income may have on the fortunes of other people. But economists have not neglected this aspect of the matter. Money is either spent or saved, and in the one case as in the other an increase or a cut in income will have repercussions on the economic actions of other individuals and of institutions. Moreover, most incomes are payments for cur-rent services of the individual or his property; hence they are "costs" to the individual or business firm or government agency that pays them. Changes in such costs also influence economic behavior.

Thus the ebb and flow in personal incomes is crucial from many points of view, and an investigation of the cyclical behavior of income cannot help but enlarge our knowledge of business cycles generally. In this Foreword to Dr. Creamer's study we select a few of his findings and attempt to show how they contribute to our understanding of this important feature of modern economic life.

In organizing the National Bureau's investigation of business cycles, Wesley Mitchell and Arthur Burns found it convenient to follow a plan that would yield answers to two questions. First, what typically happens during a business cycle? Second, what sorts of variation from this typical behavior have occurred? We shall con-sider Creamer's results in terms of these questions.

We start with the finding that recessions and revivals in general business have typically occurred at the same time as, or before, recessions and revivals in aggregate personal income for the country as a whole. In two instances since 1929 (namely, the 1933 and 1949 troughs) the turns in general business activity and in personal income came in the same month; in three instances (the 1938 and 1945 troughs and the 1948 peak) personal income turned one month earlier; and in three instances (the 1929, 1937, and 1945 peaks) income turned a month or so later. For earlier cycles, perhaps the most reliable indicator of cyclical turns in total personal income is factory payrolls (since 1929 the turns in payrolls have never differed from those in personal income by more than a month, except in the war period). The turn in factory workers' income came in the same month as that in business activity in 1924 and 1926, one month later in 1919 and 1923, two months later in 1918, three months later in 1921, and five months later in 1920 and 1927. For years before 1918 there is no dependable timing information on a monthly basis.

Of course, "general business activity" is a nebulous concept. Moreover, the measures of personal income are not beyond question. These results mean no more than that cyclical reversals in the movement of personal income have come at about the same time as, or a little later than, those in most other comprehensive measures of economic activity, such as production or employment or volume of trade. But that much is useful knowledge. Since we know that turns in many other types of time series typically precede the general turn, it appears that neither recessions nor revivals have ordinarily waited upon an actual reversal in the trend of aggregate personal income.[1] But such reversals have regularly *accompanied* general revivals and recessions, and no doubt have played a part in converting tentative and hesitant swings in economic activity into full-fledged cyclical expansions or contractions. The observer who wishes to identify the current stage of the business cycle surely cannot afford to ignore changes in income.

Creamer's analysis shows that most types or sources of income, like the total, rise and fall in fair conformity with the business cycle (Chart A and Table A). Some types may be relatively immune to

---

[1] We must leave open the question whether a slackening in the rate of rise or decline in income has regularly preceded the reversal—and what the consequences of this may have been. Ruth P. Mack's forthcoming monograph *Consumption and Business Cycles, a Case Study: The Shoe, Leather, Hide Industry*, to be published by the National Bureau of Economic Research, deals with this problem.

the shorter and milder cycles—e.g. wages and salaries from govern-ment, salary income in general, farm income, dividends, interest income, and rent—but even these usually fall in line in prolonged or severe phases. The component of total personal income that shows a closer association with the cycle, mild or severe, than any other major component is wage income in nonfarm commodity-producing industries (mining, manufacturing, and construction); it coincided precisely with the general business cycle turn in no less than six out of eight instances during 1929-1949, leading by two months at one turn (1948) and lagging by three months at another (1929). In 1953 it reached its peak precisely in the month (July) tentatively selected for the business cycle peak.[2]

Table A also shows that were it not for the synchronous timing of wages and salaries in mining, manufacturing, and construction, aggregate income would clearly lag behind the business cycle. Every other major component has tended to lag. In fact, Creamer has discovered only one income source that typically appears to lead, and this is not a component of personal income as ordinarily defined—namely, the excess of realized capital gains over losses. The table does not reveal one other type of income that lags, namely, salary income, since salaries are combined with wages in the avail-able comprehensive statistics. Nevertheless, it is quite clear from the sample series Creamer has brought together that income from salaries usually reaches cyclical turns later than wage income and later, too, than general business activity.

The second part of Table A shows how the typical lagging tendency in the several components of personal income has worked out at successive business cycle turns. At every turn but one, more components lagged than led; even at the 1948 peak, which marked the beginning of only a mild contraction, half the components lagged in the sense that they failed to contract at all. Thus business cycle recessions and revivals give rise to a sequence of changes in the various broad components of personal income. The sequences are by no means the same at every turn, but some are persistent, as Creamer's detailed review of the evidence demonstrates. In any event, it is clear that the process of change in the trend of income does not take place all at once, but is spread over a considerable

[2] So far as I am aware, this particular series was not used in determining any of the dates in the National Bureau's business cycle chronology, though of course close relatives of it, such as factory payrolls and total income, played a part, together with many other measures of economic activity.

CHART A

Specific Cycles in Total Personal Income and in Eight Components, in Relation to Business Cycles, 1929-1950

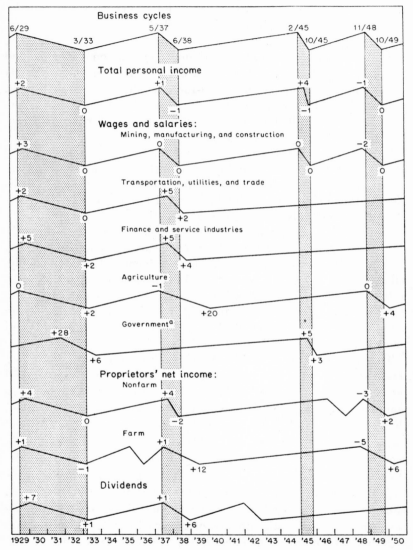

Shaded areas represent contractions of business cycles. Entries at specific cycle peaks and troughs are number of months lead (−) or lag (+) from corresponding business cycle peak or trough.

ª Excluding work relief and military.

Source: Tables 4, 7, 20.

TABLE A

Timing of Turning Points in Personal Income and in Eight Components
at Business Cycle Turning Points, 1929-1949

1. Personal Income and Components, by Type of Income

	NUMBER OF BUSINESS TURNS AT WHICH INCOME:				AVERAGE LEAD (—) OR LAG (+) (*months*)
	Leads	*Exactly* Coincides	Lags	Skips the Turn	
Total personal income	3	2	3	0	+.5
Wage and salary disbursements Mining, manufacturing, and construction	1	6	1	0	+.1
Transportation, utilities, and trade	0	1	3	4	+2.2
Finance and service industries	0	0	4	4	+4.0
Agriculture	1	2	3	2	+4.2
Governmenta	0	0	4	4	+10.5
Proprietors' net income Nonfarm	2	1	3	2	+.8
Farm	2	0	4	2	+2.3
Property income	2	0	2	4	+2.8

2. Components, by Date of Business Turning Point

	NUMBER OF COMPONENTS THAT:			
	Lead	*Exactly* Coincide	Lag	Skip the Turn
Peak				
June 1929	1	1	6	0
May 1937	2	1	4	1
February 1945	0	1	1	6
November 1948	3	1	0	4
Trough				
March 1933	1	3	4	0
June 1938	1	1	5	1
October 1945	0	1	1	6
October 1949	0	1	3	4

a Excluding work relief and military.

Source: Business turns are from the National Bureau of Economic Research business cycle chronology; other data are from Tables 4 and 7.

period. In 1937, for example, the peak in total property income was reached in April; peaks in the other components listed in Table A were distributed over the six months from April to October. No doubt a finer subdivision by type of income would show still wider dispersion.

It is not difficult to find reasons for the lagging tendencies displayed by most components of personal income. A neat illustration of the process is afforded by Creamer's materials on wage income in manufacturing. The total wage bill is a function of the number of persons employed, the average number of hours they work per week, and their average hourly earnings. If these three factors moved synchronously, with each other and with business cycles, so would the wage bill. But the typical sequence in a business recession has been first a decline in the average workweek, then a decline in the number employed, and finally a decline in hourly earnings; and a similar sequence characterizes revivals. The upshot, as the accompanying figures show, is that total wages turned in the same month as general business on five occasions during 1921-1938, and lagged behind on four.

Timing of Wages and Related Series, Manufacturing Industries, at Nine Business Cycle Turning Points, 1921-1938

	Leads	Exact Coincidences	Lags	Average Lead (—) or Lag (+) (months)
Average workweek	6	1	2	—3.1
Total man-hours	5	2	2	—1.4
Number employed	2	3	4	—1.1
Total wages	0	5	4	+1.3
Average hourly earnings	0	0	9	+8.6

Source: Table 8.

So much for the sequences among cyclical turns. Another aspect of the cyclical behavior of personal income that Creamer examines is the extent, or amplitude, of change in different types or sources of income during swings in business activity. Such measures indicate the cyclical hazards attaching to various sources of income. And they help us to analyze the factors underlying shifts in the fortunes of low income and high income recipients.

Cyclical amplitudes may be measured and compared in a variety of ways, and Creamer provides a number of such measures and comparisons. We shall summarize his results in terms of the behavior of the "shares," or percentages, of various types of income in total income. Economists have long been concerned with the reasons why these shares attain certain levels and why these levels change, and particularly with the division of income between labor and capital.

Although the available data do not exactly fit economists' concepts, they provide a rough facsimile, and have at least the merit of being observable. Table B shows the average level of the shares of several types of income at the peak and trough years of business cycles during the past four decades. Table C records the number of times a given share moved upward or downward during eleven business cycle expansions and ten contractions.

One's first impression from Table B is that business cycles have had a rather modest influence on the proportion of income derived from the several major sources or types. In prosperity and depression years alike, labor income (employee compensation, social security benefits, etc.) has constituted, on the average, somewhat more than 60 per cent of total personal income; income accruing to proprietors (farmers, independent professional people, and other business owners) has constituted about 20 per cent; and property income (dividends, interest, and rent) 17 or 18 per cent. Table C reveals that far from conforming consistently to the cycle, the shares of most of the broad types have moved rather irregularly, sometimes rising and sometimes falling during a given phase of the cycle.

But some consistencies are worth noting. Transfer payments have risen in relation to aggregate income in every contraction since 1929, and have declined relatively in every expansion. Such behavior might result merely from stability in these payments while total income changed, but in fact the dollar figures rose in every contraction, declined in two expansions, and in the remaining two expansions rose at a slower pace than in the adjacent contractions. Thus they have performed a countercyclical function, a subject to which Creamer devotes the final section of his study.

The share of property income has also moved down in expansions and up in contractions more often than not, but for a different reason. Here relative stability in the dollar figures is responsible, and the stability is imparted by interest and rent payments. Dividends are more volatile and, except in short business cycles, have usually traced out wider swings than total income. Hence the exceptions to the rule that the property income share conformed invertedly are attributable, in part, to shifts in the relative importance of the different components. One may hazard the guess that refinement of the data to obtain a truer property income total (eliminating some "rent" that is really labor income, adding some proprietors' income that is really rent, and so on) might alter the rule. Moreover, the use of a concept of personal income that would, for example, count

TABLE B

Percentage Distribution of Personal Income by Major Type and
Source of Income at Business Cycle Turning Points, 1909-1949

(*per cent*)

	AVERAGE AT:		
	Initial Troughs	*Peaks*	*Terminal Troughs*
1. Ten Cycles, 1909-1949			
Labor income, total	60.6	62.2	62.8
Wages and salaries, receipts[a]	58.4	60.3	60.0
Other labor income and transfer payments	2.3	1.9	2.9
Proprietors' net income, total	20.9	20.9	19.7
Nonfarm	12.1	11.6	11.5
Farm	8.8	9.3	8.2
Property income, total	18.5	16.9	17.5
Dividends	5.2	5.4	5.1
Interest	5.4	4.5	5.3
Rent	7.9	7.0	7.1
Total personal income	100.0	100.0	100.0
2. Three Cycles, 1932-1949			
Wages and salaries, disbursements[a]	64.6	67.3	65.1
Mining, manufacturing, and construction	22.0	27.1	24.4
Transportation, utilities, and trade	19.3	17.1	18.7
Finance and service industries	10.1	8.1	8.9
Agriculture, forestry, and fisheries	1.6	1.6	1.6
Government	11.6	13.4	11.4
Transfer payments	4.3	3.2	5.2
3. Five Cycles, 1919-1938			
Mining, manufacturing, and construction	22.8	24.8	22.0
Wages	17.6	19.7	16.8
Salaries	5.2	5.1	5.2

[a] Wage and salary receipts equal disbursements less employee contributions for social insurance.

Source: Appendix A; data for overlapping years 1919 and 1929 are averaged. Wage and salary disbursements by industry are from *National Income Supplement, 1951, Survey of Current Business*, Dept. of Commerce, and *Survey of Current Business*, July 1953. Data for wages and salaries in mining, manufacturing, and construction, 1919-1938, are from Simon Kuznets, *National Income and Its Composition, 1919-1938*, National Bureau of Economic Research, 1941. For business cycle chronology see Table 2. Data for 1909 instead of 1908 are used for the initial trough of the first cycle.

capital gains and losses and undistributed corporate profits as property income would also change the result.[3] It is possible, too,

[3] Cf. Jesse Burkhead, "Changes in the Functional Distribution of Income," *Journal of the American Statistical Association*, June 1953, pp. 192-219.

TABLE C

Conformity to Business Cycles of Percentage Shares of Major Types and Sources of Personal Income, 1909-1953

	BUSINESS EXPANSION		BUSINESS CONTRACTION		TOTAL INSTANCES OF:	
	Share Rises (1)	Share Falls (2)	Share Rises (3)	Share Falls (4)	Positive Conformity[a] (5)	Inverted Conformity[a] (6)
1. 1909-1953 (Eleven Business Expansions, Ten Contractions)						
Labor income, total	8	3	7	3	11	10
Wages and salaries, receipts[b]	8	3	7	3	11	10
Other labor income and transfer payments	4	7	7	3	7	14
Proprietors' net income, total	4	7	3	7	11	10
Nonfarm	4	7	4	6	10	11
Farm	6	5	3	7	13	8
Property income, total	4	7	8	2	6	15
Dividends	9	2	4	6	15	6
Interest	4	7	9	1	5	16
Rent	2	9	6	4	6	15
2. 1929-1953 (Four Business Expansions and Contractions)						
Wages and salaries, disbursements[b]	3	1	3	1	4	4
Mining, manufacturing, and construction	4	0	0	4	8	0
Transportation, utilities, and trade	1	3	4	0	1	7
Finance and service industries	1	3	4	0	1	7
Agriculture, forestry, and fisheries	2	2	2	2	4	4
Government	2	2	3	1	3	5
Transfer payments	0	4	4	0	0	8
3. 1919-1938 (Five Business Expansions and Contractions)						
Mining, manufacturing, and construction						
Wages	4	1	0	5	9	1
Salaries	3	2	4	1	4	6

a Column 5 is the sum of columns 1 and 4. Column 6 is the sum of columns 2 and 3.
b See Table B, note a.
Source: See Table B, source note. Data for 1953 are from *Survey of Current Business*, Dept. of Commerce, February and May 1954.

that if monthly instead of annual data were available to measure the cyclical behavior of the several types of income, the change in one type relative to another, particularly in the shorter cycles, would be altered. Thus the conclusion that property income has usually been more stable than other income during business cycles, forming a larger percentage of the total in depressed than in prosperous years, must be qualified. We can say only that this relative stability appears for property income as it is defined and measured in this study.

If the property income share moves inversely with the cycle, one might expect the labor income share to move positively. But Tables B and C belie that expectation. The labor income share has risen almost as often during business contractions as during expansions. This is true whether one takes wage and salary receipts alone or includes supplements and transfer payments, although, as already noted, the supplements and transfer payments do impart some cyclical stability.

However, if the wage and salary total could be subdivided to show wages separately from salaries, there is little doubt that the wage share would decline more frequently during contractions. That is to say, the share of wages per se in total income has probably been higher at peaks in business activity than at troughs, as a rule. This is clearly the case in mining, manufacturing, and construction, as Part 3 in Tables B and C demonstrates. Aggregate income of salaried personnel is more stable than that of wage earners, both because salary rates usually vary less than wage rates and because salaried-worker employment varies less than wage-earner employment. Although other factors are partly responsible, the relative stability of salary income is reflected in the distribution of wage and salary disbursements by industry (Part 2). In agriculture and in mining, manufacturing, and construction, wages are the dominant form of payment, and in these industries the share of wages conforms positively to the cycle in most instances. Salary payments are more important, on the whole, in the other sectors (distributive and service industries and government), and here inverse conformity of the shares is the rule. To some extent, of course, stability in an industry *permits* a salary form of payment, though many other considerations also apply.

Again, it must be recalled that the behavior of the labor income share in Tables B and C applies only to labor income as there defined. If we could include the part of proprietors' income that is a return for labor services rather than for capital, the share not only would be larger but might behave differently. Farm operators' income, which surely includes some "labor income," has moved more violently than other income more often than not, a fact that may surprise nonfarm readers. The income of nonfarm proprietors, in which group a diligent statistician would find the "typical businessman" as well as lawyers, doctors, and other professional people, has moved in swings roughly as large, percentagewise, as those in total personal income.

Changes in the distribution of income by type have far-reaching influences on the distribution of income by size, and Creamer does not neglect this aspect of the matter. Drawn from the extensive researches of Simon Kuznets, his figures suggest that some of the typical cyclical changes in the distribution of income by size can be inferred from those in the distribution of income by type. From the evidence we have just reviewed one would expect that (1) groups whose incomes depend heavily on wages or on receipts from farming would experience income fluctuations somewhat larger than those in the grand total of all incomes, so that their share in total income would conform positively to business cycles; (2) groups whose incomes consist largely of salaries plus receipts from other sources in roughly the average proportions would have relatively stable incomes, with a share in the total that would move inversely with the cycle; (3) groups whose main sources of income are salaries, dividends, and nonfarm proprietorships would have a mixed experience, since the first source would tend to moderate and the second to amplify fluctuations in income, while the third would sometimes moderate and sometimes amplify. Now our description of group 1 applies to the mass of the population, or in terms of Kuznets' statistics, the lower 93 per cent ranked according to per capita income; the income sources we have ascribed to group 2 are characteristic of those income groups just below the top—the 2nd to 7th percentage band; and our group 3 is the top income group—the upper 1 per cent (Table D).[4] And Chart B and Table E, drawn up

[4] Table D does not distinguish farm from nonfarm proprietors' income, or wage from salary income. However, the income of the lower 93 per cent comprehends virtually all farm income (Simon Kuznets, *Shares of Upper Income Groups in Income and Savings*, National Bureau of Economic Research, 1953, Chapter 8). On this assumption the share of proprietors' net income in total income of the lower 93 per cent would be split as follows:

	1920	1929	1937	1948
Farm	14	10	11	11
Nonfarm	7	6	7	6

Hence in these years 72 to 78 per cent of the income of the lower 93 per cent consisted of labor income and another 10 to 14 per cent was income from farming.

No comprehensive data are available to distinguish wage from salary income, but the proportion consisting of salaries is surely larger in the higher income brackets. Some indirect evidence is provided by Kuznets' data, which show that employee compensation of the upper groups is a larger fraction of total employee compensation at business cycle troughs than at peaks, thereby

TABLE D

Percentage Distribution of Total Income by Type, Three Income Groups and Total Population, Selected Years, 1920-1948

(*per cent*)

	TOP 1 PER CENT				2ND TO 7TH PER CENT				LOWER 93 PER CENT				TOTAL POPULATION			
	1920	1929	1937	1948	1920	1929	1937	1948	1920	1929	1937	1948	1920	1929	1937	1948
Labor income	31	28	35	32	64	58	70	60	72[a]	74	73	78	66[a]	65	68	72
Proprietors' net income	24	20	17	36	20	21	15	29	21[a]	16	18	17	21[a]	17	17	20
Dividends	28	36	35	24	5	7	7	6	1[a]	1	2	1	5[a]	7	7	4
Interest	13	13	10	5	6	8	5	3	3[a]	5	4	2	5[a]	7	5	2
Rent	4	4	3	4	5	6	3	2	3[a]	3	3	2	4[a]	4	3	2
Total	100	100	100	100	100	100	100	100	100	100	100	100	100	100	100	100

[a] Not precisely comparable with entries for later years.

Note: Details may not add to totals because of rounding.

Source: Simon Kuznets, *Shares of Upper Income Groups in Income and Savings*, National Bureau of Economic Research, 1953, Tables 114, 123, and 125. The income variant used is the "basic variant."

along the lines of Tables B and C, reveal how nicely the inferences stated above are realized. As a rule during business expansions, when employment, hours of work, wage rates, and farm prices and

CHART B

Average Percentage Shares of Three Income Groups in Total Income
during Six Business Cycles, 1919-1946

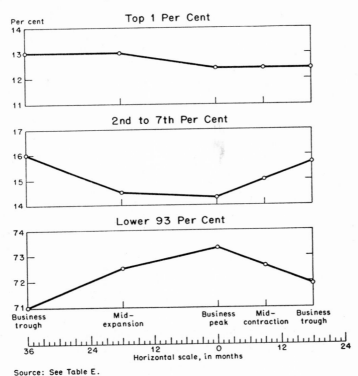

Source: See Table E.

incomes rise, the total income of the lower income group rises more rapidly than the total income of the whole population; during contractions the opposite situation prevails.[5] As we go up the income

---

exhibiting the stability characteristic of salary income (cf. Table 26 below and Kuznets' Table 23).

It is unfortunate that data are not available to make these distinctions in types of income properly, for without them one might well conclude, as Kuznets does in Chapter 3, that intertype shifts in income distribution are of relatively little consequence in accounting for cyclical shifts in the size distribution of income.

[5] We are speaking of the lower income groups in the aggregate, i.e. the lower 93 per cent. Kuznets' data, based on income tax returns, unfortunately do not

TABLE E

Percentage Shares of Three Income Groups in Total Income
during Business Cycles

1. Average Percentage Shares (Six Cycles, 1919-1946)

| | AVERAGE AT: | | |
	Initial Troughs	Peaks	Terminal Troughs
Top 1 per cent	13.0	12.4	12.4
2nd to 7th per cent	16.0	14.3	15.7
Lower 93 per cent	71.0	73.3	71.9
Total	100.0	100.0	100.0

2. Conformity (Seven or Eight Business Expansions and Contractions)

| | BUSINESS EXPANSION | | BUSINESS CONTRACTION | | TOTAL INSTANCES OF: | |
	Share Rises (1)	Share Falls (2)	Share Rises (3)	Share Falls (4)	Positive Conformity[a] (5)	Inverted Conformity[a] (6)
Top 1 per cent, 1913-1948	3	5	5	3	6	10
2nd to 7th per cent, 1918-1948	2	5	7	0	2	12
Lower 93 per cent, 1918-1948	5	2	1	6	11	3

[a] Column 5 is the sum of columns 1 and 4. Column 6 is the sum of columns 2 and 3.

Source: Simon Kuznets, *Shares of Upper Income Groups in Income and Savings*, National Bureau of Economic Research, 1953, Table 116, col. 1. The income variant used is the "basic variant."

scale greater stability in income appears, evidently due in large part to the stability of salaries; this leads to an inverted cyclical pattern in the shares of the income groups just below the top. But at the very top, dividend income becomes an important source, and imparts a certain degree of instability, particularly during the major cycles; hence the share of the top income group is less consistently inverted. This is the broad picture revealed by the statistics; the reader does not need to be reminded of the infinite variation in detail.

So far we have been concerned with the typical behavior patterns of income during business cycles revealed by Creamer's study. All this is grist for the mill of the business cycle analyst. With it he will be better prepared to describe and account for various other eco-

permit further subdivision of this group, and we therefore cannot determine how groups at various lower levels of income fare during business cycles.

nomic processes—the volume of savings, its distribution among the various investment outlets open to savers, the volume of consumer expenditures and their distribution among different classes of goods, the behavior of prices at retail, even the sources and strengths of pressures for increases in wages, in farm prices, and in interest rates. But the analyst will soon find himself needing more than the typical patterns, particularly if he is concerned with the business cycles of the future. For the mold in which business cycles are cast is neither simple nor static. Each new cycle seems to possess some of the characteristic features of its predecessors; but each also enjoys some peculiar features of its own.

Yet even the changing features of cycles are subject to analysis, and we should overlook an important contribution of Creamer's study if we did not review some of his results from this point of view. As to the fact of variation, there is no lack of evidence, as indeed we have already seen. And some knowledge of its extent is useful, whatever we can say about its ultimate causes. Consider, for example, the data on changes in total personal income during business cycles in Chart C and Table F. A noticeable uniformity appears in the rates of growth of income during business expansions. The average rate of growth during ten expansions since 1909 has been about 8 per cent per year, the most rapid growth less than twice this average, and the slowest about half. Contrast this with the business contractions. The average rate of change has been smaller than in expansions, the range of variation far wider. Of course, in some or all of the contractions in which the annual data rise, monthly data would decline and perhaps reduce the dispersion (1944-1946 is an example). But monthly (and quarterly) income data give similar results for the period they cover and so do monthly bank clearings and debits outside New York City, which move like total income and cover a much longer period. The rate of change varies much more widely from one contraction to another than from one expansion to another.

In other words, what the level of personal income will be after a year of business contraction is far more uncertain than what it will be after a year of expansion. This proposition is attested more directly in the last two columns in Part 1 of Table F.

If this phenomenon were peculiar to personal income, it would demand a special explanation. But it seems to be characteristic of a wide variety of economic processes. Consider, for example, the analyses of thirty-seven comprehensive economic series given in

TABLE F

Changes in Personal Income and in Bank Clearings or Debits
during Business Cycles, 1879-1953

1. Total Personal Income, Annual, 1909-1953

				CHANGE PER YEAR DURING:		CHANGE DURING FIRST YEAR OF:	
				Expan-	*Contrac-*	*Expan-*	*Contrac-*
			CYCLE	*sion*	*tion*	*sion*	*tion*
BUSINESS	BUSINESS	BUSINESS	BASE[a]				
TROUGH	PEAK	TROUGH	(*billions*)	(*per cent of cycle base*)			
1908	1910	1911	$ 30.4[b]	+5.3[c]	+.3		+.3
1911	1913	1914	33.6	+5.5	−1.8	+6.2	−1.8
1914	1918	1919	48.0	+12.4	+17.1	+4.8	+17.1
1919	1920	1921	65.0	+5.5	−20.6	+5.5	−20.6
1921	1923	1924	64.1	+10.5	+1.3	+6.5	+1.3
1924	1926	1927	74.8	+4.4	+.5	+5.2	+.5
1927	1929	1932	72.3	+4.4	−16.3	+2.5	−11.9
1932	1937	1938	57.6	+8.6	−9.5	−4.2	−9.5
1938	1944	1946	119.6	+13.5	+4.8	+3.5	+4.8
1946	1948	1949	193.2	+8.0	−2.1	+6.7	−2.1
1949	1953		235.1[d]	+8.2		+8.4	
Average, 1911-1949			80.9	+8.1	−3.0	+4.1	−2.5
Average deviation			33.5	2.8	8.4	2.3	7.7

2. Income Payments, 1921-1927; Personal Income, 1927-1953

				CHANGE[e] PER YEAR DURING:	
			CYCLE BASE[a]	*Expan-sion*	*Contrac-tion*
BUSINESS	BUSINESS	BUSINESS	(*billions at*	(*per cent*	
TROUGH	PEAK	TROUGH	*annual rate*)	*of cycle base*)	
3rd 1921	2nd 1923	3rd 1924	$ 61.7	+11.4	+.8
3rd 1924	3rd 1926	4th 1927	72.7	+5.5	+.7
4th 1927	2nd 1929	1st 1933	70.9	+5.5	−15.5
Mar. 1933	May 1937	May 1938	61.6	+12.7	−14.1
May 1938	Feb. 1945	Oct. 1945	116.6	+13.6	−9.3
Oct. 1945	Nov. 1948	Oct. 1949	194.1	+7.7	−5.0
Oct. 1949	July 1953		243.6[d]	+9.1	
Average, 1921-1949			96.3	+9.4	−7.1
Average deviation			39.4	3.2	5.9

Wesley Mitchell's *What Happens during Business Cycles: A Progress
Report* (National Bureau of Economic Research, 1951, pp. 326-328).
Three of the series are annual estimates of gross and net national
product and personal income; the rest are monthly or quarterly
measures of the physical volume of production, transportation,

TABLE F (continued)

3. Bank Clearings outside New York City, Monthly, 1879-1919;
Bank Debits outside New York City, Monthly 1919-1953

BUSINESS TROUGH	BUSINESS PEAK	BUSINESS TROUGH	CYCLE BASE[a] (billions at annual rate)	CHANGE[e] PER YEAR DURING: Expan- sion (per cent of cycle base)	Contrac- tion (per cent of cycle base)
Mar. 1879	Mar. 1882	May 1885	$ 13.1	+15.5	−3.8
May 1885	Mar. 1887	Apr. 1888	16.1	+16.9	−.4
Apr. 1888	July 1890	May 1891	21.2	+14.0	−9.8
May 1891	Jan. 1893	June 1894	23.7	+11.9	−19.1
June 1894	Dec. 1895	June 1897	22.6	+9.2	−2.8
June 1897	June 1899	Dec. 1900	30.3	+17.2	+5.9
Dec. 1900	Sept. 1902	Aug. 1904	41.3	+9.0	+1.9
Aug. 1904	May 1907	June 1908	53.3	+10.5	−13.1
June 1908	Jan. 1910	Jan. 1912	64.3	+14.5	+2.8
Jan. 1912	Jan. 1913	Dec. 1914	73.8	+8.1	−5.6
Dec. 1914	Aug. 1918	Apr. 1919	118.3	+20.8	+10.5
Apr. 1919	Jan. 1920	Sept. 1921	220.8	+31.5	−13.6
Sept. 1921	May 1923	July 1924	212.4	+11.3	−2.9
July 1924	Oct. 1926	Dec. 1927	264.0	+7.2	+8.3
Dec. 1927	June 1929	Mar. 1933	254.4	+7.7	−19.8
Mar. 1933	May 1937	May 1938	194.4	+12.9	−19.7
May 1938	Feb. 1945	Oct. 1945	337.2	+11.9	−4.8
Oct. 1945	Nov. 1948	Oct. 1949	602.4	+11.9	−6.5
Oct. 1949	July 1953		804.0[d]	+11.1	
Average, 1879-1949				+13.4	−5.1
Average deviation				4.0	7.3

[a] Average of all years, quarters, or months from trough to trough, trough values weighted one-half each.

[b] Average for incomplete cycle 1909-1911.

[c] Change from 1909 to 1910.

[d] Average for inverted cycle 1948-1953.

[e] Changes in monthly data are computed from three-month averages centered on business cycle trough and peak months.

Source: Business turns: National Bureau of Economic Research business cycle chronology. Personal income, annual: Appendix A. Income payments, quarterly: *Historical Statistics of the United States, 1789-1945*, Bureau of the Census, 1949, p. 321 (but note that imputed rentals, as given in Harold Barger's *Outlay and Income in the United States, 1921-1938*, National Bureau of Economic Research, 1942, Table 42, are here omitted). Personal income, quarterly and monthly: 1927-1928, estimated from income payments; 1929-1953, *National Income Supplement, 1951, Survey of Current Business*, Dept. of Commerce, and later monthly issues of *Survey of Current Business*. Bank clearings and debits: *Historical Statistics of the United States, 1789-1945*, pp. 324-325, and *Federal Reserve Bulletins*. Adjusted for seasonal variation by NBER.

wholesale prices, trade, employment and incomes, investments, deal-ings in securities, business profits and failures, bank clearings or debits, and business activity in general. Eleven series cover 3 to 5 cycles; 12 series, 6 to 14 cycles; and 14 series, 15 to 21 cycles. From the average deviations about the mean rate of change per month in successive cycles we find that:

1. The mean average deviations of the per month rates of change for all thirty-seven series are (in per cent):

Expansion
First half	1.5
Second half	1.4

Contraction
First half	2.2
Second half	2.0

2. Thirty series show greater variability from cycle to cycle (larger average deviations) in rates of change during the first half of a contraction than during the first half of an expansion, one series shows the same variability, and six show less variability.

3. Thirty series show greater variability in the second half of a contraction than in the second half of an expansion, two show the same variability, and five show less variability.

4. Thirty-three series show greater variability in an entire contraction than in an expansion, and four series show less. The four are an index of production of fuel and electricity, an index of wholesale trade sales, the value of corporate security issues, and an index of deposit activity.[6]

Does this mean that the American economy possesses an inherent tendency to expand at a rather definite rate, whereas its rate of contraction, when circumstances converge to produce a contraction, is in some sense adventitious? One additional feature of the data in Table F and Chart C is consistent with this hypothesis. The rate of change in income during an expansion seems to be correlated with the rate of change during the *preceding* contraction, but not the other way around. A sharp contraction is likely to be followed by a rapid

---

[6] One other exception to the rule appears when the series in Table F are deflated by price indexes. The average deviations of the rates of change per year are (in per cent):

	Expansion	Contraction
Deflated income (annual), 1911-1949	4.1	3.1
Deflated income (quarterly and monthly), 1921-1949	4.2	5.5
Deflated clearings and debits (monthly), 1879-1938	2.4	4.8

xxvi

CHART C
Rates of Change per Year during Business Cycle Expansions and Contractions: Personal Income, and Bank Clearings or Debits outside New York City, 1879-1953

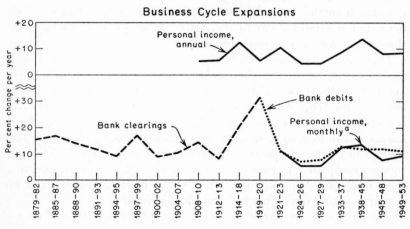

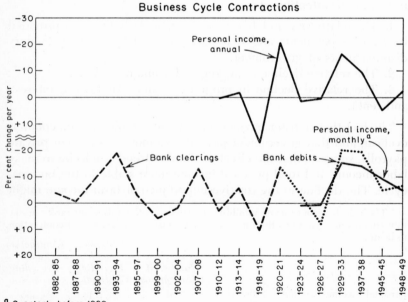

a Quarterly before 1929.
Source: Table F.

expansion and a mild contraction by a slow expansion, but no such rule applies when contractions are compared with preceding expansions.[7] Does this suggest that were it not for the variation in rates of contraction, the rates of expansion would have been even more uniform than they actually were? We cannot pursue this question here, but it would seem to merit the attention of business cycle theorists as well as economic forecasters.

There are other kinds of variation in the behavior of personal income during business cycles, and Creamer's record helps to account for some of them. At the beginning of the study he reviews secular trends in the types or sources of income. As we have seen, there are certain typical differences in both the timing and the amplitude of the several sources of income. If, then, these sources undergo secular change in relative importance, the behavior of the combination of sources comprised in total income may change also. Have fluctuations in total income in the United States become less marked on this account, or have they become more severe?

The principal secular changes in income sources that Creamer brings to our attention are:

1. The relative rise in labor income, particularly that part provided by transfer payments and that part provided by wage and salary disbursements of government.

2. The relative decline in aggregate income of farmers.

3. The relative decline in property income (dividends, interest, and rent).

The fact that transfer payments are highly stable or even countercyclical, and that government payrolls are more stable than private payrolls, suggests that the effect of the first trend would be to make labor income and total personal income more stable in the business cycle. The decline in the relative importance of farm income might

---

[7] The rule is by no means infallible, however, as the following rank correlation coefficients, based on the rates of change during expansion and contraction, indicate:

	Number of Observations	Expansion with Preceding Contraction	Contraction with Preceding Expansion
Personal income (annual), 1909-1953	10	+.71	−.55
Personal income (monthly and quarterly), 1921-1953	6	+.87	+.03
Outside clearings and debits (monthly):			
1879-1953	18	+.14	−.15
1908-1953	10	+.20	−.05
1921-1953	6	+.84	+.41

be expected to have a similar effect. But the decline in property income, insofar as it is due to the decline in interest and rent, would have a destabilizing influence on aggregate personal income.

To assess the net effect of these trends is no easy matter. One approach is illustrated by the hypothetical calculations in Table G. In 1937-1938, total personal income declined $5.5 billion, from $71.4 billion in 1937 to $65.9 billion in 1938. Using an income distribution by source that distinguishes the three trends mentioned above, and assuming the same percentage changes in income from each source that actually occurred in 1937-1938, we find that if these sources had

TABLE G

Estimated Effect of Shift in Income Distribution by Major Type and Source on Change in Total Personal Income, 1937-1938 and 1948-1949

	PERCENTAGE DISTRIBUTION OF DOLLAR TOTALS				PERCENTAGE CHANGE IN DOLLAR AMOUNTS	
	1913	1937	1948	1953	1937-1938	1948-1949
Wages and salaries, private industry	48.0	53.5	55.8	58.2	−10.2	−2.2
Wages and salaries, government	4.6	10.2	8.6	11.5	+11.0	+9.0
Other labor income and transfer payments	.9	3.4	6.4	6.4	+20.8	+10.5
Farm proprietors' net income	10.1	7.9	8.6	4.5	−21.4	−27.7
Nonfarm proprietors' net income	15.2	9.3	10.8	9.6	−4.5	−2.3
Dividends	6.0	6.6	3.5	3.3	−31.9	+4.2
Interest	4.0	5.0	2.5	2.7	−2.8	+9.8
Rent	11.2	4.3	3.7	3.8	+6.5	+2.7
Total	100.0	100.0	100.0	100.0	−7.7	−1.9

Estimated Change in Total Personal Income

	ABSOLUTE CHANGE[a] (billions)		PERCENTAGE CHANGE	
	1937-1938	1948-1949	1937-1938	1948-1949
Using 1913 weights (1st col. above)	$−5.9	$−5.5	−8.3	−2.7
Using 1937 weights (2nd col. above)	−5.5[b]	−2.9	−7.7[b]	−1.4
Using 1948 weights (3rd col. above)	−4.8	−4.0[b]	−6.7	−1.9[b]
Using 1953 weights (4th col. above)	−4.0	−1.0	−5.6	−.5

[a] Derived by applying the estimated per cent changes to total personal income at the peak, in billions, i.e. 1937: $71.4; 1948: $205.1.

[b] Actual change.

Source: Tables A-1, A-2, and A-3. For sources of 1953 data see Table C; data on employee contributions for social insurance for 1953 were supplied directly by the Department of Commerce.

had the same relative importance they had in 1913, the decline in aggregate income in 1937-1938 would have been $5.9 billion. If, on the other hand, total income had been derived as it was in 1948, the 1937-1938 decline would have been only $4.8 billion. And it would have been still smaller, $4.0 billion, if the respective sources had had the same relative importance as in 1953. Compared with 1913, the 1953 distribution effected an offset of nearly $2 billion, or about one-third of the actual decline. Results even more striking are obtained when the 1948-1949 decline is reconstructed on the basis of the 1913 and 1953 distributions, as the table shows. In dollars, the 1948-1949 contraction came to 4.0 billion; with the 1913 distribution, it might have been 5.5 million; with that of 1953, only 1.0 billion.

When the calculation is confined to labor income (divided into three components: wages and salaries, private industry; wages and salaries, government; and other labor income and transfer payments) the results are:

ESTIMATED CHANGE IN TOTAL LABOR INCOME
(*billions of dollars*)

	1937-1938	1948-1949
Using 1913 weights	—5.6	—2.1
Using 1937 weights	—3.9 (actual)	+.2
Using 1948 weights	—3.4	+.6 (actual)
Using 1953 weights	—3.1	+1.2

Here we find that the rise in importance of government payrolls and of transfer payments has clearly tended to offset the cyclical declines in private payrolls. In 1948-1949, indeed, the countercyclical movement of these two components, at their then level of importance, was sufficient to cause a rise in total labor income; whereas if they had had only the size they had in 1913, aggregate labor income would have declined. The stabilizing influence of these elements in labor income evidently continued to grow after 1948.

Such hypothetical calculations may be helpful in assessing the trends and cyclical characteristics disclosed by Creamer's study. They must, however, be interpreted with caution. Our calculations do not take into account all aspects of the distribution of income by source or type, and some neglected aspects might alter the conclusion. For example, the growing relative importance of durable-goods manufacturing industries as a source of income may have operated to enhance the variations in total income. Furthermore, in judging the influence of trends in the distribution of income by source it may be important to take account of rates of remuneration separately from volume of input. Finally, the neglect of possible indirect effects of changes in the distribution of income by source (via consumption or investment, for example) imperils any conclusion drawn from the figures.

Moreover, if the relative rise in the more stable sources of income had been a potent factor, one would have expected to see some evidence of it in Chart C. The chart reveals no clear trend toward a reduction of the swings in personal income during either expansions or contractions. However, before reaching a final judgment on whether some moderation of the cyclical swings in income is in prospect for the future, the reader should consider Creamer's analysis in Chapter 8 of certain governmental programs that offset cyclical losses in personal income. These have only recently flowered. The combined power of the unemployment compensation system, the progressive personal income tax, and the farm price-support program will not be negligible. If our estimate that shifts in the sources of income have made at least a slight contribution in the same direction is correct, there may be ground for believing that the fluctuations in income that accompany business cycles will be moderated in some degree.

ACKNOWLEDGMENT

WE OWE a special debt to Arthur F. Burns, Geoffrey H. Moore, and Millard Hastay; their comments have given shape to the inquiry and saved us from error at numerous points. We are also obligated to the National Income Division, United States Department of Commerce, for making their unpublished estimates available; without their gracious assistance much of the detail of our analysis would be lacking. We are under a similar obligation to our colleagues Daniel M. Holland, Lillian Epstein, and Elizabeth Jenks for permitting us to draw on their unpublished materials and to Harry Eisenpress for permitting us to draw on his detailed knowledge of the National Bureau's techniques for cyclical analysis of time series.

We have benefited also from comments by Lawrence Klein, Frederick C. Mills, and Anna Jacobson Schwartz. The manuscript has gained much in clarity from the work of our editorial staff and from H. Irving Forman's charts. To all our sincere thanks.

DANIEL CREAMER

CONTENTS

Foreword, by Geoffrey H. Moore   ix

Acknowledgment   xxxiii

1. Introduction   3

2. Long-Term Shifts in the Personal Income Structure   6

3. Cycles in Personal Income and Business Activity   17
    Timing of turning points   17
    Amplitude of personal income cycles   21

4. Cycles in Major Types of Income   23
    Timing of turning points   23
    Amplitude of cyclical fluctuations   29

5. Cycles in Types of Nonfarm Labor Income   34
    Timing of turns in labor income by industrial source
        before World War II   34
    Amplitude of wage and salary cycles in private sector
        before World War II   47
    Labor income during and after World War II   51

6. Cycles in Types of Property Income   60
    Cycles in dividend receipts   61
    Cycles in interest receipts   69
    Cycles in capital gains and losses   72

7. Cyclical Amplitudes in Personal Income by Size of Income   77

8. Government Offsets to Cyclical Losses in Personal Income   90
    Agricultural programs   90
    Unemployment compensation and related payments   96
    Federal personal income tax   103

9. Summary of Findings   110

APPENDIXES

A. Estimates of Personal Income 115
    1. Annual estimates of major components of personal income in current prices, 1909-1951 115
    2. Annual estimates of total personal income in 1935-1939 dollars, 1909-1951 124
    3. Monthly estimates of total personal income in 1935-1939 dollars, 1929-1950 126

B. Estimates of Factor Inputs and Returns, 1900-1950 (Chart 3) 128

C. Wage Earners and Salaried Personnel in Manufacturing, 1919-1939 136
    1. Employment of wage earners and salaried personnel in Ohio manufacturing industries, 1919-1939 136
    2. Employment and payrolls of wage earners, 1920-1939, and salaried personnel, 1922-1936, in Wisconsin manufacturing industries 137

D. Dividend Disbursements, 1884-1919, and Total Dividend Payments to Individuals, 1919-1950 145

E. Interest on Government Securities Received by Individuals, 1913-1949 149

F. Estimates of Underreporting of Dividends and Interest by Income Groups, 1939-1948 152

G. Unemployment Compensation and Losses in Income 157
    1. Payrolls, disposable income, and payments to unemployed, United States, 1945-1950 157
    2. Quarterly estimates of payrolls in private sector and payments to unemployed, twelve states, 1948-1950 158

Index 163

TABLES

A. Timing of Turning Points in Personal Income and in Eight Components at Business Cycle Turning Points, 1929-1949   xiii

B. Percentage Distribution of Personal Income by Major Type and Source of Income at Business Cycle Turning Points, 1909-1949   xvi

C. Conformity to Business Cycles of Percentage Shares of Major Types and Sources of Personal Income, 1909-1953   xvii

D. Percentage Distribution of Total Income by Type, Three Income Groups and Total Population, Selected Years, 1920-1948   xx

E. Percentage Shares of Three Income Groups in Total Income during Business Cycles   xxii

F. Changes in Personal Income and in Bank Clearings or Debits during Business Cycles, 1879-1953   xxiv

G. Estimated Effect of Shift in Income Distribution by Major Type and Source on Change in Total Personal Income, 1937-1938 and 1948-1949   xxix

1. Types of Personal Income as Percentage of Total in Peak Income Years, 1913-1951   9

2. Turning Points in Business Activity, and in Personal Income in Current and in Constant (1935-1939) Prices, 1909-1949   19

3. Amplitude of Specific Cycles in Personal Income in Current and in Constant (1935-1939) Prices, 1909-1949   21

4. Lead (—) or Lag (+) of Personal Income and of Its Major Components at Business Cycle Turning Points, 1929-1949   25

5. Turning Points in Business Activity and in Gross Farm Income, 1869-1929   28

6. Amplitude of Personal Income and of Its Major Components during Five Cycles in Personal Income, 1909-1949   32

7. Lead (—) or Lag (+) of Total Nonfarm Labor Income and of Wage and Salary Disbursements by Major Industry Group at Business Cycle Turning Points, 1929-1949   37

8. Lead (—) or Lag (+) of Factory Payrolls, Average

Hourly Earnings, and Man-Hours, and of Their Components, at Business Cycle Turning Points, 1919-1949   40

9. Lead (−) of Salaried Personnel over, or Lag (+) behind, Wage Earners at Turning Points in Employment (Ohio and Wisconsin) and in Payrolls (Wisconsin), Manufacturing Industries, 1920-1938   44

10. Amplitude of Specific Cycles in Personal and Nonfarm Labor Income and in Wage and Salary Disbursements by Major Industry Group, 1929-1938   47

11. Amplitude of Factory Payrolls, Average Hourly Earnings, and Man-Hours, and of Their Components, during Business Cycles, 1921-1949   48

12. Amplitude of Specific Cycles in Employment of Wage Earners and of Salaried Personnel, Ohio Manufacturing Industries, 1919-1938   49

13. Amplitude of Compensation of Corporate Officers, of Other Salaried Personnel, and of Factory Workers, Manufacturing Industries, during Personal Income Cycles, 1920-1938   53

14. Lead (−) of Salaried Personnel over, or Lag (+) behind, Wage Earners at Turning Points in Employment and Payrolls, Manufacturing Industries, 1945-1949   55

15. Amplitude of Personal and Nonfarm Labor Income and of Wages and Salaries by Major Industry Group during Business Cycles, 1938-1949   56

16. Changes in Components of Input and of Returns (in Current and in Constant Dollars) of Factory Labor at Business Peaks in 1937, 1945, and 1948 Relative to 1923, 1926, and 1929 Peaks   57

17. Amplitude of Specific Cycles in Employment and in Earnings of Wage Earners and of Salaried Personnel, Manufacturing Industries, 1938-1949   58

18. Amplitude of Compensation of Corporate Officers and of Other Salaried Personnel, Manufacturing Industries, during Business Cycles, 1938-1949   59

19. Turning Points in Net Profits after Taxes and in Dividend Payments to Individuals, All Corporations, 1920-1950   63

20. Lead (−) or Lag (+) of Total Dividend Payments at Business Cycle Turning Points, 1885-1949; and Am-

plitude of Specific Cycle Contractions in Deflated Bank Clearings, 1885-1919, and in Deflated Debits, 1919-1939, outside New York City   67

21. Amplitude of Corresponding Cyclical Phases in Property Income, Dividend Payments to Individuals, Total Nonfarm Labor Income, and in Farm and Nonfarm Proprietors' Net Income, 1929-1949   68

22. Personal Income and Excess of Net Capital Gains over Losses Realized by Individuals, 1917-1950   74

23. Various Types of Income as Average Annual Percentage of Total Income, Five Income Groups, Nonfarm Population, 1919-1938   81

24. Percentage Shares of Total Income, Three Income Groups, Nonfarm Population, 1913-1948   82

25. Conformity of Percentage Shares of Total Income, Three Income Groups, Nonfarm Population, to Phases in Business Cycles, 1913-1948   83

26. Percentage Shares of Various Types of Income, Three Income Groups, Nonfarm Population, at Personal Income Turning Points, 1920-1948   85

27. Percentage Shares of Total Dividends and Interest, Three Income Groups, Nonfarm Population, 1937-1948   88

28. Farm Proprietors' Net Income and Retained Government Benefit Payments, 1945-1951   91

29. Farm Proprietors' Net Income, Investment in Price-Support Operations, and Changes in Total Investment, 1946-1952   95

30. Cumulative Loss in Private Payrolls and Cumulative Compensation to Unemployed, from Seasonally Adjusted Monthly Data, 1945-1946 and 1948-1950   99

31. Cumulative Loss in Total Payrolls and Cumulative Compensation to Unemployed, from Seasonally Adjusted Monthly and Quarterly Data, 1948-1950   100

32. Cumulative Loss in Disposable Income and Cumulative Compensation to Unemployed, from Seasonally Adjusted Quarterly Data, 1948-1950   100

33. Loss in Private Payrolls, Compensation to Unemployed, and General Assistance, from Seasonally Unadjusted Quarterly Data, 1948-1950, and Change in Number Exhausting Benefits, 1948-1949, United States and Twelve States   102

34. Individual Income Tax Liabilities for Two Groups of Taxpayers, 1913-1951   105

35. Offsets to Loss in Disposable Income through Operation of Federal Personal Income Tax in Selected Contraction Periods, 1920-1949   106

A-1. Personal Income in Current Prices by Type of Income, 1909-1951   116

A-2. Percentage Distribution of Personal Income in Current Prices by Type of Income, 1909-1951   120

A-3. Wage and Salary Receipts, Government and Private Sectors, 1909-1951   122

A-4. Personal Income in Constant (1935-1939) Prices, 1909-1951   126

B-1. Indexes of Factor Inputs and Factor Returns by Type of Income, 1900-1950   129

C-1. Wage Earners and Salaried Personnel, Ohio Manufacturing Industries, 1919-1939   138

C-2. Indexes of Employment and Payrolls of Wage Earners, 1920-1939, and of Salaried Personnel, 1922-1936, Wisconsin Manufacturing Industries   141

D-1. Total Dividend Payments to Individuals, 1919-1941 and 1939-1950   146

E-1. Federal, State and Local, and Total Government Interest Received by Individuals, 1913-1949   150

F-1. Number of Taxable Income Tax Returns, and Dividends and Interest Reported as Percentage of Dividends and Interest Received, 1939-1948   153

F-2. Derivation of 1948 Accrued Interest on United States Savings Bonds, Series A to F, Received by 10 Per Cent of the Population with Highest Annual Incomes in 1947   155

G-1. Total Payments to Unemployed, Seasonally Adjusted, 1945-1950   158

G-2. Payrolls in Private Sector and Payments to Unemployed, Seasonally Unadjusted, Twelve States, 1948-1950   160

CHARTS

A. Specific Cycles in Total Personal Income and in Eight Components, in Relation to Business Cycles, 1929-1950   xii

B. Average Percentage Shares of Three Income Groups in Total Income during Six Business Cycles, 1919-1946   xxi

C. Rates of Change per Year during Business Cycle Expansions and Contractions: Personal Income, and Bank Clearings or Debits outside New York City, 1879-1953   xxvii

1. Total Personal Income in Current Prices and per Capita Personal Income in Constant (1935-1939) Prices, 1909-1951   4

2. Types of Personal Income as Percentage of Total in Peak Income Years, 1913-1951   8

3. Indexes of Factor Inputs and Factor Returns by Type of Income, 1900-1950   14

4. Personal Income in Current and in Constant (1935-1939) Prices, Monthly Data, 1929-1950   18

5. Personal Income in Current and in Constant (1935-1939) Prices, Annual Data, 1909-1951   20

6. Personal Income in Current Prices by Type of Income, Monthly Data, 1929-1950   24

7. Gross Farm Income, 1869-1937, and Farm Proprietors' Net Income, 1909-1951   27

8. Personal Income in Current Prices by Type of Income, Annual Data, 1909-1951   30

9. Nonfarm Labor Income by Major Industry Group, 1929-1951   36

10. Factory Payrolls, Average Hourly Earnings, Man-Hours, and Their Components, 1918-1951   38

11. United States Factory Employment and Wage Earners and Salaried Personnel Employed in Ohio Manufacturing Industries, 1919-1939   43

12. Employment and Payrolls of Wage Earners and Salaried Personnel, Wisconsin Manufacturing Industries, 1920-1936   45

13. Factory Payrolls, and Salaries of Corporate Officers and of Other Salaried Personnel, Manufacturing Industries, 1919-1950   52

14. Employment and Payrolls of Wage Earners and Salaried Personnel, Manufacturing Industries, 1938-1951   54

15. Net Profits after Taxes and Dividend Payments to Individuals, All Corporations, 1919-1951   62
16. Dividend Disbursements, 1884-1919, and Total Dividend Payments to Individuals, 1919-1950   66
17. Total Interest and Interest on All Government Securities Received by Individuals, 1909-1951   70
18. Individual Holdings of Federal and of State and Local Securities and Interest on Such Securities, 1913-1949   71
19. Excess of Net Capital Gains over Losses Realized by Individuals, and Absolute Annual Change in Price Index of All Common Stocks, 1917-1951   75
20. Percentage Shares of Total Income, Three Income Groups, Nonfarm Population, Three Variants, 1913-1948   80
21. Farm Proprietors' Net Income, Investment in Price-Support Operations, and Change in Total Investment, 1946-1952   94
22. Private Payrolls and Compensation to Unemployed, 1945-1946 and 1948-1950   98

Personal Income
during
Business Cycles

CHAPTER 1

INTRODUCTION

REASONABLY reliable annual estimates of aggregate income received by individuals in the United States begin with 1909. Since that date there have been two world wars and a contraction in business activity so long and severe that it is referred to as the Great Depression. It is not surprising that personal income—i.e. the income receipts of individuals[1]—has fluctuated widely in the forty-odd years since 1909. The statistical record is shown in Chart 1.

In this chart the upper curve traces the course of total personal income in current prices.[2] Personal income has been pushed up twice by major wars and inflation and pulled down twice by major depressions. On balance, however, each peak, with the exception of 1937, has been much higher than the preceding one. The picture is different if we adjust for the changing value of money, i.e. price changes, and for the continuous increase in population. The lower curve, showing per capita personal income in constant (1935-1939) prices, incorporates both adjustments. This curve fluctuates less violently but the changes are substantial. The long-term upward movement of incomes between 1909 and 1939 is less marked, and the mild recession of 1948-1949 is replaced by two recessions starting in 1944 and adding up to a decline of major proportions.[3] Aside

[1] For the detailed definition of personal income used in this study see Chapter 2.

[2] The estimates in Chart 1 comprise three discontinuous series prepared by different investigators. Although the concepts are made identical as far as possible, it seems best to present them as three discrete series, overlapping in 1919 and 1929. Since our main interest is centered in the relative movements, the differences in levels between series, which are not large in any case, do not constitute a serious problem.

[3] The 13 per cent decline in real per capita income between 1944 and 1947 may seem unduly large to those who recall those years. For those who may be inclined to attribute the largeness of the decline to faulty adjustment for price changes, we point to the following considerations, which suggest some of the factors that contributed to such a decline:

a. Labor force, including armed forces, declined from 65,890,000 in 1944 to 61,608,000 in 1947, or by 6.5 per cent (see *Statistical Abstract of the United States, 1953*, Bureau of the Census, Table 206, p. 186).

b. Average hours worked per week in nonagricultural industries declined from 46.2 in 1944 to 42.3 in 1947, or by 8.4 per cent (see *Current Population Reports—Labor Force*, Bureau of the Census, Series P-50, No. 13).

c. Population increased from 138.4 million in 1944 to 144.1 million in 1947, or by 4.1 per cent (see *Statistical Abstract of the United States, 1953*, Table 7, p. 13).

It must be noted, too, that we are discussing real income, not real consump-

from this and a similar alteration during and immediately after World War I, the cyclical configuration is much the same as in the current-price curve.

CHART 1

Total Personal Income in Current Prices and per Capita Personal Income in Constant (1935-1939) Prices, 1909-1951

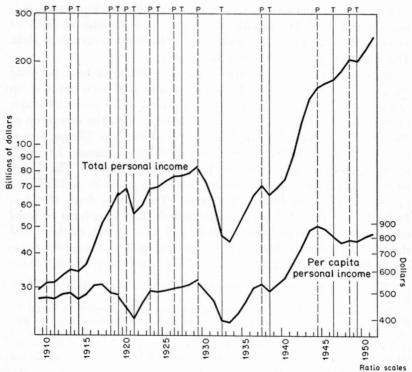

Broken and solid vertical lines represent business cycle peaks and troughs, respectively.

Source: See Appendix Table A-1 for personal income in current prices. Per capita personal income in constant prices estimated by dividing total personal income in constant (1935-39) prices (Appendix Table A-4) by population for continental United States including armed forces overseas as of July 1 (*Statistical Abstract of the United States: 1948*, Bureau of the Census, Table 7, p. 9 for 1909-1939 and *Statistical Abstract of the United States: 1953*, Table 7, p. 13 for 1940-1951).

What happens to the income structure during these swings in personal income? How do the movements in labor income during business cycles compare with those in the net income of proprietors

tion. The rise in the latter (in 1939 dollars) from $81.1 billion in 1944 to $98.3 billion in 1947 was possible because of the sharp drop in personal savings from $35.4 to $3.9 billion (see *National Income Supplement, 1951, Survey of Current Business*, Dept. of Commerce).

4

and in property income? What happens to executive salaries as compared with wages? When total income is rising, do the incomes of upper income groups increase or decline in relation to those of lower income groups? Over the years, what has happened to the relative position of families with high, with moderate, and with low incomes?

These questions suggest one of the two areas explored in this study, namely, shifts in the relative importance of the major types of income. The other is the timing of the rises and falls in personal income. While there is a consensus among economists that a fall in personal income does not usually precede a business recession, it is still necessary to ask whether the fall in personal income coincides or follows, and by how much. Similar questions may be asked about the timing of revivals in personal income and in business activity. And—perhaps of greater significance—to what extent do the major components of personal income differ from the aggregate in their timing patterns? Do these differences help to explain the behavior of the aggregate?

Since the statistics on personal income extend over four decades, we can preface the cyclical analysis with certain queries about changes in the income structure. Beginning with 1909, can we discern any long-term shifts in the relative importance of the various types of income? Have the operations of our economy over these forty years favored the owners of property, or the recipients of wages and salaries, or the independent professional people and the proprietors? Or have all marched along at the same pace? To investigate these trends is our first task.

CHAPTER 2

LONG-TERM SHIFTS IN THE PERSONAL
INCOME STRUCTURE

As NOTED above, personal income is here defined as the sum of factor returns received by individuals plus transfer payments, all measured before direct personal taxes.[1] The factor returns, i.e. earnings in public and private enterprise, are wages and salaries and their supplements (mainly compensation for injury and employer contributions to private pension and welfare funds), net income of proprietorships, and individuals' receipts of dividends, net rents, and monetary interest from nongovernmental sources. Transfer payments are income receipts unrelated to the rendering of current service, chiefly social security benefits, relief payments, and government interest.[2] In the view of some, profits and losses realized by individuals from changes in the market value of assets not regularly offered for sale (in national income terminology, realized capital gains and losses) might also be included in total personal income.[3] However, aside from the conceptual uncertainties, the statistics on realized capital gains and losses are not adequate for our purposes, since they are not available on a quarterly or monthly basis in any year and are lacking completely for the years before 1917. Hence total personal income is defined in this study to exclude realized

[1] Disposable income (personal income after direct personal taxes) is not used as the basic measure, although for some purposes it may be conceptually superior. From an operational viewpoint, estimates of disposable income have two serious limitations: estimates for a time unit shorter than a year, which are highly desirable for cyclical analysis, are available only since 1939; and it is difficult to apportion the tax liability among types of income. Moreover, the differences in the configurations of personal and disposable income before 1943 are negligible. Even from 1943 on the cyclical turns occur in the same quarters; amplitude measures differ somewhat.

[2] In its personal income series, the Department of Commerce and we include government interest under interest and dividend payments instead of under transfer payments. We exclude transfer payments originating in private business, such as consumers' bad debts, but these are not excluded from the monthly series as monthly estimates are not readily available. In 1950, business transfer payments amounted to .3 per cent of personal income according to estimates in *National Income Supplement, 1951, Survey of Current Business*, Dept. of Commerce.

[3] Unrealized capital gains can be converted into current purchasing power by various devices besides selling assets. These, however, cannot be taken into account statistically. For a discussion of these devices see Lawrence H. Seltzer's *The Nature and Tax Treatment of Capital Gains and Losses* (National Bureau of Economic Research, 1951, pp. 231-253).

6

capital gains or losses unless the contrary is specifically indicated. In brief, we use the Department of Commerce definition of personal income with minor adjustments to exclude imputed interest and business transfer payments.

The following analysis deals with three main types of income:

1. Labor income: all wages and salaries plus other labor income and transfer payments excluding government interest. A distinction is made between executive and other salaries, executive salaries being taken as equivalent to the compensation of corporate officers.

2. Net income from independent professions and from proprietorships.

3. Property income: personal receipts of dividends, monetary interest from all sources, and net rents.

These three types make up the personal income structure, and our interest is in how this structure changes over time. Here we must anticipate one of our later findings on cyclical behavior: the relative importance of each type of income varies according to the phase of the cycle in total personal income. Comparisons over time must therefore employ years similar in cyclical position. We have selected years representing peaks in personal income and, with the exception of 1937, reasonably full employment: 1913, 1920, 1929, 1937, 1948, and 1951.[4] The various types of income are expressed as percentages of total personal income in each of these years (Chart 2 and Table 1).[5]

That secular shifts occurred during the forty years is clear. Let us trace first those in the share of income going to labor. In the high-income year before World War I, labor income accounted for slightly more than half of all personal income; by 1920 its share had increased to 63 per cent, and it remained at that level in 1929, the last year of high prosperity before the Great Depression. Up to this point the movement of the wage and salary component paralleled that of the total. In 1937, the first cyclical peak after the emergence from the Great Depression, the share of labor income increased to 67 per cent, while the increase in wage and salary receipts was relatively less. The difference between the two rates of change is

---

[4] We include 1951 not merely because it is the last full year for which figures are available but also because it is a year of full employment and very high income. Our computations show that the same results are obtained from an analysis based on cycle averages.

[5] Since the estimates before and after 1929 have somewhat different conceptual bases, we present the distributions for 1929 on both bases.

CHART 2
Types of Personal Income as Percentage of Total
in Peak Income Years, 1913-1951

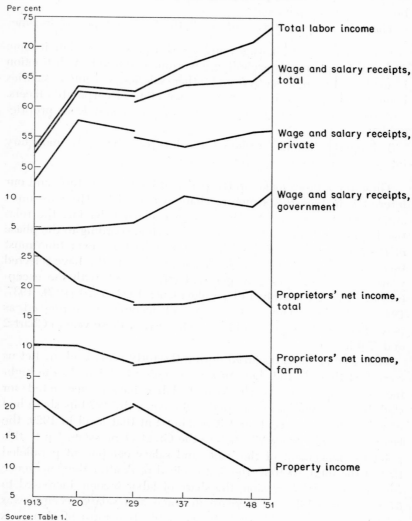

Source: Table 1.

explained largely by the enhanced importance of transfer payments, specifically direct-relief payments to the unemployed.[6] The next peak in personal income brings us to the period after World War II,

[6] Work-relief wages are included under wages and salaries.

8

TABLE 1

Types of Personal Income as Percentage of Total
in Peak Income Years, 1913-1951

(*per cent*)

	1913	1920	1929a	1929b	1937	1948	1951
TOTAL PERSONAL INCOME	100.0	100.0	100.0	100.0	100.0	100.0	100.0
Labor income	53.2	63.4	62.6	62.6	66.9	70.9	73.3
Wage and salary receipts	52.3	62.6	61.8	60.8	63.7	64.4	67.0
Corporate officers	n.a.	3.5	4.0	4.0	3.9	3.3	n.a.
Other	n.a.	59.1	57.8	56.8	59.8	61.1	n.a.
Private	47.7	57.7	56.0	54.9	53.4	55.8	56.1
Farm	2.3	2.6	1.6	1.6	1.4	1.5	1.2
Nonfarm	45.4	55.1	54.4	53.3	52.0	54.3	54.9
Government	4.6	4.9	5.8	5.8	10.2	8.6	11.0
Civilian	4.0	3.9	5.4	5.6	7.4	6.9	7.7
Military	.3	1.0	.4	.2	.4	1.8	3.3
Work relief	0	0	0	0	2.4	0	0
Other labor income	} .9c	} .9c	} .8c	.6	.7	1.3	1.7
Transfer payments				1.1	2.7	5.1	4.6
Proprietors' net income	25.6	20.4	17.3	16.9	17.1	19.4	16.8
Farm	10.1	10.0	7.2	6.9	7.9	8.6	6.3
Nonfarm	15.2	10.5	10.1	10.1	9.3	10.8	10.5
Property income	21.3	16.2	20.1	20.5	16.0	9.7	9.8
Dividends	6.0	4.6	7.6	7.0	6.6	3.5	3.6
Interest	4.0	5.3	6.7	6.4	5.0	2.5	2.6
Net rent	11.2	6.2	5.9	7.0	4.3	3.7	3.6
*Property income plus net capital gains or losses*d	n.a.	16.2	22.8	23.2	15.9	11.6	n.a.

a Comparable with preceding years.
b Comparable with following years.
c Transfer payments and other labor income are not distinguished for 1913-1929. All industries are not covered for this period.
d Property income and realized net capital gains or losses as percentage of personal income including realized net capital gains or losses.
n.a. = not available
Note: Details may not add to totals because of rounding.
Source: Based on Tables A-1 and A-3.

when, as in World War I and its aftermath, there was a substantial relative increase in labor income, amounting in 1948 to 71 per cent of total personal income. Once again, the relative rise in the wage and salary component of labor income was slight and, as before, was due to the increased importance of transfer payments. The character of these payments, however, was much altered from the prewar period, which was dominated by direct-relief payments. In 1948 the principal transfer payments besides direct relief were benefits from social insurance funds; military pension, disability, and retirement payments; and readjustment, self-employment, and subsistence allowances to veterans.[7]

Wage and salary receipts include the earnings of skilled and unskilled workers, white-collar employees, and executives. It would be interesting to show the shares of all these groups separately. Unfortunately, we can make an approximation only in the case of executives, by using the compensation (salaries and cash bonuses) of corporate officers reported to the Bureau of Internal Revenue. Thus we can compare the compensation of corporate officers in years of peak income with wages and salaries received by all other employees. The share of the former increased by a seventh during the 1920's, while the share of the latter declined slightly. During the next decade the movement was reversed: corporate executive salaries accounted for a slightly smaller percentage of total personal income in 1937 than in 1929, and other wages and salaries for a somewhat larger percentage. This trend continued during the war and postwar inflation of the 1940's: there was a further decline in the percentage of personal income paid out to executives and a modest gain in the percentage paid to other employees.

The growing importance of the government as a source of personal income shows clearly in a breakdown of wages and salaries paid by the government and by the private sector of the economy. Wages and salaries paid by private enterprise amounted to 47.7 per cent of personal income in 1913 and to 57.7 per cent in 1920, a gain of a fifth. By 1929 this share had declined slightly, and more than half of the decline was attributable to farm wages. Thereafter, in years of prosperity, this share has deviated very little from the 1929 level. Wages and salaries disbursed by government, on the other hand, accounted for a progressively larger share of personal income between 1913 and 1937, increasing from 4.6 to 10.2 per cent. This was due to the expansion of regular civilian employment and to the work-relief program. The sharp reduction of the armed forces after V-J Day and the elimination of work relief caused the government percentage to fall to 8.6 in 1948, but the remobilization connected with the Korean War brought government payrolls to 11.0 per cent of the personal income total in 1951. While the increase in military payrolls has been a significant factor, it is the expansion of the non-

[7] *National Income Supplement, 1951*, Table 36, pp. 201-202.

military functions of government that accounts for the major part of the rise between 1913 and 1948 in the share of personal income coming from the government.

Our analysis thus far clearly shows that labor income made persistent relative gains during the forty years after 1913. During the last twenty years these relative gains have been restricted entirely to wages and salaries below the highest salary bracket, to supplements to wages and salaries (other labor income), and to transfer payments. Executive salaries account for a smaller percentage of the total. Moreover, since 1920 the wages and salaries paid by private enterprise have been a virtually stable share of personal income in years of business cycle peaks, in contrast to wages and salaries paid by government, which have been an increasing share.

While the share of labor income in total personal income was rising, the shares of all other types of income were falling. The net income of proprietors (i.e. all owners of unincorporated enterprises, including farm operators and self-employed professional persons) may be said to comprise both compensation for labor and management and a return on invested capital. Since it is a mixture of labor and property income, it is treated separately from both. By 1920 the percentage of total personal income received by proprietors was down to four-fifths of its level before World War I. All of this loss was incurred in the income of nonfarm proprietors, and part of it was undoubtedly due to the conversion of proprietorships into corporations, which transforms proprietors' income into salaries, dividends, and corporate savings. A much more moderate relative decline in the net income of all proprietors occurred between 1920 and 1929, with the farm component causing most of the decrease. In 1937, and again in 1951, the shares of both farm and nonfarm proprietors stood at about the 1929 level. In 1948 both regained the 1920 level, but this may have been merely a temporary development.

The share of property income—dividends, interest, and net rent—took still another course. In 1913, property income represented slightly more than one-fifth of all personal income and in 1948 not quite one-tenth. This was the largest relative reduction found among the three major types of income. World War I and the ensuing inflation reduced the share of property income by one-fifth, but most of this was restored by 1929. The economic developments during the Great Depression and the subsequent recovery, however, did not favor property income: in 1937 its share was 16 per cent as compared with the 1929 level of 20 per cent. By 1948 its share was down

11

to about 10 per cent. Moreover, when net capital gains and losses realized by individuals are included in property income, these trends are not significantly affected.

While the percentage disbursed as dividends traced much the same course as that of total property income, the other two components had different patterns. As regards interest payments, their share increased from 1913 to 1920 and from 1920 to 1929, but by 1937 it was back at the 1920 level, and in 1948 it was only 62 per cent of the 1913 level. Net rent,[8] on the other hand, formed a declining percentage of personal income throughout the four decades, although the decline was negligible between 1920 and 1929. Again, the increased use of the corporate form in real estate management, which transforms net rent into other types of income, would be a partial explanation of its secular decline. Of the three components of property income, net rent suffered the greatest relative decline during these forty years.

In all these ways the income structure has been significantly altered during the last four decades. Wages and salaries have formed an increasing percentage of personal income. This has been accompanied by a decrease in the percentages formed by proprietors' net income and property income. Property income, particularly net rent, sustained the largest relative losses. These, together with the accompanying shifts in the distribution of income by size, constitute far-reaching structural changes.

The structural shifts just described may be viewed statistically as the net result of changes in the volume of the various productive factors and changes in the rates of return to these factors. Our materials shed some light on the question whether changes in volume of input or changes in rate of return were more important. Chart 3 presents approximations to both elements for the three main types of income; some are more accurate than others.[9] More specifically, it shows the movement in (1) the number of full-time equivalent nonfarm employees, and average annual full-time equivalent earnings per nonfarm employee; (2) the number of hired farm workers, and the composite farm wage rate; (3) the number of nonfarm proprietors, and their total net income; (4) the number of family workers in agriculture, and the total net income of farm operators;

---

[8] Estimates of net rent are perhaps more subject to error than the other estimates (see Chapter 6, note 1). To keep the record straight, we should indicate that net imputed farm rent is included in net income of farm proprietors.

[9] See Appendix B for details on sources and methods.

(5) total nonfarm reproducible wealth (other than that of house-holds, government, and nonprofit institutions) in 1929 prices, and the ratio of net dividend disbursements to corporate net worth; and (6) the yield of high-grade corporate bonds, the rent index in the Bureau of Labor Statistics Consumers Price Index, and the yield on federal government bonds.

Under labor income the input and unit returns for the farm and nonfarm components are examined separately (Panel A). In the nonfarm sector the long-run trend in numbers employed has been upward even if we omit the periods of world wars. Average annual earnings during World War I rose much faster than numbers em-ployed (both on a full-time equivalent basis). During the two inter-war decades the trend movements were suspended in both nonfarm labor input and labor return, but beginning with 1938 both rose at similar rates until 1944; thereafter, annual earnings continued to rise, but numbers employed declined for three years and then remained stable until 1949. The striking difference in the long-term movements of farm and nonfarm labor is not in the labor return (earnings) but in the numbers employed: the trend in number of hired farm workers has been slightly downward in contrast to a decidedly upward trend for the number of nonfarm employees.

We now turn to the input and returns of proprietors (Panel B). Here the measures for net income are of aggregates, in contrast to the measures for labor and property income, which are of unit rates of return. It will be recalled that the share of farm operators in total personal income has been falling since 1920. The chart indicates that this has been largely due to a relative decline in labor input. Family workers in agriculture have represented a declining percentage of the total labor force; their absolute number has been virtually con-stant over this period. Net farm income, on the other hand, shows a rising trend from 1909 to the mid-1920's. From then until World War II the movement is dominated by cyclical forces. After 1940 the net income of farm operators increased rapidly, but not fast enough to offset the relative decline in labor input and the increases in some other types of income.

The net income of nonfarm proprietors shows much the same trend as net farm income. But the number of nonfarm proprietors, in contrast to the number of family workers in agriculture, shows an upward trend; the rise, however, was less rapid than that of the total labor force. It is worth noting that the decline of one-third in the share of nonfarm proprietors in total income all occurred be-

CHART 3

Indexes of Factor Inputs and Factor Returns by Type of Income, 1900-1950

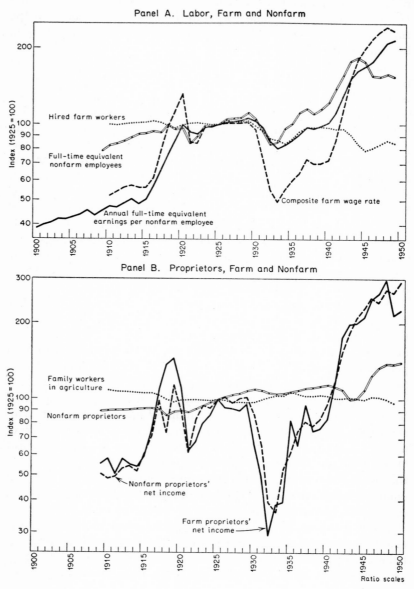

Panel A. Labor, Farm and Nonfarm

Panel B. Proprietors, Farm and Nonfarm

Ratio scales

14

CHART 3 (continued)

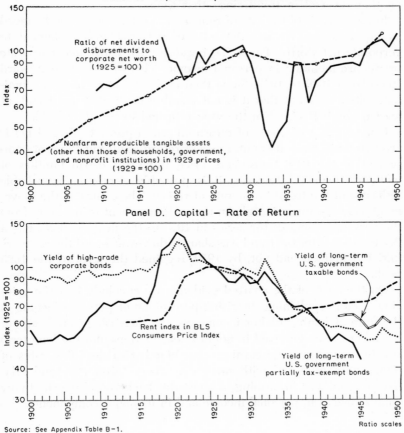

Panel C. Capital — Input and Rate of Return

Panel D. Capital — Rate of Return

Source: See Appendix Table B—1.

tween 1913 and 1920, a period during which there was virtually no change in the number of nonfarm proprietors.[10]

The measure of nonfarm reproducible wealth (other than that of households, government, and nonprofit institutions) in 1929 prices (Panel C) shows that capital in use increased from 1900 to 1929 and then declined until 1936. Thereafter capital rose, reaching the 1929 level about 1945. The various measures of rate of return on capital, however, tell a different story. The rate of return on that

---

[10] However, it must be emphasized that the estimates of numbers of nonfarm proprietors and their net income are subject to large errors during this period (see Chapter 7, note 7).

part of capital financed by debt (Panel D) increased from 1900 to 1920 and then declined until the middle 1940's. There is evidence of another reversal in trend since that time.

For a measure of the rate of return on that part of capital financed by equity funds we use the ratio of net dividends disbursed to corporate net worth (Panel C), because only distributed corporate profits are included in personal income. This ratio had an upward trend from 1909 to 1929. Since then cyclical factors have so dominated its movement that it is not possible to discern any trend, at least through 1947, when the ratio returned to the 1929 level.

Our indicator of a rate of return on rental property (Panel D) is crude indeed, since it is not a rate of return at all but the rent component of the BLS Consumers Price Index for urban families of moderate income. However, it is probably a reasonably reliable indicator of the trend in the rate of return. The course of the movement has been unequivocal. An upward movement is indicated from the very beginning of the series in 1913 to the peak in 1925. For a decade thereafter the trend was sharply downward, and the recovery initiated in 1936 had not, by 1950, regained the level of the 1925 peak.

On the basis of the charted evidence we conclude that the principal factors explaining the rising percentage of personal income in the form of nonfarm labor income are the increasing percentage of the labor force employed in nonfarm occupations and the long-term rise in annual average earnings, combined with declining rates of return on capital and with smaller numbers (absolutely and relatively) employed in farming. Against this background we shall now analyze cycles in personal income and in its major components.

CHAPTER 3

CYCLES IN PERSONAL INCOME AND BUSINESS ACTIVITY

Timing of Turning Points

How well do the cycles in personal income (see Chart 1 above) conform to cycles in business activity? One way of determining the degree of conformity is to compare the turning points in personal income and in business cycles. Since turning points can be dated more precisely by monthly data, we shall examine first the period since 1929—the period covered by the Department of Commerce in its monthly estimates of personal income (Chart 4 and Table 2).

In the two decades following 1929 there were eight turning points in business activity and eight corresponding turns in personal income. At the four troughs the upturn in personal income either coincided with or led by one month the upturn in general business. At three of the four peaks the downturn in personal income lagged one to four months behind the downturn in general business, and at the remaining peak it led by one month. On this evidence there is a one-to-one correspondence of cycles in business activity and personal income; their timing coincides roughly at the troughs, while at the peaks personal income usually lags slightly.[1]

Annual estimates of personal income give us a glimpse of its cyclical behavior during another twenty years. The starting point now is 1909. On an annual basis, cyclical fluctuations in personal income no longer show a close correspondence with cycles in business activity (Chart 5). Thus the cyclical contractions in business in 1910-1911, 1918-1919, 1923-1924, and 1926-1927 do not have a counterpart in the annual totals of personal income. To be sure, all these business cycle contractions were relatively mild, and on closer inspection there appears to have been a conformity of sorts in the slackening in the rate of increase of personal income. Moreover, real per capita income did decline in all of these cyclical contractions, except that of 1926-1927 (Chart 1).

[1] For the 1920's, also, there is evidence suggesting that the downturn in personal income lagged briefly behind the downturn in business activity. As we shall see in Chapters 5 and 6, dividends, interest, and salaries failed to trace a specific contraction between 1921 and 1929, and factory wages, which typically lead total wages, lagged at the 1920 and 1923 peaks and had a coincident turn at the 1926 peak.

CHART 4

Personal Income in Current and in Constant (1935-1939) Prices,
Monthly Data, 1929-1950

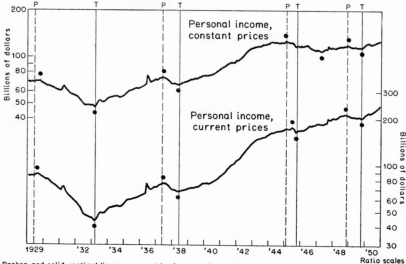

Broken and solid vertical lines represent business cycle peaks and troughs, respectively.
Source: See Appendix A; data are seasonally adjusted annual rates.

On the other hand, the contraction of business activity in 1913-1914 was fairly severe and the declines in 1920-1921 and 1929-1932 were very substantial. For each of these contractions there was a corresponding contraction in personal income. Moreover, there were no cycles in personal income that could not be matched with business cycles, and, with the exception of the 1932 trough, what turning points there were in personal income between 1909 and 1949 coincided with business cycle turns.

The statistical record for the decades immediately before and after World War I indicates, on the surface at least, that personal income continued to expand unless halted by a major downturn in business activity. This evidence of cyclical insensitivity, however, is probably spurious because of the crudity of an annual period in general and the rigidity of the calendar year in particular.[2] For this reason we contend that the behavior of the annual data does not negate the conclusion based on the monthly data: a one-to-one

[2] Note, for example, that on a monthly basis there is a contraction in personal income from June to September 1945, the first contraction after the 1938 trough; on an annual basis the first contraction did not occur until 1948.

TABLE 2

Turning Points in Business Activity, and in Personal Income in Current
and in Constant (1935-1939) Prices, 1909-1949

| | | | PERSONAL INCOME | | | |
| | BUSINESS ACTIVITY | | Current Prices | | Constant prices | |
	Monthly Date	Calendar Year Date	Monthly Date	Calendar Year Date	Monthly Date	Calendar Year Date
P		1910				
T		1911				
P		1913		1913		1913
T		1914		1914		1914
P		1918				1917
T		1919				
P		1920		1920		
T		1921		1921		1921
P		1923				
T		1924				
P		1926				
T		1927				
P	June 1929	1929	Aug. 1929	1929	Oct. 1929	1929
T	Mar. 1933	1932	Mar. 1933	1933	Mar. 1933	1933
P	May 1937	1937	June 1937	1937	June 1937	1937
T	June 1938	1938	May 1938	1938	May 1938	1938
P	Feb. 1945	1944	June 1945		Jan. 1945	1944
T	Oct. 1945	1946	Sept. 1945		Apr. 1947	1947
P	Nov. 1948	1948	Oct. 1948	1948	Dec. 1948	1948
T	Oct. 1949	1949	Oct. 1949	1949	Oct. 1949	1949

P = peak; T = trough.
Source: Business cycle turns are those in the National Bureau of Economic Research business cycle chronology; personal income turns are based on Appendix A.

correspondence between cycles in general business and personal income.

Much the same conclusion can be reached when personal income in constant prices is compared with business cycles (Chart 5 and Table 2).[3] Before 1929 the sole difference in turning points between personal income in current and in constant prices (annual data) occurred in the period of World War I and its aftermath. Personal income, whether measured in constant or in current prices, traced only one cycle, but the peak occurred in 1917 in constant prices and in 1920 in current prices. During the 1930's there was no significant difference in the timing of the turns in the two income series (monthly data) (see Chart 4).

[3] For the derivation of personal income in constant prices see Appendix A.

CHART 5

Personal Income in Current and in Constant (1935-1939) Prices,
Annual Data, 1909-1951

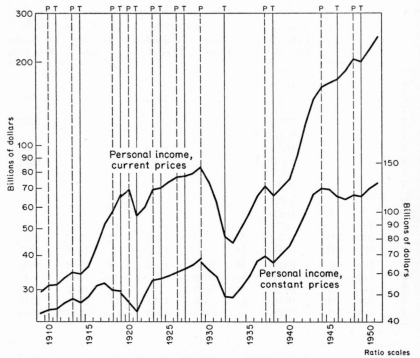

Broken and solid vertical lines represent business cycle peaks and troughs, respectively.
Source: Tables A-1 and A-4.

In World War II, timing again begins to diverge after the peak in personal income in constant prices, in January 1945 (Chart 4). The subsequent trough in personal income in current prices and in business activity was reached in September or October 1945, but personal income in constant prices continued to decline until April 1947. Thereafter until 1951 all three series had roughly coincident turning points. Thus for more than forty years the turns in personal income are virtually the same whether measured in current or in constant prices except in periods characterized by the rapid and substantial price changes that occur during war and its immediate aftermath.[4]

[4] Since consumers' prices tend to lag, one might expect personal income in constant prices to lead personal income in current prices both at peaks and at

Amplitude of Personal Income Cycles

Chart 1 served to suggest the wide swings in personal income between 1909 and 1949. The amplitude of these movements is measured more precisely in Table 3.

TABLE 3

Amplitude of Specific Cycles in Personal Income in Current
and in Constant (1935-1939) Prices, 1909-1949
(*based on cycle relatives*)

	CURRENT PRICES		CONSTANT PRICES	
PHASE	*Period*	*Amplitude*	*Period*	*Amplitude*
Expansion	1909-1913	+16.7	1909-1913	+11.8
Contraction	1913-1914	−1.8	1913-1914	−3.5
Full cycle		18.5		15.3
Expansion	1914-1920	+67.2	1914-1917	+16.4
Contraction	1920-1921	−25.5	1917-1921	−22.1
Full cycle		92.7		38.5
Expansion	1921-1929	+40.2	1921-1929	+42.1
Contraction	1929-1933	−56.2	1929-1933	−30.4
Full cycle		96.4		72.5
Expansion	1933-1937	+45.3	1933-1937	+33.4
Contraction	1937-1938	−9.1	1937-1938	−5.7
Full cycle		54.4		39.1
Expansion	1938-1948	+99.6	1938-1944	+56.8
Contraction	1948-1949	−2.8	1944-1947	−11.4
Full cycle		102.4		68.2
Expansion			1947-1948	+3.5
Contraction			1948-1949	−.7
Full cycle				4.2

Source: Based on Tables A-1 and A-4.

To measure cyclical amplitudes, we compute the average of the annual figures comprised in a cycle, and express each annual value as a percentage of this average or "cycle base." These percentages we call "cycle relatives." The difference between the cycle relatives representing the peak and the initial trough is the amplitude of

troughs. Timing differences of this sort can be tested only by monthly data, which restricts our comparison to the two decades following 1929. For this period the evidence suggests (Chart 4) that in peacetime the primary determinant of turns in real personal income is the turns in personal income in current prices; in war and postwar inflation the primary determinant becomes the turns in retail prices. For the evidence on the lag of consumers' prices see Daniel Creamer's *Behavior of Wage Rates during Business Cycles* (National Bureau of Economic Research, Occasional Paper 34, 1950, p. 21, note 14).

expansion, and the difference between the cycle relatives representing the terminal trough and the peak is the amplitude of contraction. In this way the amplitude of the rise and that of the fall are both related to a common base and can therefore be directly compared. The full cycle amplitude is the sum of the amplitudes of expansion and contraction after reversing the sign of the latter.

The amplitude of the personal income cycle (current prices) that includes the Great Depression is about as large as those of the two cycles that include war periods. The upward long-term movement is also clearly shown by these measurements. In every cycle, except the one terminated by the Great Depression, the amplitude of the expansion phase is much larger than the amplitude of the contraction phase. The same thing is true when personal income is expressed in constant prices, the 1917-1921 contraction providing the single exception. As one would expect, the full cycle amplitude is much less in constant prices than in current prices. This is not true, however, phase by phase. Whenever the movement of the BLS Consumers Price Index fails to conform in direction with the movement of personal income—i.e. declines during an expansion, as in 1921-1929, or rises during a contraction, as in 1913-1914 and 1944-1947—the amplitude of the constant-price series exceeds that of the current-price series.

Since the personal income total is an aggregate compounded of many different types of income, originating from a variety of sources, the amplitude and other cyclical characteristics of personal income represent an averaging of the cyclical characteristics of its components. These components must be analyzed if we are to gain some understanding of the cyclical behavior of the total. Hence the rest of the study is devoted to the cyclical analysis of some of the more important components.

CHAPTER 4

CYCLES IN MAJOR TYPES OF INCOME

Timing of Turning Points

As IN our analysis of trends in personal income, we shall distinguish net income of farm operators, farm wages and salaries, nonfarm labor income, property income, and net income of nonfarm proprietors. We shall look first for differences in the timing of turning points. Ordinarily this calls for the use of monthly data, which restricts our time periods to 1929-1950 (Chart 6 and Table 4). In the case of farm income, however, annual data are perhaps to be preferred, since, in many branches of farming, net income cannot be estimated within a tolerable margin of error except on an annual basis. The use of annual data for this type of income makes possible the analysis of a much longer period.

Farm income fluctuates somewhat irregularly, as one would expect of an industry whose fortunes are greatly affected by the vagaries of the weather. For example, between 1933 and 1937 the "dust bowl" drought created an extra cycle in farm income, not paralleled by one in general business. But the corresponding monthly turns in farm income and business cycles in 1929, 1933, and 1937 were virtually synchronous. Thereafter, there were substantial differences in their timing: farm income lagged a year behind the business cycle trough in 1938 and six months behind the trough in 1949; it turned down five months before the peak in 1948; and it failed to contract with general business during the 1945-1946 demobilization.

Since the net income of farm operators dominates the farm income total, it is not surprising that the two have identical turning points. Wages paid to hired farm workers, however, did not trace an extra cycle in the mid-1930's, although they, too, failed to turn downward during the period of military demobilization. The differences in timing at corresponding turns do not appear to be particularly significant.

The extent of the congruent movement in the net income of farm operators and general business may be measured by indexes of conformity. We score +100 for every expansion in general business in which net income of farm operators rises and —100 when it declines. The algebraic sum of these scores divided by the number of expansions covered is the index of conformity to expansions in general business. The index may vary from +100, signifying perfect

CHART 6

Personal Income in Current Prices by Type of Income,
Monthly Data, 1929-1950

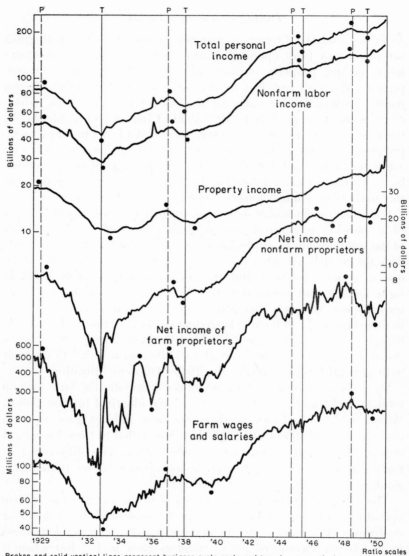

Broken and solid vertical lines represent business cycle peaks and troughs, respectively.
Source: See note to Table 4. All data are seasonally adjusted and, except for the bottom two series,
are at annual rates.

TABLE 4

Lead (−) or Lag (+) of Personal Income and of Its Major Components
at Business Cycle Turning Points, 1929-1949

(*months*)

	P June 1929	T Mar. 1933	P May 1937	T June 1938	P Feb. 1945	T Oct. 1945	P Nov. 1948	T Oct. 1949
Total personal income	+2	0	+1	−1	+4	−1	−1	0
Farm income[a]	+1	−1	+1	+12			−5	+6
Proprietors' net income[a]	+1	−1	+1	+12			−5	+6
Wages and salaries	0	+2	−1	+20			0	+4
Nonfarm labor income	+2	+1	+3	−1	+5	+4	−2	0
Nonfarm proprietors' net income[b]	+4	0	+4	−2			−3	+2
Property income	−2	+7	−1	+7				

[a] A noncorresponding peak occurred in August 1935 and a noncorresponding trough in May 1936.

[b] A noncorresponding peak occurred in August 1946 and a noncorresponding trough in August 1947.

P = peak; T = trough.

Source: Business cycle turns are those in the National Bureau of Economic Research business cycle chronology; personal income turns are based on published and unpublished estimates in current prices of the National Income Division, Department of Commerce.

positive conformity, to −100, signifying perfect inverse conformity. Conformity to contractions in general business is measured similarly, +100 being scored for a decline in the net income of farm operators during a contraction in general business and −100 for a rise. A third index, full cycle conformity, measures the frequency with which the rate of change per month during a contraction in general business is algebraically lower than the rate of change during the preceding and following expansions in general business; +100 means there have been no exceptions.[1]

Our indexes indicate a high degree of cyclical conformity between farm operators' net income and general business during the two decades 1929-1949, with indexes of +100, +50, and +100, respectively, for expansions, contractions, and full cycles in general business. The lapse from perfect conformity to business contractions is due to the failure of farm income to decline in 1945. No doubt this high conformity is the result, at least in part, of the unusually

[1] For a fuller discussion of indexes of conformity see Arthur F. Burns and Wesley C. Mitchell's *Measuring Business Cycles* (National Bureau of Economic Research, 1946, pp. 31-33).

large amplitudes of the business cycle movements of the 1930's and 1940's.

The high conformity evident in recent years is not found in earlier decades. By using estimates on an annual basis we can view farm operators' net income back to 1909, and by reference to a kindred series, gross income of farm operators back to 1869 (Chart 7 and Table 5). Since for overlapping years most of the turning points are identical for both series, and since there is a one-to-one correspondence in the specific cycles of the two series, we have analyzed the longer series, gross farm income.

In all decades from 1870 to 1930 there is evidence that the factors that cause cycles in farm income frequently operate independently of factors that cause cycles in general business. Thus in the middle 1870's there was a cycle in farm income that had no counterpart in general business. In the next decade the business cycle trough of 1888 coincided with a peak in farm income, and similar inversions of turning points occurred in 1891 and 1892. Another sign of independent movement is skipped cycles: between 1896 and 1911, general business traced four cycles and farm income only one. Cycles were skipped also in the early and middle 1920's. Low conformity is indicated by the conformity indexes: +50, +6, and +25, respectively, for expansions, contractions, and full cycles in general business.

Note that the conformity index for farm income is significantly higher in the expansion phase of the business cycle than in the contraction phase. This might be because the influence of business conditions on agricultural income is more apparent in business expansions than in contractions, particularly when annual data are used, since the expansion phases have usually been longer than contractions. The upward trend in farm income over the decades also is conducive to such a result.

While the low conformity indexes indicate a lack of regularity in the relations between cyclical movements in the agricultural sector and in general business, and do not reveal in which direction the relations have run, no doubt there have been occasions when changes in farm income have had a significant influence on the course of business cycles, as well as vice versa. The agricultural sector apparently helped to lift the entire economy out of several depressions in the latter half of the nineteenth century.[2] Crop failures abroad

[2] See, for example, Wesley C. Mitchell's interpretation of the business contractions of 1873-1878, 1890-1891, and 1895-1896 in his *Business Cycles* (Uni-

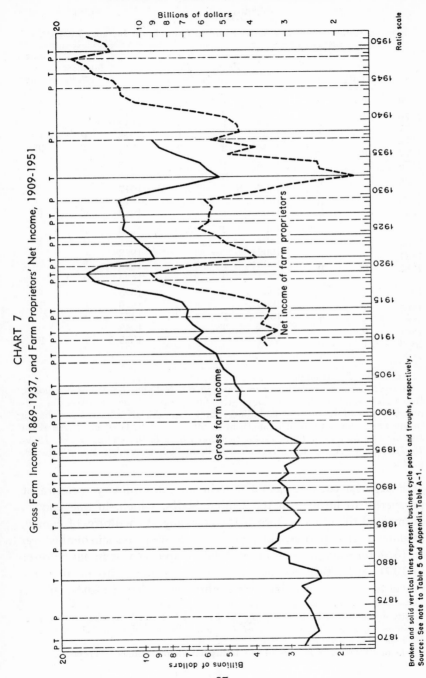

CHART 7

Gross Farm Income, 1869-1937, and Farm Proprietors' Net Income, 1909-1951

Billions of dollars

Ratio scale

Net income of farm proprietors

Gross farm income

Billions of dollars

Broken and solid vertical lines represent business cycle peaks and troughs, respectively.

Source: See note to Table 5 and Appendix Table A-1.

TABLE 5

Turning Points in Business Activity and in Gross Farm Income, 1869-1929

	Business Activity	Gross Farm Income		Business Activity	Gross Farm Income		Business Activity	Gross Farm Income
1869	P		1890	P		1910	P	P
1870	T		1891	T	P	1911	T	T
1871		T	1892	P	T	1912		
1872			1893		P	1913	P	P
1873	P		1894	T	T	1914	T	T
1874			1895	P	P	1915		
1875		P	1896	T	T	1916		
1876		T	1897			1917		
1877		P	1898			1918	P	
1878	T	T	1899	P		1919	T	P
1879			1900	T		1920	P	
1880			1901			1921	T	T
1881			1902			1922		
1882	P	P	1903	P		1923	P	
1883			1904	T		1924	T	
1884			1905			1925		P
1885	T		1906			1926	P	T
1886		T	1907	P		1927	T	
1887	P		1908	T		1928		
1888	T	P	1909			1929	P	P
1889		T						

P = peak; T = trough.

Source: Business cycle turns are those in the National Bureau of Economic Research business cycle chronology; gross farm income turns are based on estimates of gross farm income including "omitted products," adjusted for change in inventory values of meat animals, in F. Strauss and L. H. Bean, *Gross Farm Income and Indices of Farm Production and Prices in the United States, 1869-1937*, Dept. of Agriculture, Technical Bulletin 703, December 1940, Table 8, p. 24.

and large harvests at home brought an extraordinary measure of prosperity to farmers in the United States, which, in due course, permeated the other sectors of the economy. Agriculture, of course, assumes more importance in our economy as we go back in our history. In 1870, for example, half of our total manpower was in agriculture; in 1900, agriculture accounted for only about a third of all manpower and thirty years later for slightly more than a fifth.[3] Agricul-

versity of California Press, 1913, pp. 45, 51, and 60) and *What Happens during Business Cycles: A Progress Report* (National Bureau of Economic Research, 1951, p. 58).

[3] Daniel Carson, "Changes in the Industrial Composition of Manpower since

tural income now accounts for only about one-tenth of total personal income; hence its influence on general business is much less than it was eighty years ago. The high conformity of agricultural income to business cycles in recent decades must largely reflect the influence of business cycles on the demand for farm products.

While farm income follows a more independent course, labor income (nonfarm) mirrors the ebb and flow of general business. The cycles of nonfarm labor income were in one-to-one correspondence with business cycles in the two decades following 1929. Short lags predominated—five out of eight turns—and at the other turns there were one coincidence and two leads not exceeding two months (Table 4).

During the 1930's the net income of nonfarm proprietors lagged four months behind the business cycle at each of the two peaks and either coincided with it or led by two months at the troughs. In the brief postwar period the timing has been reversed: nonfarm proprietors' income led the 1948 peak in general business by three months and lagged two months behind at the next trough.[4] However, one cannot place much confidence in these observations, since the estimates of this type of income are subject to large errors on account of the dearth of data.

Property income between 1929 and 1939 led the business cycle at peaks and lagged at troughs. Equally notable is the fact that since January 1939, property income has expanded continuously, unaffected by the business contraction accompanying the brief period of demobilization. The business contraction of 1948-1949 is reflected only in a slackening of the rate of expansion in property income.

As is true of total personal income, no component systematically leads the turns in business cycles, except possibly property income at peaks. Moreover, the few leads have been short. The more typical relationship is either coincidence or a brief lag.

Amplitude of Cyclical Fluctuations

In this section we shall use as common reference cycles the five cycles in total personal income traced by annual data from 1909 to 1951. We shall measure the amplitude of expansion, of contraction,

the Civil War," *Studies in Income and Wealth, Volume Eleven,* National Bureau of Economic Research, 1949, p. 47.

[4] We should note also a peak in August 1946 and a trough in August 1947, neither of which can be construed as corresponding to business cycle turning points.

and of the full cycle in various types of income during the periods defined by the turning points in total personal income (Chart 8 and Table 6).

CHART 8

Personal Income in Current Prices by Type of Income, Annual Data, 1909-1951

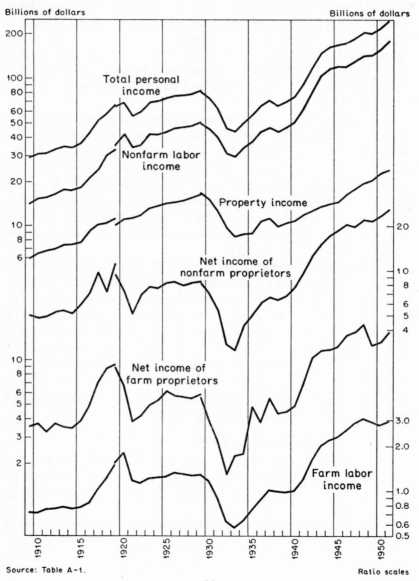

Source: Table A-1.

Ratio scales

Let us first observe, for each major type of income, the average full cycle amplitude (the total movement during expansion and contraction after reversing the sign of the latter) over the five cycles. The largest amplitude occurs in the net income of farm operators:

	All Cycles	Excluding War Cycles
Net income of farm proprietors	101	78
Net income of nonfarm proprietors	80	67
Farm wages and salaries	78	48
Nonfarm wages and salaries	74	55
Property income	55	56
Transfer payments and other labor income	49	2
Total personal income	73	56

When we exclude from the averages the two cycles 1914-1921 and 1938-1948, which include wars, the amplitude of all types except property income is reduced. The reduction is particularly marked in transfer payments and other labor income, because in both war expansions the rise in this type of income exceeded that of all other types, whereas in peacetime its cyclical changes have usually been relatively small.

Of equal significance is the average amplitude of expansion compared with the average amplitude of contraction (Table 6). For each of the three primary types of income the rise was substantially larger than the fall. This was true not only on the average but in every cycle of personal income except the one encompassing the Great Depression. This excess of expansion over contraction is in keeping, of course, with the rising secular trend in personal income. Table 6 also shows that nonfarm labor income had the largest average net rise (algebraic sum of the amplitudes of expansion and contraction) over the period, exceeding the net rise in property income (the next largest) in four of the five cycles.

Finally, we must note the continuous expansion in transfer payments and other labor income. In each of the five contractions in personal income these supplementary payments continued to rise. The largest increases occurred during the expansions that included war and a postwar transition. In 1921-1938 these payments moved countercyclically in the sense that they rose at a more rapid rate during the contractions than during the expansions; during this period they were dominated by relief payments.

TABLE 6

Amplitude of Personal Income and of Its Major Components during Five Cycles in Personal Income, 1909-1949

(based on cycle relatives)

| PERSONAL INCOME CYCLE | | TOTAL PERSONAL INCOME | LABOR INCOME | | | PROPRIETORS' NET INCOME | | PROPERTY INCOME |
| Phase | Period | | Wages and Salaries | | Other Labor Income and Transfer Payments | | | |
			Farm	Nonfarm		Farm	Nonfarm	
Expansion	1909-1913	+16.7	+8.2	+22.2	+21.6	−.7	+7.3	+20.9
Contraction	1913-1914	−1.8	−3.0	−1.7	+1.1	−1.5	−5.1	+.3
Full cycle		+18.5	+11.2	+23.9	+20.5	+.8	+12.4	+20.6
Net change over cycle		+14.9	+5.2	+20.5	+22.7	−2.2	+2.2	+21.2
Expansion	1914-1920	+67.2	+86.7	+78.6	+118.8	+56.6	+45.0	+48.0
Contraction	1920-1921	−25.5	−53.2	−26.7	+9.6	−48.3	−33.0	+1.7
Full cycle		+92.7	+139.9	+105.3	+109.2	+104.9	+78.0	+46.3
Net change over cycle		+41.7	+33.5	+51.9	+128.4	+8.3	+12.0	+49.7
Expansion	1921-1929	+40.2	+11.0	+39.7	+12.4	+45.0	+48.5	+40.6
Contraction	1929-1933	−56.2	−61.5	−51.3	+26.7	−76.0	−70.8	−61.9
Full cycle		+96.4	+72.5	+91.0	−14.3	+121.0	+119.3	+102.5
Net change over cycle		−16.0	−50.5	−11.6	+39.1	−31.0	−22.3	−21.3
Expansion	1933-1937	+45.3	+54.9	+43.2	+21.8	+82.9	+59.5	+29.6
Contraction	1937-1938	−9.1	−4.0	−8.2	+22.4	−29.7	−9.8	−14.6
Full cycle		+54.4	+58.9	+51.4	−.6	+112.6	+69.3	+44.2
Net change over cycle		+36.2	+50.9	+35.0	+44.2	+53.2	+49.7	+15.0

32

TABLE 6 (continued)

(based on cycle relatives)

PERSONAL INCOME CYCLE		TOTAL PERSONAL INCOME	LABOR INCOME			PROPRIETORS' NET INCOME		PROPERTY INCOME
Phase	Period		Wages and Salaries		Other Labor Income and Transfer Payments			
			Farm	Nonfarm		Farm	Nonfarm	
Expansion	1938-1948	+99.6	+103.0	+97.0	+150.3	+121.7	+106.6	+68.4
Contraction	1948-1949	-2.8	-5.6	-.9	+18.1	-42.6	-14.4	+5.7
Full cycle		+102.4	+108.6	+97.9	+132.2	+164.3	+121.0	+62.7
Net change over cycle		+96.8	+97.4	+96.1	+168.4	+79.1	+92.2	+74.1
Average, all cycles								
Expansion		+53.8	+52.8	+56.1	+65.0	+61.1	+53.4	+41.5
Contraction		-19.1	-25.5	-17.8	+15.6	-39.6	-26.6	-13.8
Full cycle		+72.9	+78.3	+73.9	+49.4	+100.7	+80.0	+55.3
Net change over cycle		+34.7	+27.3	+38.3	+80.6	+21.5	+26.8	+27.7
Average excluding war cycles, 1914-1921 and 1938-1949								
Expansion		+34.1	+24.7	+35.0	+18.6	+42.4	+38.4	+30.4
Contraction		-22.4	-22.8	-20.4	+16.7	-35.7	-28.6	-25.4
Full cycle		+56.5	+47.5	+55.4	+1.9	+78.1	+67.0	+55.8
Net change over cycle		+11.7	+1.9	+14.6	+35.3	+6.7	+9.8	+5.0

Source: Based on Table A-1. The reference cycles are cycles in personal income in current prices.

33

CHAPTER 5

CYCLES IN TYPES OF NONFARM LABOR INCOME

THE importance of labor as a source of personal income—in recent decades it formed about two-thirds of the total—suggests that we cannot be content simply with analyzing the aggregate of nonfarm labor income. By analyzing its components we can see the dispersion about the average, and the pattern of dispersion may provide more illuminating insights.

Timing of Turns in Labor Income by Industrial Source before World War II

Total labor income was defined above as the sum of wages, salaries, their supplements, and transfer payments, excluding those paid by business, minus employee contributions for social insurance. However, in dealing with individual industries or industry groups, we must use figures on wages and salaries alone, since supplements and transfer payments are not available by industrial source. The monthly record of wages and salaries begins with 1929. Following the Department of Commerce in its published estimates, with minor adjustments, we distinguish four broad groups of industries. The percentages of wages and salaries paid to each during the 1929-1937 period are as follows:

Commodity-producing industries excluding agriculture (mining, manufacturing, and construction)   37 per cent
Distributive industries (transportation, public utilities, and trade)   31 per cent
Service industries (finance, insurance, real estate, and other services)[1]   17 per cent
Government, including work relief   16 per cent

PRIVATE SECTOR—WAGES AND SALARIES

Labor income in each of the three private-industry groups in the prewar decade conforms to the cycles in general business. Differences in turning points, however, appear. In the commodity-producing industries, for example, the turns coincide with the turns

---

[1] The monthly and even the annual estimates of payrolls in most of the service trades between 1929 and 1939 are not well grounded in statistical materials, especially in the noncensus years.

34

in general business, while brief lags characterize the distributive industries, and still longer lags are found in the service industries (Chart 9 and Table 7).

While it is hazardous to base a conclusion on four observations, these differences among the three industry groups seem to be valid ones; in any case they accord with expectations. The differences may be traced in part to fluctuations in man-hours worked, since there is good reason to believe that wage rates in all industry groups typically lag behind turns in man-hours.[2] In many of the distributive and service trades the number employed is conditioned by the need to meet daily or weekly peak demands. Aggregate demand or activity may change moderately and yet peak demands may not be affected enough to justify altering the working force. This situation is much less common in commodity-producing industries. This factor, moreover, would be operative at both peaks and troughs. It would tend to create lags in employment and man-hours, and therefore in payrolls, since wage rates also lag.

At peaks, differences in the economic character of the output of these three groups also contribute to the differences in the observed lags. It is well known that consumers are reluctant to alter their standard of living immediately upon suffering a reduction of income.[3] Therefore, industries that deal directly with final consumers are likely to react more slowly to downturns in general business than industries that deal directly with other enterprises and only indirectly with consumers. The service industries largely receive their income directly from the final consumer; this is less true of the distributive industries, and still less true of the commodity-producing industries. Hence at peaks we should expect labor income to show a longer lag in service than in distributive industries, and in distributive than in commodity-producing industries. However, the statistical findings, based on two turning points between 1929 and World War II, confirm only one of our expectations, namely, that wage and salary disbursements of the service industries lag behind the commodity-producing industries.

Labor income originating in the commodity-producing industries

[2] This was shown to be the case in manufacturing and rail transportation in Daniel Creamer's *Behavior of Wage Rates during Business Cycles* (National Bureau of Economic Research, Occasional Paper 34, 1950).

[3] See the argument to this effect by Franco Modigliani in his "Fluctuations in the Saving-Income Ratio: A Problem in Economic Forecasting," in *Studies in Income and Wealth, Volume Eleven* (National Bureau of Economic Research, 1949, pp. 384-388).

CHART 9

Nonfarm Labor Income by Major Industry Group, 1929-1951

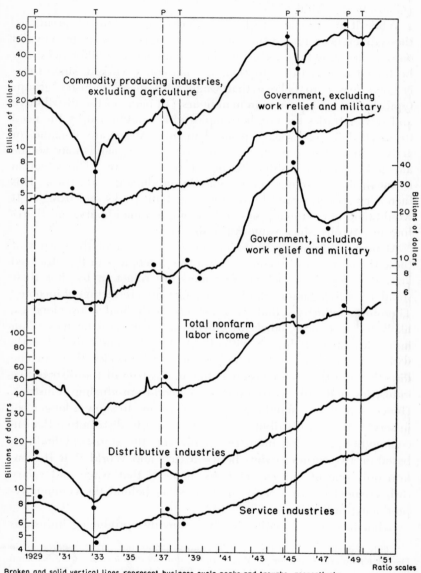

Broken and solid vertical lines represent business cycle peaks and troughs, respectively.
Source: See note to Table 7. All data are seasonally adjusted annual rates.

TABLE 7

Lead (−) or Lag (+) of Total Nonfarm Labor Income and of Wage and Salary Disbursements by Major Industry Group at Business Cycle Turning Points, 1929-1949

(*months*)

	P June 1929	T Mar. 1933	P May 1937	T June 1938	P Feb. 1945	T Oct. 1945	P Nov. 1948	T Oct. 1949
Total nonfarm labor income	+2	+1	+3	−1	+5	+4	−2	0
Nonfarm wage and salary disbursements								
Nonagricultural commodity-producing industries	+3	0	0	0	0	0	−2	0
Distributive industries	+2	0	+5	+2				
Service industries	+5	+2	+5	+4				
Government								
Including work relief and military[a]	+30	−3	−6	−7	+5	+23		
Excluding work relief and military	+28	+6			+5	+3		

[a] A noncorresponding cycle occurred between 1937 and 1939 due to the inclusion of work relief. The work-relief programs, started in 1930 and ended in 1942, produced an inverted response in government payrolls in the 1937-1938 contraction.

P = peak; T = trough.

Source: Business cycle turns are those in the National Bureau of Economic Research business cycle chronology; turns in nonfarm labor income and in disbursements are based on published and unpublished estimates of the National Income Division, Department of Commerce.

(excluding agriculture) has turned at virtually the same time as general business, while labor income in the other groups has typically lagged. It therefore seems worthwhile to examine the main component of this type of income, namely, labor income in manufacturing industries, which accounted for about four-fifths of all labor income in nonfarm commodity-producing industries and for nearly one-fifth of all personal income in 1929-1937.

The monthly record for our purposes begins with 1918 and covers wages of production workers (Chart 10 and Table 8), not wages and salaries. During the subsequent two decades there were twelve turning points in general business. Factory payrolls had turning points corresponding with each of these. At five of the twelve turning points there was strict coincidence and at the others lags up to five months, but only at four turns did the lag exceed two months. Thus the typical timing pattern for factory payrolls is coincidence

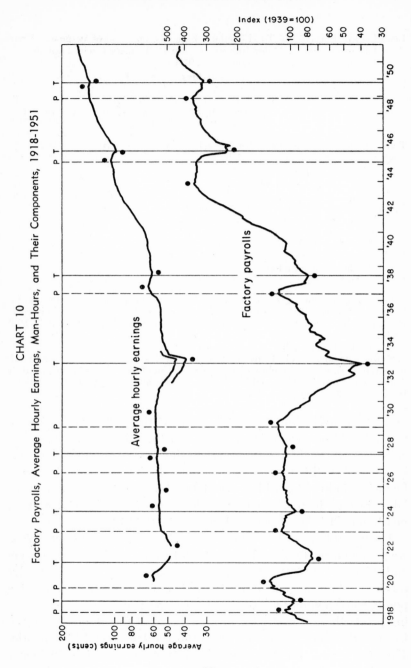

CHART 10

Factory Payrolls, Average Hourly Earnings, Man-Hours, and Their Components, 1918-1951

Index (1939=100)

Factory payrolls

Average hourly earnings

Average hourly earnings (cents)

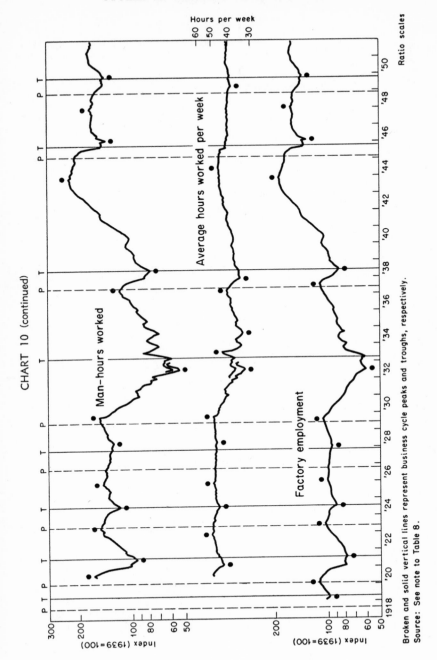

CHART 10 (continued)

Hours per week

Man-hours worked

Average hours worked per week

Factory employment

Index (1939=100)

Index (1939=100)

Ratio scales

Broken and solid vertical lines represent business cycle peaks and troughs, respectively.

Source: See note to Table 8.

39

TABLE 8

Lead (−) or Lag (+) of Factory Payrolls, Average Hourly Earnings, and Man-Hours, and of Their Components, at Business Cycle Turning Points, 1919-1949

(*months*)

Business Cycle Turn	Factory Payrolls (1)	Average Hourly Earnings (2)	Man-Hours (3)	Number Employed (4)	Average Hours Worked per Week[a] (5)
P Aug. 1918	+2				
T Apr. 1919	+1				
P Jan. 1920	+5				
T July 1921	+3	+12	−1	0	−5
P May 1923	+1	+18	−1	+1	−6
T July 1924	0	+14	0	0	0
P Oct. 1926	0	+10	−11	−9	−11
T Nov. 1927	+5	+3	+5	+2	+5
P June 1929	+3	+10	+4	+2	+4
T Mar. 1933	0	+3	−8	−8	−7
P May 1937	0	+5	−1	+2	−2
T June 1938	0	+2	0	0	−6
P Feb. 1945	−15	+1	−15	−15	−8
T Oct. 1945	+4	−1	+4	+4	
P Nov. 1948	0	+8	−11	−10	
T Oct. 1949	+1	+1	+1	+1	
Average					
Aug. 1918–June 1938					
P	+1.8				
T	+1.5				
July 1921–June 1938					
P	+1.0	+10.8	−2.2	−1.0	−3.8
T	+1.6	+6.8	−.8	−1.2	−2.6
July 1921–Oct. 1949					
P	−1.8	+8.7	−5.8	−4.8	
T	+1.9	+4.9	+.1	−.1	

[a] A noncorresponding peak occurred in July 1933 and a noncorresponding trough in September 1934.

P = peak; T = trough.

Source: Business cycle turns are those in the National Bureau of Economic Research business cycle chronology. Data for all series except factory payrolls and employment begin in 1920, but the first full cycle begins in 1921. Columns 1 and 4—Bureau of Labor Statistics; columns 2 and 5—National Industrial Conference Board for 1920-1933, BLS from 1932; column 3—NICB for 1920-1933, from 1932 derived by multiplying average hours worked per week by number employed.

with, or brief lags behind, turns in general business[4]—on the average a lag of 1.5 months at the troughs and 1.8 at the peaks. It is significant that there was not a single instance where turns in aggregate factory payrolls led turns in general business during the two decades before World War II.

It is possible to show how this average timing pattern for factory payrolls results from the timing patterns of labor input and unit labor returns. Here also the analysis is restricted to the years between the two World Wars. Labor input is measured by man-hours worked (number employed multiplied by average hours worked per week) and unit labor returns by average hourly earnings. Unit labor returns lag consistently and by a number of months behind turns in business activity—a half year at the troughs and more than ten months at the peaks, on the average.[5] Labor input (man-hours), however, typically coincides with or briefly leads the turns in business activity. Thus wage income turns up or down with, or shortly behind, business activity because the prompt changes in labor input just about offset the lagging changes in unit labor returns.

The timing pattern of labor input can be explained by examining the turns in its two constituent elements—number employed and average hours worked per week. The latter typically lead at both troughs and peaks, while the number employed tends to coincide with business activity at upturns and to lag a few months at downturns. As the low point is approached, part-time employment is reduced before larger numbers are employed; and overtime work is curtailed before the peak is reached and before wage earners are laid off.

PRIVATE SECTOR—SALARY DISBURSEMENTS

Wages disbursed to production workers obviously are not the whole of labor income in manufacturing. The salaries of nonproduction workers also must be taken into account. According to census surveys of 1929 and 1939, these have formed about a fourth of total labor income in manufacturing; they have amounted to about a third of factory wages.

Salaried personnel in manufacturing enterprises perform functions that are best described as overhead operations. Hence, the number

[4] Two of the longer lags are associated with the rapid and substantial changes in wage rates in 1919-1921, which tend to reverse direction only after a considerable lag, and another with the unusually mild business contraction in 1926-1927.

[5] For a fuller discussion see Creamer, *op. cit.*

so employed may be expected not to vary with minor changes in production. Moreover, fluctuations in the employment of salaried personnel, when they do occur, may be expected to lag behind corresponding movements in production or factory employment, and to have a smaller amplitude. The available data, though fragmentary, support these expectations, but perhaps not in the degree expected.

To our knowledge there are only three statistical fragments on a monthly basis pertaining to the interwar decades. The longest statistical record relates to the number of salaried personnel (bookkeepers, stenographers, office clerks, and salespeople, excluding traveling salesmen) employed in Ohio manufacturing industries. This source, however, does not provide information on salary payments. Only for Wisconsin manufacturing industries do we have monthly series on salaried and wage-earner employment and payrolls. These cover a shorter period than the Ohio series and are less well grounded. Moreover, the series for Wisconsin salaried personnel have several gaps, one of which occurs at months critical for establishing a turning point. Nonetheless, these data serve to point up the essential differences in the cyclical pattern of wages and salaries.

Employment of factory wage earners and salaried personnel in Ohio manufacturing industries, 1919-1939, and United States factory employment, 1919-1939, are plotted in Chart 11. The similarity of the cyclical movements of factory employment in Ohio and in the United States, as measured by turning points and by amplitude, suggests that the cyclical movements in Ohio salaried personnel are a reasonably good approximation to the cyclical movements of salaried employees in all United States manufacturing for 1919-1939.

These series support the proposition that mild fluctuations in the employment of wage earners do not have a counterpart in the employment of salaried workers. Thus the moderate decline in 1923-1924 and the still more moderate recession of 1926-1927 in wage-earner employment do not appear in the curve for salaried personnel except as a slowing in the rate of growth.[6] On the other hand, the pronounced turns in 1920, 1921, 1929, 1933, 1937, and 1938 are clearly marked in the employment of salaried workers. While wage-earner employment went through five cycles in the three decades,

[6] There is some evidence of an absolute contraction between June 1927 and January 1928. The decline is so slight, however, that it does not qualify as a specific cycle according to National Bureau criteria.

CHART 11

United States Factory Employment and Wage Earners and
Salaried Personnel Employed in Ohio Manufacturing Industries,
1919-1939

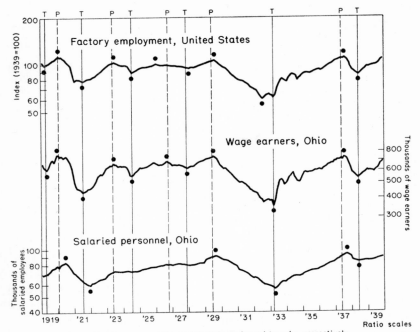

Broken and solid vertical lines represent business cycle peaks and troughs, respectively.
Source: Ohio data from Appendix Table C-1; index of United States factory employment
published by Bureau of Labor Statistics.

employment of salaried workers traced only two complete cycles
and the contraction phase of a third.

With rare exceptions, the turning points in Ohio wage-earner
employment coincide, either precisely or roughly, with the turning
points in general business. Employment of salaried personnel tends
to lag behind wage-earner employment at the turns, and thus behind
general business (Table 9). But in Ohio this lag was substantial at
only two of the six corresponding turning points from 1919 to 1938;
at the four remaining turns there was one coincidence and three
lags not exceeding two months.

These findings are supported by the data on employment in Wisconsin manufacturing industries. The mild contractions in factory
employment of wage earners in the mid-1920's, for example, appear
in the employment of salaried workers as a slowing up in the rate

TABLE 9

Lead (−) of Salaried Personnel over, or Lag (+) behind, Wage Earners at
Turning Points in Employment (Ohio and Wisconsin) and in
Payrolls (Wisconsin), Manufacturing Industries, 1920-1938

(*months*)

| | CORRESPONDING BUSINESS CYCLE TURN | EMPLOYMENT | | PAYROLLS |
		Ohio	*Wisconsin*	*Wisconsin*
P	Jan. 1920	+6	a	a
T	July 1921	+5	a	a
P	May 1923			
T	July 1924			
P	Oct. 1926		+22	
T	Nov. 1927		+2	
P	June 1929	+1	+7	+11
T	Mar. 1933	+1	0	+1
P	May 1937	+2	a	a
T	June 1938	0	a	a

a No data available for salaried employment and payrolls for these years.
P = peak; T = trough.
Source: Business cycle turns are those in the National Bureau of Economic
Research business cycle chronology; other turns are based on data in Tables C-1
and C-2.

of growth (Chart 12). Moreover, at the corresponding turning
points, of which there were only four, employment of salaried
workers lagged behind the employment of wage earners at three
and coincided at the fourth. The two long lags occurred at the two
peaks, while at the two troughs there was no lag at all or a short one.

Can these findings on employment be translated into the cyclical
movements of salary payments? If salary scales were unaltered
during a business cycle, and if we make the further assumption that
part-time or overtime employment is a negligible consideration for
this group, then total salary payments would obviously have the
same configuration as employment of salaried workers. It follows
that the turning points in salary disbursements would also lag
behind the reversals in general business. However, a more realistic
assumption would be that salary scales probably do change during
business cycles of at least moderate amplitude and duration, and
that the lag in the reversals of salary rates has probably been at least
as long as the lag in the reversals of wage rates, which we know is
substantial.[7] Even this assumption makes it likely that salary payments lag behind wage payments at cyclical turning points.

[7] See Creamer, *op. cit.*

44

The Wisconsin monthly index of salary payments supports this expectation (Chart 12). During the mild business recession of 1926-1927 there was no recession in the payrolls of salaried employees, despite a slight recession in their employment. The turning points

CHART 12

Employment and Payrolls of Wage Earners and Salaried Personnel, Wisconsin Manufacturing Industries, 1920-1936

Broken and solid vertical lines represent business cycle peaks and troughs, respectively.
Source: Appendix Table C-2.

in employment of and total payments to salaried personnel were identical at the single corresponding peak in the two series and virtually so at the single corresponding trough. However, total salaries lagged behind factory wages by eleven months at the 1929 peak and by one month at the end of the Great Depression.

GOVERNMENT SECTOR

Labor income originating in government followed a cyclical course during the 1930's different from that of labor income originating in the private sector. The onset of the Great Depression had no immediate effect on government payrolls; indeed, carried forward by the secular growth in governmental functions, they continued to increase for another thirty months.[8] However, as the depression deepened, the tax base also contracted and the resulting financial stringency caused temporary reductions in salary scales and minor curtailment in the number employed. As severe depression continued, another factor appeared: relief of the unemployed by work programs. The wages disbursed under these programs are included in government payrolls, and the cyclical variations in this segment of government labor income are reflected in total government payrolls (Chart 9 and Table 7). Work-relief wages also explain the fact that turns in government payrolls led the three turning points in general business activity after the initial long lag. Work-relief wages, like unemployment, trace an inverted cycle, but the turns lag behind those in general business because of administrative delays. As the business contraction deepened, a work-relief program was instituted which boosted government payrolls just before the upturn in general business. Late in 1936, when expansion was well advanced, the work-relief program was curtailed, causing the government payroll to turn down before the 1937 downturn in general business.

This was the sequence during the 1933-1937 expansion and the subsequent contraction: The peak in work-relief wages was reached in September 1936, eight months before the peak in business activity, and work-relief wages did not begin to rise again until December 1937, seven months after the business contraction started and six months before it ended. That is, inverted turns that lag appear as positive turns that lead. In a period of full employment, work-relief programs would not be in operation and government payrolls would probably turn down later than general business.

If we exclude work-relief wage disbursements from the government total, we find that government labor income lagged more than two years behind the 1929 peak and six months behind the 1933 trough. For the rest of the decade, government labor income increased more or less continually.

[8] For an extended account of this growth see Solomon Fabricant's *The Trend of Government Activity in the United States since 1900* (National Bureau of Economic Research, 1952).

Amplitude of Wage and Salary Cycles in Private Sector before World War II

Some of the reasons adduced to explain the differences in the timing of turning points in labor income according to industrial source also help to explain differences in amplitude. For example, one would expect the industries most directly dependent on final consumers to show the least severe fluctuations during a given cyclical phase. The amplitude measurements in Table 10 conform

TABLE 10

Amplitude of Specific Cycles in Personal and Nonfarm Labor Income and in Wage and Salary Disbursements by Major Industry Group, 1929-1938

(based on cycle relatives)

BUSINESS CYCLE		PERSONAL	NONFARM LABOR	WAGE AND SALARY DISBURSEMENTS		
Phase	*Period*	INCOME	INCOME	*Commodity-Producing*[a]	*Distributive*	*Service*
Contraction	June 1929– Mar. 1933	−69.9	−57.7	−98.2	−63.4	−51.9
Expansion	Mar. 1933– May 1937	+53.2	+49.2	+79.2	+44.9	+33.5
Contraction	May 1937– June 1938	−14.6	−11.3	−35.4	−8.6	−5.0

[a] Excluding agriculture.

Source: Business cycle phases are those in the National Bureau of Economic Research business cycle chronology; amplitudes are estimated from published and unpublished data of the National Income Division, Department of Commerce.

to this expectation: in the expansion and the contractions the smallest amplitudes are found in the service industries and the largest in the commodity-producing group. The differences, moreover, are substantial.

Fluctuations in factory payrolls, much the most important component of wages of the commodity-producing industries, have been traced in greater detail. We can measure, for example, the cyclical amplitudes in labor input (man-hours) and in unit labor returns (average hourly earnings). Since the product of the two equals payrolls of production workers, we can determine the relative importance of each in accounting for fluctuations in labor income in manufacturing industries.

In Chart 10 (see above) and Table 11 we compare the amplitudes of man-hours, average hourly earnings, and factory payrolls during the course of four business cycles from 1921 to 1938. Man-hours worked show deeper swings than the other components of the wage bill, and these differences were substantial during business cycle expansions and even more pronounced during contractions. The differences occurred not only on the average but in each phase.

TABLE 11

Amplitude of Factory Payrolls, Average Hourly Earnings, and Man-Hours, and of Their Components, during Business Cycles, 1921-1949

(*based on cycle relatives*)

		FACTORY PAYROLLS	AVERAGE HOURLY EARNINGS	MAN-HOURS	NUMBER EMPLOYED	AVERAGE HOURS WORKED PER WEEK
BUSINESS CYCLE						
Phase	Period	(1)	(2)	(3)	(4)	(5)
Expansion	July 1921–May 1923	+36.0	+8.0	+31.1	+24.9	+6.5
Contraction	May 1923–July 1924	−17.2	+3.5	−21.8	−13.5	−8.2
Full cycle		+53.2	+4.5	+52.9	+38.4	+14.7
Expansion	July 1924–Oct. 1926	+15.2	+2.1	+14.5	+9.3	+5.5
Contraction	Oct. 1926–Nov. 1927	−3.8	+.6	−6.1	−4.3	−1.8
Full cycle		+19.0	+1.5	+20.6	+13.6	+7.3
Expansion	Nov. 1927–June 1929	+12.7	+2.5	+15.5	+11.1	+2.6
Contraction	June 1929–Mar. 1933	−88.4	−23.1	−82.4	−49.8	−35.4
Full cycle		+101.1	+25.6	+97.9	+60.9	+38.0
Expansion	Mar. 1933–May 1937	+92.7	+39.1	+59.4	+51.4	+18.8
Contraction	May 1937–June 1938	−47.1	−.1	−41.5	−25.7	−20.3
Full cycle		+139.8	+39.2	+100.9	+77.1	+39.1
Expansion	June 1938–Feb. 1945	+123.3	+51.7	+83.5	+61.6	+25.7
Contraction	Feb. 1945–Oct. 1945	−53.5	−7.6	−40.3	−28.6	−9.4
Full cycle		+176.8	+59.3	+123.8	+90.2	+35.1
Expansion	Oct. 1945–Nov. 1948	+40.2	+31.3	+9.5	+13.2	−4.0
Contraction	Nov. 1948–Oct. 1949	−12.7	+.2	−11.4	−10.7	−.8
Full cycle		+52.9	+31.1	+20.9	+23.9	−3.2
Average July 1921–June 1938						
Expansion		+39.2	+12.9	+30.1	+24.2	+8.4
Contraction		−39.1	−4.8	−38.0	−23.3	−16.4
Full cycle		+78.3	+17.7	+68.1	+47.5	+24.8
June 1938–Oct. 1949						
Expansion		+81.8	+41.5	+46.5	+37.4	+10.8
Contraction		−33.1	−3.7	−25.8	−19.6	−5.1
Full cycle		+114.9	+45.2	+72.3	+57.0	+15.9

Source: Business cycle phases are those in the National Bureau of Economic Research business cycle chronology. Data for all series except factory payrolls and employment begin in 1920, but the first full cycle begins in 1921. Columns 1 and 4—Bureau of Labor Statistics; columns and 5—National Industrial Conference Board for 1920-1933, BLS from 1932; column 3—derived by multiplying the cycle relatives of average hours worked per week by those of number employed.

Labor input, or man-hours worked, is a product of the number employed and the average number of hours worked per week. Here again we can see which of the two is the more important determinant. It is clear that the number employed fluctuates much more widely than the average hours worked per week, both on the average during upswings and downswings and during each phase of these four business cycles. Thus we find that the most important single cause of cycles in labor income, in manufacturing industries at least, has been cycles in employment. In business cycle expansions, changes in hourly earnings have on the average been more important than changes in hours worked per week; during contractions the relative importance of these two factors has been reversed.

Our presumption (see pages 41-42) that the cyclical fluctuations of salaried employment would be less than those of wage-earner employment finds support in the Ohio data (Table 12). There are four corresponding phases in the employment of production and of non-production workers, three contractions and one expansion. In the contractions the average amplitude of the declines was —48.4 for wage earners and —29.3 for salaried personnel. In the one expansion the amplitude of the rise was +59.9 for wage earners and +48.4

TABLE 12

Amplitude of Specific Cycles in Employment of Wage Earners and of Salaried Personnel, Ohio Manufacturing Industries, 1919-1938
(*based on cycle relatives*)

Phase	CORRESPONDING BUSINESS CYCLE Period	WAGE EARNERS	SALARIED PERSONNEL[a]
Expansion	Apr. 1919–Jan. 1920	+20.5	[b]
Contraction	Jan. 1920–July 1921	—48.6	—30.0
Expansion	July 1921–May 1923	+37.8	
Contraction	May 1923–July 1924	—17.0	
Expansion	July 1924–Oct. 1926	+18.6	
Contraction	Oct. 1926–Nov. 1927	—8.9	
Expansion	Nov. 1927–June 1929	+19.6	
Contraction	June 1929–Mar. 1933	—65.0	—46.1
Expansion	Mar. 1933–May 1937	+59.9	+48.4
Contraction	May 1937–June 1938	—31.7	—11.9

[a] There was a continuous expansion in employment of salaried personnel from December 1921 to August 1929.

[b] Data insufficient for measuring amplitude of this phase.

Source: Business cycle phases are those in the National Bureau of Economic Research business cycle chronology; amplitudes are estimated from data in Appendix C.

for salaried personnel. Much the same amplitude differences appear in the Wisconsin data, as far as they go. In terms of man-hours the differences would be even more striking. Since wage earners may be retained on a workweek varying from part-time to overtime, man-hours worked fluctuate more sharply than number employed. For salaried personnel, on the other hand, deviations from the standard workweek are exceptional, which means that there would be little difference between the fluctuations of hours worked and those of number employed. Thus salary payments, compared with factory payrolls, would show smaller amplitudes over the cycle, even if the fluctuation in salary rates were as large as that in wage rates, which is probably not the case.

Salary payments fluctuate more sharply than employment of salaried personnel, to judge by the Wisconsin data. A comparison is possible for only one phase, the Great Depression, when employment declined 32 per cent from peak to trough and salary payments 51 per cent. This was caused by cyclical changes in basic salary rates and probably also by the shifting importance of subgroups of industries. The Wisconsin data suggest also a wide disparity in amplitude between salary payments and wage payments. At the 1933 trough, salary payments had declined by 51 per cent from the preceding peak while wage payments had declined by 72 per cent. The difference in the relative recoveries by January 1936, when our index of salaries ends, is even larger than the differences in the relative declines of the Great Depression.

Aggregate salary disbursements may well be too broad a category, for among salaried personnel there are much wider differences in the terms of employment and compensation than among factory wage earners. The difference between what a clerk and a highly paid executive earn annually is many times greater than the difference between the annual earnings of a common laborer and a skilled mechanic. It is desirable therefore to analyze the salaries of executives separately. Some annual data for the executive group can be brought to bear by assuming that the movements in salary payments to corporate officers are representative of the fluctuations in salary receipts of all senior executives and professional personnel.

Statistics of Income gives the annual compensation of corporate officers in manufacturing industries for all years from 1919 to 1938, except 1925-1927, when this item was not reported separately. This series has been compared with salaries, other than those of corporate officers, in manufacturing and with the Bureau of Labor Statistics index of wage payments to factory workers (Chart 13 and Table 13). These annual data on salaries and wages confirm our findings based on monthly data for Ohio and Wisconsin. Salary payments, unlike wage payments, did not trace the mild cycles of the middle 1920's, and salary payments, whether expanding or contracting, usually fluctuated much less than wage payments. When we look only at salaried personnel, however, we find that from 1920 to 1937 the earnings of corporate officers, and therefore of senior executives and professional personnel, typically fluctuated considerably less than the earnings of other salaried employees. But from 1937 to 1938 the earnings of corporate officers contracted more than those of other salaried employees.

Frequently a substantial fraction of a corporate officer's compensation takes the form of a bonus that varies with profits or sales, and in family-owned corporations profits are often distributed in the form of salaries to officers. Since profits fluctuate more sharply than general salaries during cycles in business activity, we might expect the *per capita* annual compensation of corporate officers to trace, on the average, larger cyclical amplitudes than do *per capita* annual salaries of other salaried employees. There are, however, no statistics with which to test this inference. The smaller amplitudes noted in *total* compensation of corporate officers compared with *total* salaries of other salaried employees are probably due to the steadier employment of the former. On this latter point John C. Baker reached the same conclusion in his analysis of sample corporations: "After a study of what happened to executive employment and aggregate compensation among a group of 100 industrial companies from 1928 to 1932, the following points stand out clearly: (a) an amazing steadiness in the employment of executives; (b) an equally amazing steadiness in their salary; . . . (d) wide fluctuation in bonus payments. . . ."[9]

Labor Income during and after World War II

Nonfarm labor income during the 1930's, as we have noted, conformed perfectly to cycles in general business, and this was true also

[9] John C. Baker, *Executive Salaries and Bonus Plans*, McGraw-Hill, 1938, p. 27. Mr. Baker reports the following figures (in thousands) for all executives in the 100 industrial companies (p. 20):

	1928	1929	1930	1931	1932
Salaries	$22,650	$24,495	$25,837	$24,598	$22,102
Bonuses	13,313	17,815	14,639	7,325	3,124
Total compensation	35,963	42,310	40,476	31,923	25,225

CHART 13

Factory Payrolls, and Salaries of Corporate Officers and of
Other Salaried Personnel, Manufacturing Industries,
1919-1950

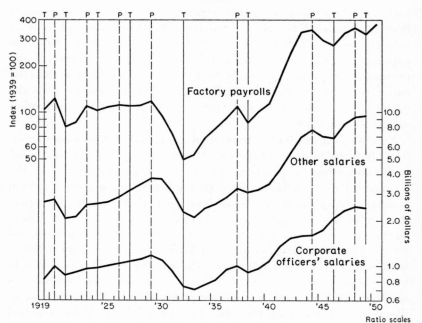

Broken and solid vertical lines represent business cycle peaks and troughs, respectively.
Source: See note to Table 13.

of labor income in each of the major industrial groupings in the
private sector of the economy. During and after World War II the
components of nonfarm labor income did not conform perfectly to
cycles in general business. With the two business cycles between
1938 and 1949 can be matched two cycles in total nonfarm labor
income and two in wage and salary disbursements by nonfarm commodity-producing industries. There have been, however, no cycles—
indeed, not a single cyclical turning point—since 1938 in wage and
salary disbursements by the distributive and service industries
(Chart 9 and Table 7).

In the 1940's the turning points in total nonfarm labor income
continued to coincide roughly with, or lag slightly behind, the
corresponding turns in business cycles. In nonfarm commodity-
producing industries the turns in labor income coincided perfectly
or roughly, as in the prewar decade. Cycles in factory wages again

TABLE 13

Amplitude of Compensation of Corporate Officers, of Other Salaried
Personnel, and of Factory Workers, Manufacturing Industries,
during Personal Income Cycles, 1920-1938
(*based on cycle relatives*)

PERSONAL INCOME CYCLE		CORPORATE OFFICERS	OTHER SALARIED PERSONNEL	FACTORY WORKERS
Phase	Period			
Contraction[a]	1920-1921	−11.8	−23.6	−42.4
Expansion	1921-1929	+29.8	+60.4	+39.0
Contraction	1929-1933	−47.4	−59.8	−67.8
Expansion	1933-1937	+34.4	+42.1	+67.1
Contraction	1937-1938	−10.6	−6.2	−29.1

[a] Computed on base of inverted cycle in personal income, 1920-1921-1929.
Source: Phases of personal income in current prices are based on data in
Table A-1. Compensation of corporate officers is reported in *Statistics of Income*
(Bureau of Internal Revenue) except for 1925-1927; a straight-line interpolation was used to obtain estimates for these missing years. Compensation of other
salaried personnel was derived by subtracting compensation of corporate officers
from compensation of all salaried personnel. Estimates of the latter for 1919-
1929 are from Simon Kuznets, *National Income and Its Composition, 1919-1938*
(National Bureau of Economic Research, 1941, Table M-7, p. 582); for all
other years from unpublished estimates of the National Income Division,
Department of Commerce. The Bureau of Labor Statistics index of factory payrolls was used for compensation of factory workers.

paralleled those in labor income in the nonfarm commodity-producing group, except in the case of the long lead before the wartime
peak (Table 8).

The cyclical movements of salaried income during these years are
based on data for all United States manufacturing industries (Chart
14 and Table 14). Both employment and payrolls of salaried workers
lagged behind those of wage earners only at the peaks, while at the
two troughs they led them briefly.[10]

For the prewar decade we found it helpful to separate the work-
relief payroll from the regular government payroll; for the war and
postwar decade we need to separate military from civilian payrolls.
The payroll of the armed services continued to rise until V-J Day
in the third quarter of 1945. The subsequent decline was precipitous,
coming to a halt in the first quarter of 1948; the following rise was
at a moderate rate until the Korean War, when it accelerated greatly.

[10] There was some growth during the war and postwar years, as indicated by
the fact that salaried personnel as a percentage of all employees increased from
16.0 in 1939 to 16.5 in 1947. See *Census of Manufactures, 1947*, Bureau of the
Census, Volume I, p. 69.

CHART 14

Employment and Payrolls of Wage Earners and Salaried Personnel,
Manufacturing Industries, 1938-1951

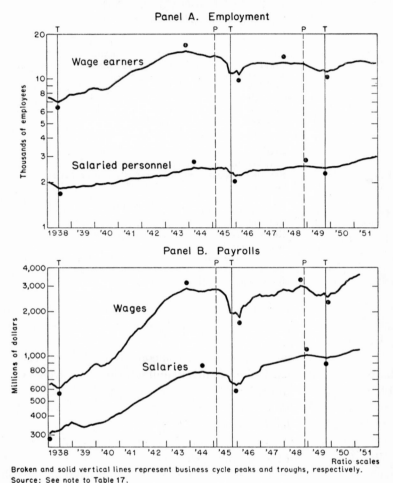

Panel A. Employment

Panel B. Payrolls

Broken and solid vertical lines represent business cycle peaks and troughs, respectively.
Source: See note to Table 17.

The salaries disbursed to the civilian branch of government also continued to expand from a trough in 1933 until July 1945, virtually the end of World War II. The ensuing contraction was reversed after six months by upward adjustments in salary scales.[11] Thereafter,

[11] According to the seasonally adjusted series in a Federal Reserve Board release of October 1950, the number of civilian employees in government declined from December 1944 to September 1947. The changes in federal

TABLE 14

Lead (−) of Salaried Personnel over, or Lag (+) behind, Wage Earners
at Turning Points in Employment and Payrolls,
Manufacturing Industries, 1945-1949
(*months*)

Corresponding Business Cycle Turn		Employment	Payrolls
P	Feb. 1945	+4	+8
T	Oct. 1945	−2	−2
P	Nov. 1945	+11	+3
T	Oct. 1949	−1	−1

P = peak; T = trough.
Source: Business cycle turns are those in the National Bureau of Economic
Research business cycle chronology. Employment of salaried personnel is the
difference between Bureau of Labor Statistics estimates of all employees in
manufacturing industries and BLS estimates of production workers. Salaried
payrolls and payrolls of wage earners are unpublished estimates of the National
Income Division, Department of Commerce.

civilian government payrolls continued to rise through 1949, reflect-
ing the 1948-1949 contraction in general business only by a slackening of the rate of increase. These payrolls showed the same limited
conformity to business cycles in the prewar decade.

The order of amplitudes of labor income according to industrial
sources found in the 1930's was repeated to a certain extent during
the war and postwar cycles. Since no specific cycles were traced by
wages and salaries in the distributive and service industries, it is
impossible to compare specific cycle amplitudes. It is possible, however, to get some idea of the relative movements by measuring the
amplitude of fluctuations during the cycles in general business
(Table 15). In the private sector, much the largest rise during the
war expansion occurred in the nonfarm commodity-producing industries, for the obvious reason that economic incentives were used to
obtain a rapid and vast production of war goods. The smallest rise
was in the service industries, and this was also true in the 1930's.
In the 1945 contraction, wage and salary disbursements declined
substantially in the commodity-producing industries but continued
to expand in the other two groups. In the first postwar cycle, while
wages and salaries in the nonfarm commodity-producing industries

government salary scales during this period are given in "Federal Classified
Employees: Salary Trends, 1939-1950," in the *Monthly Labor Review* (Bureau
of Labor Statistics, May 1951, pp. 537-540).

TABLE 15

Amplitude of Personal and Nonfarm Labor Income and of Wages and Salaries by Major Industry Group during Business Cycles, 1938-1949

(*based on cycle relatives*)

| BUSINESS CYCLE | | PERSONAL INCOME | NONFARM LABOR INCOME | WAGES AND SALARIES | | | |
| | | | | *Private* | | | |
Phase	*Period*			Commodity-Producing[a]	Distribu-tive	Service	Govern-ment[b]
Expansion	June 1938–Feb. 1945	+91.5	+98.8	+109.3	+64.3	+51.0	+149.2
Contraction	Feb. 1945–Oct. 1945	−6.1	−8.7	−38.2	+8.0	+10.9	−8.9
Expansion	Oct. 1945–Nov. 1948	+23.6	+22.4	+43.7	+39.5	+31.4	−73.9
Contraction	Nov. 1948–Oct. 1949	−5.1	−2.3	−11.8	−1.5	+3.6	+5.1

a Excluding agriculture.
b Including work relief and military.
Source: Business cycle phases are those in the National Bureau of Economic Research business cycle chronology; amplitudes are estimated from published and unpublished data of the National Income Division, Department of Commerce.

again had the largest amplitudes and those in the service industries the smallest, the excess of the rise and fall in commodity-producing industries over the rise and fall in the other two groups was much less than before the war.

When we consider labor input and unit labor returns (Table 11), we find that in the war and postwar years man-hours on the average fluctuated more than hourly earnings, repeating the prewar pattern. There is a single deviation from the average pattern that is especially interesting: in the first postwar expansion the rise in average hourly earnings was more than three times the rise in man-hours. Fluctuations in employment continued to be a more important determinant of fluctuations in labor input than changes in average hours worked per week.

A break with the past, however, is evident when we view the war and postwar changes against the background of the preceding two decades: in 1948, peak man-hours were up only 12 per cent from what they were in the 1920's, but real wages (discounting for the price rise) had more than doubled. This can be seen in Table 16, where we set out indexes of factory payrolls for production workers, their labor input, and unit returns, at peaks in business cycles, using as the index base the average standing at the cyclical peaks in 1923, 1926, and 1929. The 12 per cent rise in labor input (man-hours) shown in this table is the result of a 50 per cent rise in number employed and a 25 per cent *decline* in average hours worked per week. By contrast, unit labor returns (average hourly earnings) in 1948 were two and two-thirds times as large as in the 1920's and real hourly earnings were nearly double.

This comparison leaves no doubt that the prime cause of the long-term rise in factory labor income was the rise in average hourly earnings. While the above illustration is drawn from manufacturing industries, there is a strong presumption that in other sectors of the economy labor input and unit returns have played the same role, both in cyclical movements and in long-term fluctuations, that they have in manufacturing.

The prewar relationship between amplitudes of change in wages and in salaries in manufacturing industries was repeated during the war cycle, but not during the first postwar cycle (Chart 14 and Table 17). The rise in salaries during the war expansion was only about two-thirds of the rise in wages, while the following contraction in salaries was less than half of the fall in wages. In the next expansion phase, however, the rises were virtually the same despite

TABLE 16

Changes in Components of Input and of Returns (in Current and in Constant Dollars) of Factory Labor at Business Peaks in 1937, 1945, and 1948 Relative to 1923, 1926, and 1929 Peaks
(*index numbers*)

| | | AVERAGE HOURS | | AVERAGE HOURLY EARNINGS IN: | | PAYROLLS IN: | |
| BUSINESS PEAK | NUMBER EMPLOYED | WORKED PER WEEK | MAN-HOURS | Current Dollars | Constant Dollars | Current Dollars | Constant Dollars |
	(1)	(2)	(3)	(4)	(5)	(6)	(7)
May 1923 ⎫ Oct. 1926 ⎬ June 1929 ⎭	100.0	100.0	100.0	100.0	100.0	100.0	100.0
May 1937	106.2	74.5	79.1	122.8	147.4	102.8	123.4
Feb. 1945	171.1	84.2	144.1	205.9	199.3	302.5	292.8
Nov. 1948	151.0	74.0	111.7	269.7	191.5	312.7	222.1

Source: See note to Table 8. Constant-dollar hourly earnings and payrolls were obtained by deflating current-dollar series by Bureau of Labor Statistics Consumers Price Index. The product of the index of man-hours and the index of hourly earnings does not equal the index of factory wages because each is derived from a different sample.

TABLE 17

Amplitude of Specific Cycles in Employment and in Earnings
of Wage Earners and of Salaried Personnel,
Manufacturing Industries, 1938-1949

(*based on cycle relatives*)

| BUSINESS CYCLE | | WAGE EARNERS | | SALARIED PERSONNEL | |
Phase	Period	*Employ-ment*	*Wages*	*Employ-ment*	*Salaries*
Expansion	June 1938–Feb. 1945	+70.7	+127.1	+31.1	+87.1
Contraction	Feb. 1945–Oct. 1945	−36.8	−52.1	−10.6	−23.9
Expansion	Oct. 1945–Nov. 1948	+15.1	+39.4	+12.5	+40.5
Contraction	Nov. 1948–Oct. 1949	−13.4	−14.3	−2.8	−4.5

Source: Business cycle phases are those in the National Bureau of Economic Research business cycle chronology. Salaried personnel were derived as the difference between all employees and production workers (wage earners), both estimated by the Bureau of Labor Statistics and seasonally adjusted by the Division of Research and Statistics, Board of Governors of the Federal Reserve System. Wages and salaries are from unpublished tables of the National Income Division, Department of Commerce.

the fact that the increase in employment of salaried personnel was only 80 per cent of the increase in wage-earner employment. This suggests that during a period of sustained full employment, salaried personnel were able to make up for the partial suppression of salary raises during the war. Thus from the June 1938 trough to the February 1945 peak in business activity, wages per production worker increased by 130 per cent and salaries per nonproduction worker by 76 per cent. However, between the February 1945 and November 1948 peaks the respective percentage gains were 18 and 27. During the 1948-1949 contraction the decline in salaries was only a third of the fall in wages, and the fall in salaried employment was about a fifth of that for wage earners. Over the whole postwar cycle the net gain in salaries exceeded the net gain in wages by more than two-fifths.[12] If we use a prewar base, however, we find that the rise in average salary was still lagging behind the rise in average wage—the latter having increased by 165 per cent between June 1938 and October 1949 and the former by 121 per cent.

When we distinguish executive and professional salaries, i.e. compensation of corporate officers, from other salaries, we find much the same difference in amplitude as between salaries and wages (Table 18). During the war the amplitude of the rise in executive salaries was 44 per cent less than in other salaries. (The amplitude

[12] It is the force of this expansion in salaries that explains the timing of the turning points vis-à-vis wages noted above.

TABLE 18

Amplitude of Compensation of Corporate Officers and of Other Salaried
Personnel, Manufacturing Industries, during Business Cycles,
1938-1949

(*based on cycle relatives*)

BUSINESS CYCLE		CORPORATE OFFICERS	OTHER SALARIED PERSONNEL
Phase	*Period*		
Expansion	1938-1944	+48.5	+86.6
Contraction	1944-1946	+33.5	−16.8
Full cycle		+15.0	+103.4
Net change over cycle		+82.0	+69.8
Expansion	1946-1948	+16.9	+28.2
Contraction	1948-1949	−2.0	+2.9
Full cycle		+18.9	+25.3
Net change over cycle		+14.9	+31.1
Addenda: Percentage change, 1938-1949		+165.7	+209.7

Source: Business cycle phases are those in the National Bureau of Economic
Research business cycle chronology. Compensation of corporate officers is reported in *Statistics of Income* (Bureau of Internal Revenue) for appropriate
years; compensation of other salaried personnel was derived by subtracting
compensation of corporate officers from compensation of all salaried personnel
as given in unpublished tables of the National Income Division, Department
of Commerce.

of the rise in all salaries was 31 percent less than the amplitude of
the rise in wages, shown in Table 17 above.) In the transition to
peace, a period of contraction, unemployment among the lower-
salaried personnel led to a fall in other salaries, while the removal
of controls opened the way for such a rapid expansion in the
compensation of corporate officers that the net gain in their compensation over the cycle exceeded that for other salaried employees
by 17 per cent. In the next expansion, however, the relative rise in
other salary payments far outstripped the relative rise in compensation of officers, and in the 1948-1949 contraction other salaries
continued to rise slightly while compensation of corporate officers
declined slightly. Between 1938 and 1949 compensation of corporate
officers increased by 166 per cent and other salaries by 210 per cent.
This suggests that during World War II and the early postwar
years the larger relative gains in labor income were received by
wage earners and salaried employees below the executive level.[13]

[13] This agrees with our findings on secular changes; compare Chapter 1.
Compensation of corporate officers includes cash bonuses but excludes bonuses
in the form of stock or stock options and company contributions to pension and
retirement funds established for corporate officers. We do not know of any estimate of their quantitative importance, but we can be sure that it has increased.

CHAPTER 6

CYCLES IN TYPES OF PROPERTY INCOME

Turns in property income cycles, according to the findings in Chapter 4, lead business cycle peaks by one or two months but lag behind the business cycle troughs. On an over-all average, in both expansions and contractions, the amplitudes of property income cycles are smaller than those for any other type of income. But this is not the case in every cyclical phase. In the expansion of 1921-1929 and in the contractions of 1929-1933 and 1937-1938 the amplitude in property income was larger than that in other major types of income.

Has each component of property income followed the same cyclical course, or is the pattern of the aggregate an average of diverse patterns of the individual components? Although property income is defined as the sum of receipts by individuals of net rent, interest, and dividends, detailed analysis must be restricted to interest and dividends, since the estimates of net rent are rather arbitrarily derived even on an annual basis, except in the years in which there was a census of housing, as in 1930 and 1940.[1]

Interest receipts by individuals are largely based on ownership of long-term debt issued by corporations or governments, or by firms or individuals on real estate and other fixed assets. Since such debts are long-term contracts, there is little advantage in using monthly instead of annual estimates. The latter, moreover, are well grounded in data for a long period, at least for corporation and government interest. Monthly estimates of dividend receipts, on the other hand, are reasonably accurate and are adequate for measures of timing and amplitude beginning with 1919 and for timing alone beginning with 1884.[2]

[1] The National Income Division, Department of Commerce, assesses its estimates of net rent in the following terms: ". . . the final estimates [of net rent] are often calculated as the difference between much larger items which, in turn, are also obtained as residuals. Even small errors made at the various stages of the estimating procedure may significantly affect the final results. Both as to general level and relative movement the rental estimates must be regarded as among the least satisfactory of national income statistics." *National Income Supplement, 1951, Survey of Current Business,* Dept. of Commerce, p. 79.

[2] The monthly estimates of dividends received by individuals in 1919-1939 are prepared by adjusting monthly data on dividend disbursements reported in the *Journal of Commerce* to the level of annual totals derived from *Statistics of Income* (Bureau of Internal Revenue) (dividends paid minus dividends received by corporations); for years since 1939 we use the estimates of the

Cycles in Dividend Receipts

It is a commonplace that in an individual corporation, dividend disbursements lag behind profits. Profits are determined only after the close of the accounting period in which they were actually earned. The board of directors, which must approve a decision to pay dividends, meets still later to consider the accounting report. There is an additional time lapse of at least several weeks between the directors' decision to pay dividends and the actual disbursement of dividends to stockholders. Some lag, therefore, is inherent in the process of distributing dividends.

Policy decisions, however, may prolong the inherent procedural lag. There are many reasons why corporate management often prefers to withhold part of corporate profits from stockholders in periods of prosperity; one of them is a desire to maintain dividend payments in the earlier stages of contraction, when profits decline, without violating the legal injunction not to impair the capital structure by distributing dividends.[3] This practice obviously could affect the cyclical turning points at the peaks. In business revivals corporate management may find it advantageous to finance some part of its growing requirements for inventories, accounts receivable, and plant expansion by retaining a larger fraction of net profits, which have now begun to reappear or to increase. Such a policy might reinforce the procedural lag at the troughs in general business.

The relation between timing of dividends and profits for an individual corporation will apply to all corporations if the cyclical movement of total corporate profits is well defined, which proves to be the case.[4] It is no surprise, therefore, to find that the lag of dividend disbursements behind profits is confirmed by the statistical record (Chart 15 and Table 19).

Department of Commerce, but only after applying our own seasonal correction. For years before 1919, annual control totals are nonexistent; only the monthly compilations of the *Journal of Commerce* and its predecessors are available. This series relates to all dividends paid out and is not restricted to dividends paid to individuals. Tests presented in Appendix D suggest that for the determination of cyclical turning points in dividend disbursements we may have confidence in the monthly series unadjusted to annual totals.

[3] Some of the factors affecting the distribution of profits to stockholders are discussed by Sergei P. Dobrovolsky in his *Corporate Income Retention, 1915-43* (National Bureau of Economic Research, 1951).

[4] See, for example, Thor Hultgren, *Cyclical Diversities in the Fortunes of Industrial Corporations*, National Bureau of Economic Research, Occasional Paper 32, 1950, p. 12.

CHART 15

Net Profits after Taxes and Dividend Payments to Individuals, All Corporations, 1919-1951

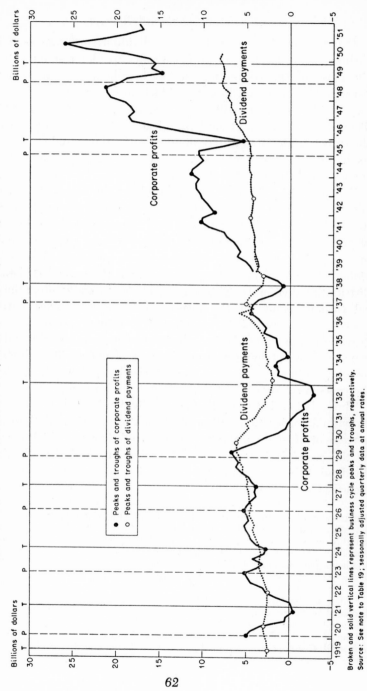

● Peaks and troughs of corporate profits
○ Peaks and troughs of dividend payments

Broken and solid vertical lines represent business cycle peaks and troughs, respectively.

Source: See note to Table 19; seasonally adjusted quarterly data at annual rates.

62

TABLE 19

Turning Points in Net Profits after Taxes and in Dividend Payments
to Individuals, All Corporations, 1920-1950

CORRESPONDING BUSINESS CYCLE TURN		NET PROFITS		DIVIDENDS		LAG OF DIVIDENDS BEHIND NET PROFITS
Quarter of Year	Year	Quarter of Year	Year	Quarter of Year	Year	(quarters)
P	1st	1920	1st	1920[a]	3rd	1920	2
T	3rd	1921	2nd	1921	2nd	1922	4
P	2nd	1923	2nd	1923			
T	3rd	1924	3rd	1924			
P	3rd	1926	3rd	1926			
T	4th	1927	4th	1927			
P	2nd	1929	3rd	1929	1st	1930	2
T	1st	1933	3rd	1932	2nd	1933	3
P			1st	1934			
T			3rd	1934			
P	2nd	1937	4th	1936	2nd	1937	2
T	2nd	1938	2nd	1938	4th	1938	2
P			3rd	1941	4th	1941	1
T			1st	1942	4th	1942	3
P	1st	1945	1st	1944			
T	4th	1945	4th	1945			
P	4th	1948	3rd	1948			
T	4th	1949	2nd	1949			
P			4th	1950			

[a] Tentative.

P = peak; T = trough.

Source: Business cycle turns are those in the National Bureau of Economic
Research business cycle chronology. Quarterly net profits for 1920-1938 are
from Harold Barger, *Outlay and Income in the United States, 1921-1938*
(Studies in Income and Wealth, Volume Four, NBER, 1942); thereafter the
estimates are those of the National Income Division, Department of Commerce,
as reported in *Survey of Current Business* (Dept. of Commerce). For dividends
see Appendix D.

Not every turn in profit cycles is matched by a corresponding turn
in dividend payments; they failed to coincide at some of the turns
marking cycles of only moderate amplitude and duration. At the
eight corresponding turning points during 1920-1950, dividends
turned one to four quarters, but typically two quarters, after corporate profits.

The data in Table 19 indicate also that since 1920 the turning
points in corporate profits typically have either coincided with or
led the corresponding turns in general business. This must mean
that dividend payments turned later than general business. This

timing relationship, however, can be tested over a longer period on the basis of monthly dividend disbursements (Chart 16 and Table 20). From 1884, the initial date of our dividend series, to 1949, general business traced seventeen cycles while dividend payments traced only ten. Every turning point in dividends can be matched with one in general business, except two during World War II; in the fifty-five years before World War II there never was a turn in dividends that did not accompany a corresponding turn in general business.

Dividends did not decline during eight business contractions, viz. those of 1890-1891, 1895-1897, 1899-1900, 1910-1912, 1923-1924, 1926-1927, 1945, and 1948-1949. In all such cases the decline in general business was modest and in most cases the business contraction was relatively brief (Table 20).[5]

That dividend payments turned after general business throughout this long period is clear. At fifteen of the seventeen corresponding turning points[6] dividends lagged behind general business; at one turn dividends led; and at one they coincided. The lead occurred at the peak of general business in August 1918. The decline in dividends, however, appears to have been relatively slight. This was undoubtedly because of the uncertainties attending the entrance of the United States into World War I and because of the proposals for higher corporate taxes. Although corporate profits after taxes were at the same level in 1917 as in 1916, they were about 45 per cent lower in 1918.[7] Corporate income taxes increased from $.2 billion in 1916 to $2.1 billion in 1917 and to $3.2 billion in 1918.

Thus the one instance of an earlier turn in dividend payments occurred under exceptional circumstances. And special circumstances also explain some of the shorter lags. When contractions, for example, were ushered in by severe financial panics, as in 1893 and 1907, the lags were brief, three and four months respectively. At the 1933

[5] The relative decline in business activity is measured by deflated clearings or debits (after 1918) outside of New York City for the years 1885 to 1939, when the series ends. For the relative severity of the 1948-1949 contraction see Geoffrey H. Moore's *Statistical Indicators of Cyclical Revivals and Recessions* (National Bureau of Economic Research, Occasional Paper 31, 1950, p. 69).

[6] The gap in the dividend series for 1904 and 1905 makes it impossible to determine the dates of two turning points. The data are sufficient, however, to indicate that a contraction took place sometime during those two years. There are, therefore, ten cycles with only seventeen corresponding turning points and, during World War II, two noncorresponding turning points.

[7] According to *Statistics of Income*, corporate net profits after taxes were $7.9 and $8.0 billion in 1916 and 1917 and $4.5 billion in 1918.

trough and the 1937 peak the lags were even shorter: only one month. At both of these turning points corporate net profits turned two quarters earlier than general business. In such circumstances the normal lag of dividends behind net profits would result in a rough coincidence with turns in general business.

When we shift attention from the exceptional cases to the average timing pattern, we find that the average lag of dividend payments at the seventeen corresponding turning points in general business between 1884 and 1949 is 6.0 months. While lags are predominant in all periods, the average lag tends to decrease as we approach the most recent period. For 1884 to the outbreak of World War I the average lag is 10.2 months, and for 1919-1949 it is 4.4 months. This trend toward a diminishing lag may be partly explained by the growing practice of making quarterly and semiannual dividend declarations instead of annual declarations.[8] More frequent review of profits and dividends means that dividend declarations can be more quickly adjusted to fit changes in profits or profit outlook.

With the growth of business and the ever-increasing use of the corporate form of organization, there has been a strong secular rise in the aggregate amount of dividends disbursed. This growth factor would be expected to accentuate the lags at peaks and to reduce the lags at troughs if the procedural and policy factors acted with the same force at both the upper and the lower turning point of the dividend cycle. However, the opposite appears to have been true, with an average lag at peaks of 4.4 months, and at troughs of 7.4 months.[9] Whether this means that procedural and especially policy factors vary from one turning point to another, or points to some discontinuities in our monthly samples of corporations paying dividends, we do not know.

[8] This change in frequency of dividend payments is inferred from the change in the seasonal movements. Until the turn of the century there were pronounced concentrations of dividend payments in January and July of each year. From shortly thereafter until 1936, the heavy concentration of dividend payments occurred in four months of each year, January, April, July, and October. These four seasonal peaks are roughly of the same magnitude. Conceivably, of course, this shift in seasonal pattern could be due to a redistribution in the terminal dates of fiscal years. The first interpretation is supported by the fact that as we approach the present the number of quarterly income statements published by corporations increases. Beginning with 1936 still another seasonal pattern emerges: dividend disbursements are highest in December with secondary "highs" occurring in the terminal and initial months of the other three calendar quarters.

[9] If the lead at the peak is excluded, the average at peaks is 7.0 months.

CHART 16

Dividend Disbursements, 1884-1919, and Total Dividend Payments to Individuals, 1919-1950

Panel A. Dividend Disbursements

Panel B. Total Dividend Payments to Individuals

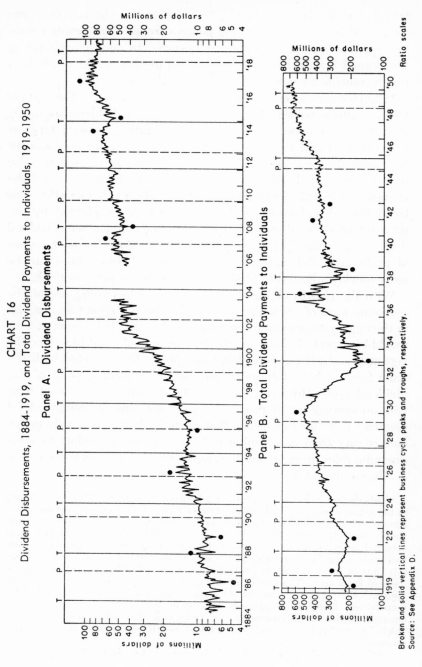

Broken and solid vertical lines represent business cycle peaks and troughs, respectively.
Source: See Appendix D.

TABLE 20

Lead (−) or Lag (+) of Total Dividend Payments at Business Cycle Turning Points, 1885-1949; and Amplitude of Specific Cycle Contractions in Deflated Bank Clearings, 1885-1919, and in Deflated Debits, 1919-1939, outside New York City

	Business Activity Turn	Dividends[a] (months)	Bank Clearings and Debits[b] (based on cycle relatives)
T	May 1885	+15	
P	Mar. 1887	+14	
T	Apr. 1888	+13	−6.5
P	July 1890		
T	May 1891		−8.0
P	Jan. 1893	+3	
T	June 1894	+17	−26.0
P	Dec. 1895		
T	June 1897		−9.7
P	June 1899		
T	Dec. 1900		−6.2
P	Sept. 1902	+8[c]	
T	Aug. 1904	[d]	−5.9
P	May 1907	+4	
T	June 1908	0	−25.0
P	Jan. 1910		
T	Jan. 1912		−3.3
P	Jan. 1913	+16	
T	Dec. 1914	+3	−11.9
P	Aug. 1918	−14	
T	Apr. 1919	+2	−4.9
P	Jan. 1920	+4	
T	July 1921	+10	−10.9
P	May 1923		
T	July 1924		−5.7
P	Oct. 1926		
T	Nov. 1927		0
P	June 1929	+7	
T	Mar. 1933	+1	−54.7
P	May 1937	+1	
T	June 1938	+6	−13.5
P	Feb. 1945		
T	Oct. 1945		
P	Nov. 1948		
T	Oct. 1949		

a After 1938 there were a noncorresponding peak in December 1941 and a noncorresponding trough in December 1942.

b Series ends in November 1939.

c Data sufficient to establish a minimum lag of eight months but insufficient for a precise measurement. This entry is excluded from averages.

d Data insufficient or unavailable for determining turning point.

P = peak; T = trough.

Source: Business cycle turns are those in the National Bureau of Economic Research business cycle chronology; for total dividend payments see Appendix D; deflated bank clearings and debits are based on data in NBER files.

Dividends are sensitive to general business cycles of more than mild amplitude. Our measures show that they fluctuate more sharply than most other types of income. For the 1920's we are obliged to measure the amplitude of nonfarm labor income in terms of annual data, over the cycle measured from peak to peak and bounded by its turning points in 1920, 1921, and 1929. For comparability we measure dividends in the same unit and manner. Although in their 1920-1921 contraction the fall (in terms of specific cycle relatives) in nonfarm labor income was 18.0 and in dividends 5.9, in their 1921-1929 expansion the rise in dividends (78.8) was twice that in nonfarm labor income (38.5). This relationship persisted throughout the 1930's: the amplitudes of the two contractions (1929-1933 and 1937-1938) and of the one expansion (1933-1937) were larger in dividend payments than in total nonfarm labor income (Table 21, Part A).[10] Indeed, only the net income of proprietors, both farm

TABLE 21

Amplitude of Corresponding Cyclical Phases in Property Income, Dividend Payments to Individuals, Total Nonfarm Labor Income, and in Farm and Nonfarm Proprietors' Net Income, 1929-1949

	BUSINESS CYCLE	DIVIDENDS	PROPERTY INCOME	TOTAL NON-FARM LABOR INCOME	PROPRIETORS' NET INCOME Nonfarm	Farm
	A. Total Rise (+) or Fall (−) in Specific Cycle Relatives					
Contraction	June 1929–Mar. 1933[a]	−115.9	−70.2	−57.7	−122.5	−134.3
Expansion	Mar. 1933–May 1937	+86.6	+32.4	+49.2	+91.0	+117.6[b]
Contraction	May 1937–June 1938	−56.0	−18.1	−11.3	−16.1	−45.3
	B. Total Rise (+) or Fall (−) in Business Cycle Relatives					
Expansion	June 1938–Feb. 1945	+32.8	+36.9	+98.8	+102.0	+94.3
Contraction	Feb. 1945–Oct. 1945	+15.9	+8.3	−8.7	+14.0	+9.6
Expansion	Oct. 1945–Nov. 1948	+38.5	+25.9	+22.4	+9.8	+27.9
Contraction	Nov. 1948–Oct. 1949	−1.8	−.3	−2.3	−8.1	−33.5

[a] The amplitudes for this reference cycle contraction are computed on the base of the peak-to-peak cycle 1929-1937. The amplitudes for the other two phases are computed on the base of the trough-to-trough cycle 1933-1938.

[b] For the purpose of this comparison the extra cycle in this series that occurs between 1933 and 1936 was ignored.

Source: Business cycle phases are those in the National Bureau of Economic Research business cycle chronology; amplitudes are estimated from published and unpublished data of the National Income Division, Department of Commerce.

[10] The relative cyclical instability of dividends compared with labor income may be somewhat unexpected because we more often contrast the stability of dividends with the instability of corporate savings or profits. For the latter comparison see Chart 15 and the analysis by Dobrovolsky (op. cit.).

and nonfarm, showed larger fluctuations (and this component includes the highly volatile element of business savings). This was limited to the first two of the three phases. However, the rise in dividends during their 1933-1937 expansion and the fall during their subsequent contraction were accentuated by the undistributed profits tax, which undoubtedly precipitated more dividend payments at the peak than would otherwise have been disbursed.[11]

Between 1938 and 1949, dividend payments did not have turning points corresponding to those in other types of income. Hence for this period our comparison of amplitudes is based on cycles in general business (Table 21, Part B). During the business expansion of World War II the amplitude of the rise in dividends, and in property income in general, was only about a third of that in labor income and in the net income of proprietors. Although dividend receipts continued to increase during the contraction of the transition period and labor income declined, the net gain in labor income over the 1938-1945 cycle exceeded the net rise in dividends by 85 per cent.

In the first cycle after World War II there is some indication of a reversion to the prewar relation of amplitudes in dividends and labor income. In any case, the amplitude of the rise in dividends during the expansion phase was about 70 per cent larger than that in labor income, although the amplitude of the fall during the 1948-1949 contraction was about equal for both types.

Cycles in Interest Receipts

Usable estimates of interest received by individuals are available on an annual basis from 1909 (Chart 17). The striking feature of the fluctuations in this type of income is their low conformity to cycles in business activity. Between 1909 and 1950, general business had twenty turns and interest receipts only two—a peak in 1929 and a trough in 1943. Of all the types of income studied, interest receipts have shown the least sensitivity to business cycles. Monthly estimates of interest receipts probably would not provide more evidence of specific cycles. However, it is possible for one or more components of the total to trace cycles not found in the total, and this, in fact, is the case with interest received by individuals holding government debt, the only component that can be estimated with reasonable accuracy (Chart 17 and Appendix E).[12]

[11] For evidence see George E. Lent, *The Impact of the Undistributed Profits Tax, 1936-1937*, Columbia University Press, 1948, pp. 31-33 and Table 3, p. 34.
[12] The National Income Division of the Department of Commerce has monthly estimates of government interest receipts by individuals beginning with

CHART 17

Total Interest and Interest on All Government Securities
Received by Individuals, 1909-1951

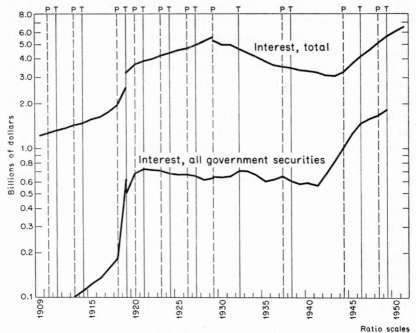

Ratio scales

Broken and solid vertical lines represent business cycle peaks and troughs, respectively.
Source: Total interest from Appendix Table A-1; interest on all government securities from
Appendix Table E-1.

The amount of interest paid to individual owners of government debt is, of course, the product of the volume of government debt held by individuals (Chart 18) and the average interest rate on this debt. Both interest rates (at least on federal bonds) and individual holdings of government debt (federal, state, and local) reached a peak in 1921.[13] Thereafter, interest rates declined until 1944, and government debt in the hands of individuals contracted until 1928 despite the fact that individuals held ever-increasing amounts of state and local debt. The decrease in the amount of federal debt

---

1929. We believe, however, that the concept used is inappropriate and prefer our own annual estimates. For an explanation see Appendix E.

[13] For interest rates on the federal debt see *Statistical Abstract of the United States, 1950*, Bureau of the Census, Table 384, p. 340. For holdings of government debt see source and notes to Appendix Table E-1.

CHART 18

Individual Holdings of Federal and of State and Local Securities
and Interest on Such Securities, 1913-1949

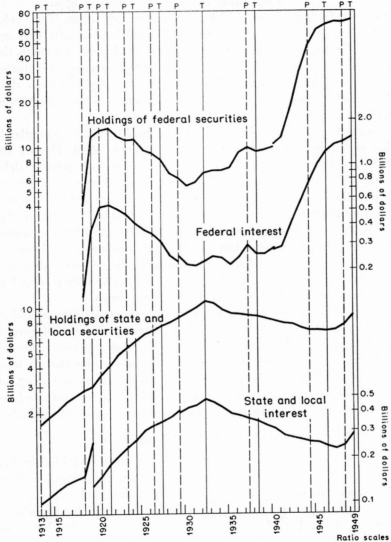

Broken and solid vertical lines represent business cycle peaks and troughs, respectively.
Source: See Appendix E; holdings are as of June 30

held by individuals more than offset the gains in holdings of state and local debt. After 1932 these trends were reversed: individuals held ever-diminishing amounts of state and local debt from 1932 to 1946 and, with the exception of 1938, ever-increasing amounts of federal debt from 1930 to 1949, the end of our series. The cycles in total government interest during the 1930's and until 1941 are caused by the cycles in interest on the federal debt. Although the trend in government debt owned by individuals was upward during this period, interest received by individuals on government debt continued downward because of the sustained decline in interest rates.

Interest on private debt followed a cyclical course very similar to that of interest on state and local government debt. During the 1920's, individuals owned ever-larger amounts of private debt, especially corporate bonds and real estate mortgages, and interest from this source more than offset the decline in government interest. The rise in interest from private debt was halted in 1929, and during the ensuing decade its downward course reinforced the downward movement in government interest. It is this decline in total interest receipts during the 1930's, and presumably in net rent also, that explains why the timing of the turns of property income, noted in Chapter 4, was that of a secularly declining series.

By 1941 the deficit financing of the rearmament program and of World War II had sharply reversed the downward course of government interest received by individuals. The rise continued through 1950 and in itself was sufficient to account for the rise in total interest receipts during World War II. In the years following, an expanding private debt and a reversal in the falling interest rate have contributed to the postwar rise in interest received by individuals.[14]

Cycles in Capital Gains and Losses

So far we have been concerned with the income yielded by the use of capital assets. Now we turn to the cycles in the gains realized by individuals on sales of capital assets. Gains made through the disposal of capital assets may be regarded as enhancing one's command over goods and services; the realization of capital losses, on

[14] The tremendous expansion in the volume of federal bonds held by individuals during and after World War II may give a misleading impression of the importance of federal interest received by individuals in total personal income. Individual receipts of federal interest amounted to .3 per cent of personal income in 1939 and .8 per cent ten years later.

the other hand, reduces one's command over goods and services. Such gains and losses could affect spending and investing habits and hence have some impact on business activity.[15] It is highly relevant, therefore, to indicate their magnitude and ascertain the degree to which they conform with movements in general business.

The measurement of their relative importance, however, poses some problems. Capital gains might be measured as a percentage either of total personal income or of the value of personally owned capital assets. But statistics on personally owned capital assets are not available, so we are obliged to rely on the former measure exclusively. We shall use the comprehensive estimates of net capital gains and losses realized by individuals prepared for the National Bureau of Economic Research under the supervision of Lawrence H. Seltzer.[16] These estimates are based on individual tax returns reporting the net difference between gains and losses from sales of capital assets. The results measure the extent to which personal income is supplemented by net gains or offset by net losses (Table 22).

During the thirty-four years 1917-1950 the largest amount of realized capital gains relative to personal income occurred in 1928— nearly 6 per cent. In six of the nineteen years in which net gains were realized they represented less than 1 per cent of personal income. Capital losses show the same kind of pattern: in 1932 they amounted to 6 per cent of income, but in eight of the fifteen years in which net losses occurred they amounted to less than 1 per cent of personal income.[17]

The fact that the year of largest gains coincides with high stock-market prices and the year of largest losses coincides with low stock-market prices suggests a high correlation between changes in

[15] This much can be said without taking sides in the difficult theoretical argument on whether realized capital gains and losses are a part of income.

[16] See Lawrence H. Seltzer, *The Nature and Tax Treatment of Capital Gains and Losses*, National Bureau of Economic Research, 1951, Appendixes One and Two.

[17] For certain income groups, however, these transactions in capital assets are very important. Seltzer's analysis discloses, for example, that "for 1917-46 as a whole . . . [net capital gains] accounted for nearly a third of the aggregate net income of individuals with statutory net incomes of $100,000 or more, and half of the total for those with $1 million or more" (*ibid.*, pp. 122-123). Of course, many individuals have these high incomes in a given year by virtue of having realized capital gains. This situation has obtained although the greater part of net capital gains has been realized by taxpayers in other than the highest income groups (*ibid.*, p. 124). With respect to net capital losses Seltzer finds "some evidence that the largest net losses in relation to total income are sustained neither by the top nor the bottom group filing income tax returns" (*ibid.*, p. 128).

TABLE 22

Personal Income and Excess of Net Capital Gains
over Losses Realized by Individuals, 1917-1950
(*dollars in millions*)

	Excess of Net Capital Gains over Losses (1)	Personal Income (2)	Percentage Change in Personal Income from Net Change in Realized Capital Values (Col. 1 ÷ Col. 2 × 100) (3)
1917	$ 248	$ 52,199	+.5%
1918	—68	58,017	—.1
1919	263	66,165	+.4
1919	263	65,574	+.4
1920	—16	69,153	a
1921	—639	55,787	—1.1
1922	232	60,000	+.4
1923	192	69,264	+.3
1924	1,037	70,118	+1.5
1925	2,572	73,962	+3.5
1926	2,166	76,704	+2.8
1927	2,618	77,135	+3.4
1928	4,504	78,949	+5.7
1929	2,893	83,401	+3.5
1929	2,893	82,310	+3.5
1930	—1,360	73,507	—1.9
1931	—2,718	62,106	—4.4
1932	—2,682	46,607	—5.8
1933	—1,403	44,179	—3.2
1934	—630	50,729	—1.2
1935	—89	57,414	—.2
1936	589	65,803	+.9
1937	—105	71,380	—.1
1938	—342	65,892	—.5
1939	—269	70,102	—.4
1940	—437	75,836	—.6
1941	—896	92,645	—1.0
1942	—380	119,912	—.3
1943	1,057	147,374	+.7
1944	1,602	162,686	+1.0
1945	4,267	168,430	+2.5
1946	6,644	173,967	+3.8
1947	4,384	186,988	+2.3
1948	4,382	205,061	+2.1
1949	3,100	201,055	+1.5
1950	5,768	221,015	+2.6

a Less than .05 per cent decrease.

Source: Net capital gains or losses: *1917-1946*—Lawrence H. Seltzer, *The Nature and Tax Treatment of Capital Gains and Losses*, National Bureau of Economic Research, 1951, p. 367; *1947-1950*—preliminary estimates by NBER. Personal income: *1917-1919*—based on estimates by Willford Isbell King and Simon Kuznets; *1919-1929*—by Kuznets; *1929-1950*—by Department of Commerce (see Appendix A).

stock prices and the amount of realized capital gains and losses, although the exact period over which price changes should be reckoned is in doubt. This relationship is supported by the general agreement of the courses of year-to-year changes in stock-market prices and of realized gains and losses depicted in Chart 19, as well as by Seltzer's analysis for 1936.[18] It follows that cycles in realized net gains and losses conform with cycles in general business, since this is true also of changes in stock prices. Because cyclical turns in

CHART 19

Excess of Net Capital Gains over Losses Realized by Individuals, and Absolute Annual Change in Price Index of All Common Stocks, 1917-1951

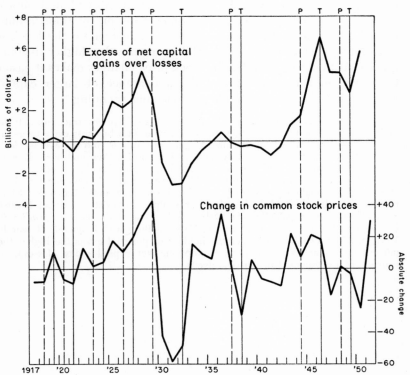

Broken and solid vertical lines represent business cycle peaks and troughs, respectively.
Source: Net capital gains or losses from Table 22; data for common stock prices are available in National Bureau of Economic Research files.

[18] "In 1936, the only year for which comprehensive data are available, 79 per cent of the total net gain and 68 per cent of the total net loss were reported as derived from stocks and bonds" (*ibid.*, p. 145).

stock-price changes typically lead turns in business activity,[19] it is possible that net realized capital gains and losses typically lead turns in general business. Our annual data on net capital gains and losses strongly suggest this. During 1918-1938 each of the five peaks in the excess of capital gains over losses preceded the corresponding business cycle peak by one year; four of the six troughs preceded the corresponding business trough by one year and the other two were coincident. We must remember, however, that annual data provide only a crude measure of timing.

In the light of this relationship the typical lead of stock-price changes at peaks in general business could have a double-barrelled effect on the course of the business cycle. The decline of stock prices limits the funds available to finance new investment and simultaneously, by reducing realized capital gains or by transforming them into losses, could have a depressing influence on the level of consumption expenditures, especially among the higher income groups. At the trough the lead in stock-price changes makes it easier to finance new investment and the appearance of larger capital gains probably immediately affects consumer spending.[20]

[19] A National Bureau analysis discloses that stock prices trace nine turning points between 1919 and 1938 that correspond with business cycle turns; at seven turns stock prices lead the turns in general business, and the average lead at all nine turns, based on monthly data, is 4.8 months. Presumably stock-price changes, computed over an appropriate interval, would also show leads.

[20] Unfortunately, empirical work in this particular area is very meager. In a cross-sectional analysis of a small sample of spending units Lawrence Klein reports, "We have established within our sample the existence of an inverse asset effect on savings" ("Assets, Debts, and Economic Behavior," *Studies in Income and Wealth, Volume Fourteen,* National Bureau of Economic Research, 1951, p. 226). That is, the larger the holding of personal assets the higher the percentage of income spent on consumption. Net capital gains (losses), of course, are a component of personal assets.

CHAPTER 7

CYCLICAL AMPLITUDES IN PERSONAL INCOME
BY SIZE OF INCOME

THE effort to understand cycles in personal income has led us to examine the cycles in the various types of income that make up the whole. Incomes may also be classified according to their size. How have increases in income during business expansions, and decreases during contractions, been distributed among the high, moderate, and low income groups? Our analysis of income by type is of some assistance in answering this question. Looking at nonfarm personal income, we can say that:

1. Except for the expansion after World War II, salaries have expanded and contracted less than wages.
2. The compensation of corporate officers, i.e. the higher-paid executives, typically expands and contracts less than the compensation of other salaried personnel.
3. Supplements to wages and transfer payments show a secular increase, rising during contractions as well as expansions in personal income.
4. The net income of nonfarm proprietors has larger relative upswings and downswings than nonfarm labor income.
5. Dividend disbursements to individuals between 1921 and 1938 also show larger fluctuations than nonfarm labor income.
6. Interest payments to individuals have a low conformity to cycles in general business and in personal income. From 1900 through 1929 they rose steadily during both contractions and expansions in personal income; during the 1930's they dropped without interruption regardless of the phase of the income cycle.

These findings mean that we can with some qualifications deduce the cyclical amplitudes of high, moderate, and low incomes (nonfarm) if we know, for each income-size group, what proportion of total income came from wages, dividends, and the other main types. This information is supplied by Kuznets' analysis.[1] The estimates in

---

[1] Simon Kuznets, *Shares of Upper Income Groups in Income and Savings*, National Bureau of Economic Research, 1953. It must be clear to any student of the subject that this section can make little claim to originality either in the development of data or in interpretation. It is based almost entirely on Kuznets' researches. The only reason for its inclusion in this study is to round out the discussion of the cyclical behavior of personal incomes. The analysis is restricted

Table 23 are averages for the period 1919-1938 for the nonfarm population and are adapted from Kuznets' study, where income per tax return by net income classes is reduced to income per capita. Starting with the net income classes receiving the highest per capita incomes in each year, Kuznets distinguishes, among others, the top 1 per cent of the nonfarm population, 2nd and 3rd per cent from the top, 4th and 5th per cent from the top, 6th and 7th per cent from the top, and the lower 93 per cent. The individuals included in a given percentage band vary from year to year. Those in the top 1 per cent we shall designate as the highest income group, those in the 2nd to 7th percentage band the middle income group, and those in the lower 93 per cent the lowest income group.[2]

Although Kuznets distinguishes between three income variants—basic, economic, and disposable[3]—we shall restrict our discussion to the "basic variant," since the longest record is available in this variant and only in this variant can estimates of shares of types of income by total income size be prepared. To sketch the broad outlines, which is our purpose, this narrow definition of personal income is adequate (see Chart 20).

Table 23 reveals striking differences in the composition of the three groups. In the lowest income group, for example, employee compensation (wages, clerical salaries, and transfer payments, in the main) constitutes about 80 per cent of all income; proprietors' net income about 10 per cent; combined shares of dividends, interest, and rent about 10 per cent. All this is in sharp contrast to the income composition of the top 1 per cent. For this group, employee com-

---

to the nonfarm population because of the severe limitations that attach to the estimates of farm income by size.

[2] It is helpful to know the absolute level of income per capita in the three groups (nonfarm population, basic variant):

	TOP 1 PER CENT		2ND TO 7TH PERCENTAGE BAND		LOWER 93 PER CENT	
	Range	Average	Range	Average	Range	Average
1920	$3,364 & over	$ 9,773	$1,176–$3,363	$1,631	$1,175 & under	$ 606
1929	4,051 & over	11,488	1,491– 4,050	1,984	1,490 & under	585
1937	2,966 & over	8,330	1,189– 2,965	1,543	1,188 & under	486
1948	6,143 & over	12,894	2,186– 6,142	3,161	2,185 & under	1,233

Source: Based on data in *ibid.*, Tables 117 and 119.

[3] The "basic variant" as used by Kuznets signifies that net realized capital gains or losses have been excluded from the income total and the income total is taken before all deductions other than business expenses; economic income is basic income plus compensation of employees of state and local governments and imputed rent on nonfarm homes; and disposable income equals economic income minus federal income taxes plus gains over losses from sales of assets.

pensation, which we here identify with executive and professional salaries, accounts for nearly a third of total income received, and dividends constitute another third. The next largest source is net income of proprietors, which amounts to less than a fifth, slightly exceeding the combined share of interest and rent.

The income structure of the middle income group follows still another pattern. Somewhat more than half of this group's income comes from employee compensation and more than a fifth from proprietorships. Dividends contribute less than 10 per cent, and interest and rents combined about 13 per cent.[4]

The most striking feature of the long record of 1913-1948 is the sharp secular decline in the share of income received by the top 1 per cent—a decline of nearly half between 1913 and 1948, from 16 to 9 per cent (Chart 20 and Table 24). This decline is largely attributable to the fact that property income accounts for half of this group's income; this type of income has sustained a sharp relative fall, as our discussion in Chapter 1 has shown. The most pronounced decreases in the share of the top 1 per cent occurred during World Wars I and II and their immediate aftermaths and during the Great Depression, i.e. decreases have occurred alike in periods of severe inflation and in periods of prolonged deflation.

The strong trend movements, of course, have their effect on the cyclical changes in each size group. During the 1913-1914 contraction the share of the top 1 per cent was reduced by one-eighth. In the early part of World War I this group regained its income loss, but by 1918, the wartime peak, its share of income was slightly below what it had been in the 1914 depression year. At the 1920 peak it dropped again, about 7 per cent. But in the swift deflation of the following year the share of the top group was higher by 5 per cent. Although this group's share of personal income continued to rise through most of the 1920's, even at the 1929 peak it was 1 percentage point below what it had been in 1913. This gradual expansion during the 1920's is consistent with our finding that salaries, dividends, and interest receipts failed to contract during the brief and mild business cycle contractions between 1921 and 1929.

The Great Depression, unlike the 1920-1921 contraction, caused this top group's share of income to drop by 14 per cent, and the next expansion restored less than one-third of the absolute loss. The

[4] For trend changes in the structure of incomes of various sizes see Geoffrey H. Moore's "Secular Changes in the Distribution of Income" (Papers and Proceedings, *American Economic Review*, May 1952, pp. 527-544).

CHART 20

Percentage Shares of Total Income, Three Income Groups, Nonfarm
Population, Three Variants, 1913-1948

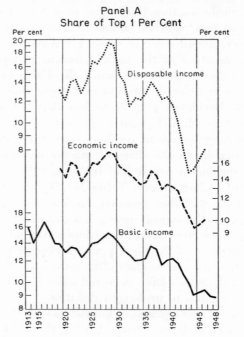

Panel A
Share of Top 1 Per Cent

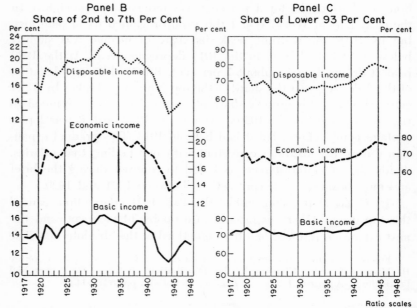

Panel B
Share of 2nd to 7th Per Cent

Panel C
Share of Lower 93 Per Cent

Ratio scales

Source: For basic income variant, Table 24; for economic and disposable variants, Simon Kuznets,
Shares of Upper Income Groups in Income and Savings, National Bureau of Economic Research,
1953, Table 122. For definition of variants, see note 3 in text.

TABLE 23

Various Types of Income as Average Annual Percentage of Total Income,
Five Income Groups, Nonfarm Population, 1919-1938

(*per cent*)

		INCOME GROUP				
	Total Nonfarm	*Top 1 Per Cent*	*2nd and 3rd Per Cent*	*4th and 5th Per Cent*	*6th and 7th Per Cent*	*Lower 93 Per Cent*
Employee compensation	70.1	31.1	53.6	60.8	64.4	79.8
Proprietors' net income	12.0	18.4	23.3	20.5	18.8	8.9
Property income						
Rent	3.4	3.8	5.0	5.4	5.3	3.0
Interest	7.3	13.6	8.7	7.6	7.1	6.0
Dividends	7.1	33.0	9.5	5.7	4.4	2.3
Total income	100.0	100.0	100.0	100.0	100.0	100.0

Note: Not all details add to 100.0 because of rounding.
Source: Simon Kuznets, *Shares of Upper Income Groups in Income and Savings*, National Bureau of Economic Research, 1953, Table 8, p. 27. Computed by use of basic variant; for definition see text, note 3, above.

1937-1938 contraction cut this group's income share by another 12 per cent. The start of World War II, like that of World War I, initiated another period of sustained and significant reductions in this group's share of income. This decline continued until 1948 (the end of our record), except for a small spurt during the 1945-1946 transition from war to peace. The World War II reduction in this group's share of income was much sharper than the decline in World War I—a reduction of a third between 1937 and 1944 compared with an eighth between 1913 and 1918.

To the middle income group (2nd to 7th percentage band) also, both the lean years following 1932 and the inflated years of World War II brought a steady decrease in its share of total income. This group had benefited by a modest increase in the 1920's, and its share reached a peak in 1932. After this peak the middle income group's share declined, reaching a trough in 1944. But there is evidence of another reversal in direction in the first postwar years.

The history of the lowest income group (the lower 93 per cent) is the direct reverse of what happened to the top income group. Over the prosperous years from 1920 to 1929, this group's share of income gradually diminished. But over the fifteen-year period ushered in by the Great Depression, it steadily increased. At the 1944 peak the lowest income group's share was 7 per cent above

TABLE 24

Percentage Shares of Total Income, Three Income Groups,
Nonfarm Population, 1913-1948
(*per cent*)

	INCOME GROUP		
	Top 1 Per Cent	*2nd-7th Per Cent*	*Lower 93 Per Cent*
1913	15.93	n.a.	n.a.
1914	13.95	n.a.	n.a.
1915	15.32	n.a.	n.a.
1916	16.73	n.a.	n.a.
1917	15.39	13.72	70.89
1918	13.89	13.63	72.48
1919	13.87	14.04	72.09
1920	12.87	12.90	74.23
1921	13.49	15.12	71.39
1922	13.41	14.56	72.03
1923	12.37	13.59	74.04
1924	13.04	14.75	72.21
1925	13.99	15.20	70.81
1926	14.06	14.96	70.98
1927	14.66	15.25	70.09
1928	15.19	15.60	69.21
1929	14.76	15.29	69.95
1930	13.83	15.34	70.83
1931	13.06	16.41	70.53
1932	12.62	16.44	70.94
1933	12.01	15.91	72.08
1934	12.07	15.55	72.38
1935	12.26	15.35	72.39
1936	13.65	15.06	71.29
1937	13.27	14.74	71.99
1938	11.63	15.77	72.60
1939	12.09	15.55	72.36
1940	12.23	14.56	73.21
1941	11.79	14.20	74.01
1942	10.63	12.33	77.04
1943	9.88	11.60	78.52
1944	9.00	11.25	79.75
1945	9.19	11.89	78.92
1946	9.37	12.78	77.85
1947	8.86	12.37	78.77
1948	8.81	12.95	78.24

n.a. = not available.

Source: Simon Kuznets, *Shares of Upper Income Groups in Income and Savings*, National Bureau of Economic Research, 1953, Table 116. Computed by use of basic variant; for definition see text, note 3, above. Kuznets' series for 1919-1938 was extrapolated backward by Willford Isbell King's data with a splicing ratio based on 1919, and extrapolated forward by Department of Commerce series with a splicing ratio based on 1936-1938.

what it had been in 1920. In the first few years after World War II, its share seemed to be stabilized just below the 1944 peak.

This absence of a firm pattern in the cyclical movements of the several shares is confirmed by indexes of conformity to business cycles (Table 25).[5] For both the high and the low income group the conformity indexes are low in expansions as well as in contractions, although they are consistently negative for the highest incomes and consistently positive for the lowest incomes. Thus the top group's share of income tends to decline during the upswings in business activity and to increase during downswings. The share of the lowest income group, on the other hand, tends to move in an opposite direction to that of the high income group. But these tendencies are not strong for either group.

TABLE 25

Conformity of Percentage Shares of Total Income, Three Income Groups, Nonfarm Population, to Phases in Business Cycles, 1913-1948

(*index of conformity*)[a]

BUSINESS CYCLE PHASE AND PERIOD	INCOME GROUP		
	Top 1 Per Cent	*2nd-7th Per Cent*	*Lower 93 Per Cent*
Average, 1918-1948			
Expansion	−14	−14	+43
Contraction	−14	−100	+43
Full cycle	−38	−100	+54
Average, 1913-1948			
Expansion	−25	n.a.	n.a.
Contraction	0	n.a.	n.a.
Full cycle	−27	n.a.	n.a.

[a] For definition see pages 23 and 25.
n.a. = not available.
Source: Business cycle phases are those in the National Bureau of Economic Research business cycle chronology; other data are based on Table 24.

Only the share received by the middle income group has high conformity indexes. The indexes mean that in every contraction this group increased its share of income, and that although in three out of seven expansions this group also increased its share, the increase was always at a lower rate than in the adjacent contractions.

This diverse record gives no simple answer to how business cycles affect the shares of income received by the highest, middle, and lowest groups. And for this particular question it makes little dif-

[5] See pages 23 and 25 for a definition of the index of conformity.

ference which income variant is used. Although the rates of change in the shares of the various groups differ according to the income variant used, the general configuration of movement is similar for all three variants (Chart 20).[6]

The absence of perfect conformity in the shares must be due, at least in part, to the conflicting trends and varying cyclical amplitudes of the several types of income. The incomes of the upper income groups are more heavily weighted by dividend receipts, interest payments, salary income, and proprietors' income than are those of the lower income groups, where wages, wage supplements, and transfer payments predominate. But although dividend disbursements and net income of nonfarm proprietors have a larger amplitude than nonfarm labor income in most cycles, interest payments and high salaries have a smaller amplitude. And wage supplements and transfer payments, with a small cyclical amplitude, have a rapidly rising trend, which must have tended to reduce the amplitude of changes in low incomes in recent cycles.

Some cyclical uniformities, however, do emerge from an analysis of the short-run changes in the share of a given type of income received by each income size group. From Table 26 we can see, for each type of income, the change in the share of each size group between a trough in total income and the preceding and succeeding peaks, yielding three sets of peak-trough-peak comparisons.

The share of the highest income group (top 1 per cent) in employee compensation, composed largely of executive and professional salaries, is higher at the troughs than at the preceding and following peaks. This is also true for the middle income group. But the share received by the lowest income group (lower 93 per cent), composed of wages and clerical salaries, is lower at the troughs than at the preceding and following peaks. This is in line with our finding that wages fluctuate more than salaries in response to business cycles, although we must recall that the different percentage bands do not refer to fixed groups of individuals.

Regardless of income size, there is less consistency in the cyclical shifts of shares in proprietors' net income. Thus the shares received by the highest and middle income groups at the 1921 trough were slightly higher than those received at the 1920 peak but lower than

---

[6] The basic variant, the one used above, shows the smallest changes in the share received by the top 1 per cent; and the disposable income variant, the largest changes (see Kuznets, *op. cit.*, Chapter 2).

TABLE 26

Percentage Shares of Various Types of Income, Three Income Groups,
Nonfarm Population, at Personal Income Turning Points,
1920-1948

(*per cent*)

	P 1920	T 1921	P 1929	T 1933	P 1937	T 1938	War-time P 1944[a]	Post-war P 1948
Total income								
Top 1 per cent	12.87	13.49	14.76	12.01	13.27	11.63	9.00	8.81
2nd-7th per cent	12.90	15.12	15.29	15.91	14.74	15.77	11.25	12.95
Lower 93 per cent	74.23	71.39	69.95	72.08	71.99	72.60	79.75	78.24
Employee compensation								
Top 1 per cent	5.27	6.06	5.56	6.54	6.00	6.12	3.16	3.58
2nd-7th per cent	10.07	12.22	12.14	15.67	13.46	14.50	8.86	9.54
Lower 93 per cent	84.66	81.72	82.30	77.79	80.54	79.38	87.98	86.88
Proprietors' net income								
Top 1 per cent	23.24	24.07	24.32	16.84	19.99	17.70	34.55	22.96
2nd-7th per cent	25.10	26.91	29.54	20.41	22.55	20.76	27.89	31.86
Lower 93 per cent	51.66	49.02	46.14	62.75	57.46	61.54	37.56	45.18
Interest								
Top 1 per cent	30.06	27.65	28.80	19.06	22.28	20.01	20.15[b]	13.91
2nd-7th per cent	15.49	17.91	19.40	12.61	12.00	12.89	11.71[b]	11.49
Lower 93 per cent	54.45	54.44	51.80	68.33	65.72	67.10	68.14[b]	74.60
Dividends								
Top 1 per cent	68.40	61.92	63.31	53.65	61.81	54.12	46.87[b]	48.22
2nd-7th per cent	15.98	20.04	14.34	12.94	15.22	17.07	11.88[b]	16.10
Lower 93 per cent	15.62	18.04	22.35	33.41	22.97	28.81	41.25[b]	35.68

[a] There was not a "true" peak in personal income in 1944; the year was selected to show the structure of personal income by type and size in the last full year of war. It also contained a peak in general business.

[b] For 1943.

P = peak; T = trough.

Source: Simon Kuznets, *Shares of Upper Income Groups in Income and Savings*, National Bureau of Economic Research, 1953, Tables 116 and 124. Computed by use of basic variant; for definition see text, note 3, above. Continuous series derived as explained in source of Table 24.

those received at the 1929 peak. However, their shares at the 1933 and 1938 troughs were less than at the preceding and following peaks. The share of the low income group, which receives the remainder, traced movements opposite in direction, of course, to those of the upper income groups. We can rationalize the 1929-1938 movements by saying that when business activity is at a high level, relatively more proprietors acquire incomes that take them out of the low income group. When business activity falls off, many of these again find themselves with a low income.[7]

In the case of dividend receipts we find a higher degree of consistency in cyclical changes, at least for the highest and lowest income groups. The highest income group received a smaller share of dividends at the end of a contraction than at the preceding or succeeding peaks during the interwar decades; the share of the lowest income group, on the contrary, was generally higher at the troughs than at the surrounding peaks. Interest shares showed virtually the same pattern. The trough-peak changes in the share of dividends and interest received by the moderate income group are not like the pattern of either of the other two groups.[8]

Part of this apparent stability in the investment income of the low income group is due to a defect in the data. The investment income of nonprofit organizations is included in the dividend and interest receipts of the lower 93 per cent.[9] Such organizations invest with an eye to stability of current income, while many individuals in the upper income groups invest with an eye to capital gains. Another contributing factor is the fact that the investment income of retired persons must constitute an important segment of the dividends and interest received by the lower income group, and their investment objective would also be stability of income.

[7] Since the share changes between 1920 and 1921 are small for all three groups, little importance can attach to these movements in view of the large errors of estimate of the country-wide total of nonfarm proprietors' income in those years. One need only point out that the first year covered by the census of distribution and service establishments was 1929.

[8] We refrain from analyzing the cyclical movement in the shares of rent by income size because the errors of estimate of the country-wide aggregate are much too large. Thus the use of Kuznets' country-wide aggregate for 1919-1938 yields a pattern that differs significantly from the one given by the use of Department of Commerce estimates for 1929-1938 extrapolated to 1919 by Kuznets' estimates. The Department of Commerce estimates for the 1929-1938 period are preferred since more data were available to the Department than to Kuznets. The Department, however, holds no brief for its own estimates (see Chapter 6, note 1).

[9] The estimating procedures are as follows: The country-wide total of dividends is the difference between dividends paid out by corporations and dividends received by corporations, all based, with minor exceptions, on corporate income tax returns. Since nonprofit organizations do not file corporate income tax returns, their receipts of dividends are counted as being received by individuals. Dividends received by the lower 93 per cent are computed by taking the difference between the country-wide total and the dividend receipts of the upper income groups reported on personal income tax returns. Corporate bond interest is estimated similarly.

Our final comparison shows how the war and postwar inflation affected the share of each type of income received by each of the three income-size groups. The previous discussion of how the compensation of production and nonproduction workers has fluctuated prepares us for the finding that the share of the lower 93 per cent in employee compensation increased by nearly 10 per cent between 1937 and the wartime peak of 1944 but lost a fraction of this gain by 1948. This gain was offset by drastic declines in the share of employee compensation received by the highest and middle income groups.

In the case of proprietors' net income, however, the relative gains in wartime were scored by the upper income groups. The general prosperity caused many small businessmen to shift from the low to the upper income groups. The postwar prosperity was less favorable to the top 1 per cent, and the respective shares of the three groups in 1948 reverted to the 1929 distribution.

The reasons for the shifts in the shares of dividends and interest are not entirely clear. The lower 93 per cent increased its share of dividends by 80 per cent between 1937 and 1943,[10] while the share of the top 1 per cent declined by a quarter and that of the middle income group by 22 per cent (Table 27). By 1948 the lowest income group had lost 30 per cent of its absolute gain, which accrued chiefly to the share of the middle income group. The obvious inference is that during the decade following 1937 the lowest income group increased its ownership of equities faster than the highest and middle income groups. Unfortunately, there is no independent evidence to confirm or contradict this inference. But there is evidence that dividends and interest were not fully reported to the tax authorities in this period, and that the share of the top 7 per cent in dividends and interest was actually higher than would appear from the published data (see Appendix F). Because of this defect in the data, which statistical procedures cannot obviate, we believe that Kuznets' estimates of the distribution of property income among the three income-size groups are somewhat inaccurate, and that it would be closer to reality to assume that the distributions in 1944 and 1948 were the same as that in 1937.

On this assumption, what can be said about the impact of war and postwar inflation on the distribution of total income among the

[10] It is necessary to substitute 1943 data for 1944 since only the composite of dividends and interest was tabulated by the Bureau of Internal Revenue in 1944 and 1945.

TABLE 27

Percentage Shares of Total Dividends and Interest, Three Income Groups,
Nonfarm Population, 1937-1948
(*per cent*)

	TOP 1 PER CENT		2ND-7TH PER CENT		LOWER 93 PER CENT	
	Dividends	*Interest*	*Dividends*	*Interest*	*Dividends*	*Interest*
1937	61.81	22.28	15.22	12.00	22.97	65.72
1938	54.12	20.01	17.07	12.89	28.81	67.10
1939	56.04	21.61	14.67	13.71	29.29	64.68
1940	57.06	20.99	14.39	14.85	28.55	64.16
1941	51.75	22.25	15.99	15.20	32.26	62.55
1942	47.14	22.88	11.21	13.09	41.65	64.03
1943	46.87	20.15	11.88	11.71	41.25	68.14
1944	n.a.	n.a.	n.a.	n.a.	n.a.	n.a.
1945	n.a.	n.a.	n.a.	n.a.	n.a.	n.a.
1946	45.47	16.89	16.67	14.28	37.86	68.83
1947	45.02	15.18	13.82	11.63	41.16	73.19
1948	48.22	13.91	16.10	11.49	35.68	74.60

n.a. = not available.

Source: Simon Kuznets, *Shares of Upper Income Groups in Income and Savings*, National Bureau of Economic Research, 1953, Table 124. Computed by use of basic variant; for definition see text, note 3, above. Continuous series derived as explained in source of Table 24.

three income-size groups of the nonfarm population? It is clear from the following computations that the basic trend is unaltered, although the rate of change is modified slightly. The reservations mentioned above on the estimated shifts in property income do not call into question the underlying trend during the war and postwar years, but only whether the shifts in the distribution of property income paralleled those in employee compensation.

	PER CENT OF TOTAL INCOME RECEIVED BY:		
	Top 1 Per Cent	2nd to 7th Percentage Band	Lower 93 Per Cent
1937	13.27	14.74	71.99
1944			
Unrevised	9.00	11.25	79.75
Revised	10.13	11.33	78.54
1948			
Unrevised	8.81	12.95	78.24
Revised	9.83	12.85	77.32

The persistent rise in the percentage of income received by the lower 93 per cent reflects the very large weight of employee compensation in the income of this group and the pronounced increase in the relative importance of this type of income. As we noted in Chapter 5, the main cause of the long-term rise in wage disbursements was the rise in average hourly earnings.

CHAPTER 8

GOVERNMENT OFFSETS TO CYCLICAL LOSSES IN PERSONAL INCOME

THE severity of the Great Depression and the slowness and partial character of the recovery before World War II brought to the fore governmental schemes designed to inject purchasing power into the income stream at ebbs in the economic tides. At much the same time there developed a literature on "built-in" stabilizers of income— quasi-automatic programs—that come into play to bolster income when it begins to sag and to restrain the rise in income when inflationary pressures become serious. It is not our purpose to review or appraise this literature.[1] Our aim is an empirical one: to determine whether the programs we can readily analyze are in fact countercyclical and to measure their importance during the recent past in supporting personal income once it begins to fall. We have selected three programs for discussion: the farm price-support program, unemployment compensation and related programs, and the federal personal income tax. Only the second and third lend themselves readily to measurement.

Agricultural Programs

In recent years the federal government's program for maintaining farm income has had two main facets: cash benefits and price support.[2]

Cash benefits are paid directly to farm operators, primarily to encourage conservation practices and to provide incentives for production control through withdrawal of acreage from cultivation for specified crops. Did these benefit payments follow a countercyclical course with respect to net farm income after World War II? If so, the year-to-year change in volume of cash disbursed should be opposite in direction to the annual change in the net income of farm operators. This is a minimum condition if the program is to

[1] For a discussion of these problems and a brief bibliography see A. G. Hart, *Money, Debt and Economic Activity* (2nd ed., Prentice-Hall, 1953, Chapter 28).

[2] Both programs were initiated in 1933. During the 1930's the main objective was to raise the income of farmers—countercyclical only in a broad sense—and during the war years it was to expand production. It seems appropriate, therefore, to look for countercyclical behavior only in the postwar years. However, see pages 94-96 for a brief comment on the complications that arise from countercyclical measures when cycles in net farm income do not conform to cycles in general business.

qualify as countercyclical. According to the data in Table 28, the annual changes in net income and in cash benefits were opposite in direction in only two out of the six year-to-year changes. Cash

TABLE 28

Farm Proprietors' Net Income and Retained Government Benefit Payments, 1945-1951

(*millions of dollars*)

	Net Income	Government Benefit Payments
1945	12,528	659
1946	14,790	688
1947	15,589	277
1948	17,666	227
1949	12,776	161
1950	13,348	249
1951	15,568	251

Source: Net income of farm proprietors: *Survey of Current Business*, Dept. of Commerce, July 1952, Table 1, pp. 12-13. Government benefit payments retained by farm operators: *Farm Income Situation*, Bureau of Agricultural Economics, August-September 1952, Tables 9 and 13, pp. 35 and 39.

benefits failed to increase during the first year that net farm income showed a decline (1949), and increased by only $88 million in the second year (1950), when net income was reduced by $4,318 million below the 1948 peak. Moreover, in 1951, when net farm income again increased, cash benefits remained virtually unchanged. We conclude that this program has not been an important offset to loss of farm income in the postwar period. This was partly intentional, of course, since some of the objectives of the program are long-run, not short-run, in character.

In the price-support program, farmers receive cash directly from nonrecourse loans made or guaranteed by the Commodity Credit Corporation of the Department of Agriculture and from its direct purchases of commodities. The CCC, however, on occasion disposes of some or all of its holdings through the commercial market in competition with farmers. The inventories of the CCC represent the net purchases (purchases less sales) plus the collateral acquired from farmers defaulting on loans. The federal government's cumulated investment (actual and contingent) in the price-support program on a given date is the sum of the loans held by the CCC, loans held by private lending agencies with CCC guarantee, purchase agreement obligations, and inventories of the CCC.

This investment by the federal government is *not* a measure of the financial benefit received by farmers (offset to loss of net income) from the price-support program. A measure of this benefit would be the difference between (1) actual farm receipts from sales in commercial markets plus sales to and net loans from the CCC and (2) what farm receipts would have been from commercial sales without a price-support program—assuming that farm production expenses are the same with or without price supports. Since 2 is a hypothetical quantity, it is bound to be characterized by large errors of estimate, and for this reason no annual estimates of this offset to loss of farm net income have been attempted.[3] However, *changes* in the government's investment in price-support operations are an *indicator* of the direction of change in the amount of the offset provided by this program to loss in net farm income. If the change in the government's investment rises or falls, we may infer that the amount of the offset does the same. By analyzing changes in the government's investment, therefore, we can determine whether the program has in fact been operating in a countercyclical manner.

The offset provided by this program (Chart 21 and Table 29) has shown a higher degree of countercyclical conformity since the war than the crop control program, but the conformity has been less than perfect. If this device were a fully effective stabilizer of farm income, the series on quarterly changes in the amount of the government's outstanding investment would rise when farm income recedes and decline when farm income expands. Assuming that the investment is to be liquidated sometime in the course of the cycle, we might expect that the changes in total outstanding investment would pass from positive to negative values sometime in mid-expansion, and from negative to positive values sometime in mid-contraction. By this test, the program has shown only partial countercyclical conformity. The peak in quarterly changes in the government's investment (based on a four-quarter moving average to eliminate seasonal fluctuations) occurred at the end of the fourth quarter of 1948, although the contraction of farm income continued until the fourth quarter of 1949. Similarly, in the following expansion, the trough in the decline of the government's investment was reached at the end of the fourth quarter of 1950, although farm income continued to expand until the fourth quarter of 1951. Finally, the change from negative to positive values occurred very shortly after the peak

[3] In note 4, below, such an estimate for 1949 is presented for its illustrative value.

in farm income, and the converse change occurred after the trough in farm income.

From the point of view of stabilization, one might say that the program responded too promptly to cyclical developments, exerting its maximum countercyclical effect in early expansion and early contraction, instead of toward the end of these phases. This tendency is clearly revealed in the figures on the government's total outstanding investment in the program, which reached its peak and troughs almost synchronously with the trough and peaks of farm income, rather than roughly half a phase later, as an ideal program might be expected to do. Thus, in effect, the program failed to provide increased support to the agricultural market during the worst stages of the contraction, and operated to damp the ensuing revival at its inception rather than when it was well under way. These observations, of course, apply only to a single contraction and revival, and it is not therefore clear whether this limited success in stabilization is an inherent feature of the mechanics and objectives of the program, or merely reflects circumstances peculiar to the postwar period. It must be repeated that since we do not measure the absolute amount of the offset, we cannot say anything about its relative importance in compensating farmers for the loss of income.[4]

[4] As already noted, the amount of the offset is difficult to measure because of the necessity of determining what prices and commercial sales would have been without the price-support program. George Mehren has attempted such estimates for 1949 ("Comparative Costs of Agricultural Price Support in 1949," Papers and Proceedings, *American Economic Review*, May 1951, pp. 717-746). Using his estimates of prices and commercial sales with and without price-support operations, we can prepare a rough estimate of the offset for 1949:

	(millions of dollars)
a. Farm receipts with price-support operations	
Actual commercial sales (from Mehren)	17,437
Sales to CCC (*Agricultural Statistics, 1950*, Dept. of Agriculture, Table 756)	917
New loans minus repayments (*ibid.*, Table 755)	1,850
Total	20,204
b. Farm receipts without price-support operations	
Hypothetical commercial sales (from Mehren)	16,066
c. Offset to loss of net farm income (a — b)	4,138
d. Hypothetical loss in net farm income between 1948 and 1949 if there had been no price-support operations (change in net income of farm operators between 1948 and 1949 [see Table 28] minus c)	9,028
e. Offset as per cent of loss in net farm income (c ÷ d)	46%

Because of the potentially large margins of error that must attach to estimates of hypothetical prices and commercial sales without price supports, our computation must be taken as having only illustrative value.

CHART 21

Farm Proprietors' Net Income, Investment in Price-Support Operations, and Change in Total Investment, 1946-1952

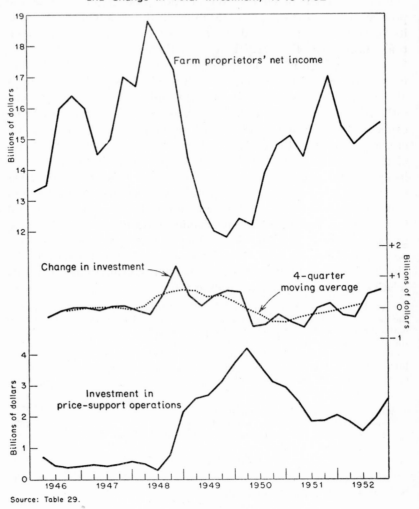

Source: Table 29.

Since the offset provided by the price-support operations is geared to cycles in net income of farm operators, the program would not be countercyclical with respect to personal income if the cycle in net farm income did not conform with the cycle in personal income. In recent decades there has been at least one instance, 1925 to 1926, when net farm income was declining while personal income was

TABLE 29

Farm Proprietors' Net Income, Investment in Price-Support Operations, and Changes in Total Investment, 1946-1952

			INVESTMENT IN PRICE-SUPPORT OPERATIONS[b]			
					Total Investment	
YEAR AND QUARTER		FARM PROPRIETORS' NET INCOME[a] (billions of dollars)	Inventories	Outstanding Loans and Purchase Agreement Obligations	Amount	Change from Previous Quarter
				(m i l l i o n s o f d o l l a r s)		
1946	1st	13.3	562	150	712	
	2nd	13.5	398	48	446	−266
	3rd	16.0	351	29	380	−66
	4th	16.4	291	120	411	+31
1947	1st	16.0	256	200	456	+45
	2nd	14.5	294	121	415	−41
	3rd	15.0	311	174	485	+70
	4th	17.0	286	279	565	+80
1948	1st	16.7	209	281	490	−75
	2nd	18.8	150	144	294	−196
	3rd	18.0	202	573	775	+481
	4th	17.2	322	1,841	2,163	+1,388
1949	1st	14.4	326	2,269	2,595	+432
	2nd	12.8	1,082	1,610	2,692	+97
	3rd	12.0	1,656	1,456	3,112	+420
	4th	11.8	1,725	1,976	3,701	+589
1950	1st	12.4	1,855	2,372	4,227	+526
	2nd	12.2	2,624	1,004	3,628	−599
	3rd	13.9	2,174	924	3,098	−530
	4th	14.8	1,926	979	2,905	−193
1951	1st	15.1	1,717	739	2,456	−449
	2nd	14.4	1,501	334	1,835	−621
	3rd	15.8	1,363	480	1,843	+8
	4th	17.0	1,265	756	2,021	+178
1952	1st	15.4	1,098	703	1,801	−220
	2nd	14.8	1,131	372	1,503	−298
	3rd	15.2	1,124	846	1,970	+467
	4th	15.5	1,118	1,443	2,561	+591

[a] Seasonally adjusted annual rates.

[b] End of quarter.

Source: Net income of farm proprietors: *National Income Supplement, 1951, Survey of Current Business*, Dept. of Commerce, Table 41, p. 205, and *Survey of Current Business*, July 1952, Table 41, p. 29, and February 1953, p. S-1. Inventories and outstanding loans and purchase agreement obligations: *Charts*, multilithed, Commodity Credit Corporation, December 1951, Table 7, for data for 1946 to 1950; and monthly issues of *Report of Financial Condition and Operations*, CCC, for data for 1951 and 1952.

expanding. In such circumstances offsetting the loss in net farm income adds to the inflationary pressures in the economy at large. In the opposite situation—rising net farm income with declining personal income—this program would add deflationary pressures to an economy that was already contracting.

Unemployment Compensation and Related Payments

The offset to the loss of labor income provided by unemployment benefits has been less than complete, in part by legislative design. For administrative reasons and to prevent malingering, a waiting period is imposed, weekly benefits are computed at about half of the former weekly wage, and the number of benefit payments in a fifty-two-week period is limited. Moreover, not all unemployed persons are eligible to draw benefits, and it is not the intention of the system to compensate for loss of labor income resulting from the loss of overtime work, reduction in the normal workweek,[5] or cuts in wage rates. By measurement, however, we can determine how much of the loss in labor income has been offset by unemployment benefits and related payments. Since it was not until 1939 that all states were paying unemployment compensation benefits,[6] their adequacy can be tested only by the two recessions in labor income (wages and salaries) since 1938—those in 1945-1946 and 1948-1949— neither of which was severe or prolonged. Initially we eliminate from our analysis labor income originating in government, in order to circumvent the special problem of loss of labor income resulting from the demobilization of the armed forces.[7]

On this basis the first recession in labor income adjusted for seasonal movements began in February 1945; labor income continued to decline until October of that year, and by April 1946 had more than recovered the level of the initial peak. In the second recession the peak is September 1948, and the trough is October

---

[5] In all states except Montana some partial unemployment is compensated. The provisions usually stipulate that when partial unemployment reduces the weekly wage of a worker below what his weekly benefit would be were he fully unemployed, the difference plus an increment varying from $2 to $8, depending on the state, will be paid as a benefit. See *Significant Provisions of State Unemployment Insurance Laws, October 1, 1951,* multilithed, Dept. of Labor, Bureau of Employment Security.

[6] *Social Security Yearbook, 1941,* Federal Security Agency, 1942, Table 1, p. 168.

[7] The system of compensation to unemployed veterans following discharge from service was an *ad hoc* arrangement that does not qualify as part of a built-in system of income stability.

1949; by May 1950 the level of the initial peak had been exceeded. The loss in labor income in a given month (quarter) is the difference between labor income in the peak month (quarter) and the given month (quarter). We accumulate the loss between the initial peak and trough and between the initial peak and the return to the level of the initial peak. The relative loss in labor income is the cumulative loss expressed as a percentage of the labor income that would have been disbursed if labor income in the peak month (quarter) had been maintained in all months (quarters) comprised in the recession or recession and recovery.

The cumulative amounts paid out each month (quarter) as unemployment benefits and general assistance minus the amounts paid out in the month (quarter) of the payroll peak—all computations based on seasonally adjusted data—constitute the offset to loss of labor income.[8] The relative offset is the cumulative offset expressed as a percentage of the cumulative loss in labor income.

In the first of these contractions of private wages and salaries, compensation to the unemployed offset only 6 per cent of the payroll loss; but in the second contraction, it offset as much as 17 per cent (Chart 22 and Table 30). If we cover the period between the peak and the return to the level of the initial peak, the relative offsets are much higher, 12 per cent in the first period and 20 per cent in the second. In the 1945-1946 contraction and recovery, general assistance accounted for about 2.5 per cent of the offset, and in the 1948-1950 period for about 8 per cent. This suggests that the longer the recession and recovery period, the more important is general assistance in offset payments.

For some purposes it is more appropriate to compare compensation to the unemployed with the loss in all payrolls (private and government) or with the loss in disposable income (excluding compensation to the unemployed). The offset to loss in total payrolls has been computed for 1948-1950 on a monthly and quarterly basis, and the offset to loss in disposable income on a quarterly basis (Tables 31 and 32).

[8] Unemployment benefits include those paid to railroad employees as well as to all other covered workers. We include general assistance, despite the fact that assistance payments are often received by unemployables, because unemployed workers ineligible for unemployment benefits may also receive general assistance. Moreover, assistance payments may be extended to supplement unemployment benefits that are deemed too low to provide a family with minimum subsistence. Like benefits, general assistance payments increase during contractions and decrease during expansions.

CHART 22

Private Payrolls and Compensation to Unemployed, 1945-1946 and 1948-1950

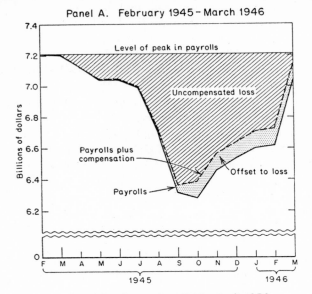

Panel A.   February 1945 – March 1946

Panel B.   September 1948 – April 1950

Source: See Appendix G, section 1.

On the basis of monthly data, the ratio of offset to loss in total payrolls was 20 per cent (peak to trough) and 24.5 per cent (peak to level of initial peak), as compared with 17 and 20 per cent respectively in the case of private payrolls. This is because government payrolls continued to increase during this recession, so that the

98

TABLE 30

Cumulative Loss in Private Payrolls and Cumulative Compensation to
Unemployed, from Seasonally Adjusted Monthly Data,
1945-1946 and 1948-1950

(*dollars in millions*)

	Peak to Trough, Feb. 1945– Oct. 1945	Peak to Initial Peak Level, Feb. 1945– Mar. 1946	Peak to Trough, Sept. 1948– Oct. 1949	Peak to Initial Peak Level, Sept. 1948– Apr. 1950
Loss in private payrolls	$2,958	$5,750	$5,008	$7,450
Total compensation to unemployed	$173	$698	$832	$1,504
Unemployment benefits	168	682	776	1,383
General assistance	5	16	56	121
Total compensation as percentage of payroll loss	5.8%	12.1%	16.6%	20.2%
Unemployment benefits	5.7	11.9	15.5	18.6
General assistance	.2	.3	1.1	1.6

Source: Appendix G, section 1.

loss in total payrolls was smaller than in private payrolls, and the
given offset was relatively higher.[9] In this period the relative offset
based on quarterly data is slightly lower than the offset based on
monthly data.[10]

That the cumulative payroll loss on a quarterly basis is generally
less than on a monthly basis is clear. Since the peak value is the
basis for computing the loss, the lower the peak value, the lower the
loss. The value of the peak month by definition is higher than the
monthly average for the quarter in which the peak month falls

[9] The amount of the offset differs slightly in Tables 30 and 31 because the
1948 peak occurs a month later and the terminal date a month earlier in the
latter table.

[10] Using quarterly data and dealing with the identical period, Ida Merriam
estimates the ratio of the offset of unemployment compensation (state and
railroad) to the loss in civilian wages and salaries as 24.3 per cent ("Social
Security Programs and Economic Stability," *Policies to Combat Depression*,
to be published by Princeton University Press for the National Bureau of
Economic Research, Table 2). This is identical with the relative offset presented
above in Table 31. Our computations, however, are based on total payrolls
including pay to the military, which continued to rise during this period (see
above, page 53), and on compensation to the unemployed that includes general
assistance. That is, if the only differences were those in definition of payrolls and
of compensation to the unemployed, the relative offset computed by Mrs.
Merriam would be lower than ours. The identity of the results indicates the
presence of other differences, which we presume to be differences in the seasonal
adjustment of payrolls and of compensation to the unemployed.

TABLE 31

Cumulative Loss in Total Payrolls and Cumulative Compensation to
Unemployed, from Seasonally Adjusted Monthly and Quarterly Data, 1948-1950
(*dollars in millions*)

| | PEAK TO TROUGH | | PEAK TO INITIAL PEAK LEVEL | |
	Monthly, Oct. 1948– Oct. 1949	*Quarterly, 4th 1948– 3rd 1949*	*Monthly, Oct. 1948– Mar. 1950*	*Quarterly, 4th 1948– 1st 1950*
Loss in total payrolls	$4,275	$3,183	$5,992	$5,192
Compensation to unemployed	$857	$595	$1,466	$1,261
Compensation as percentage of payroll loss	20.0%	18.7%	24.5%	24.3%

Source: Appendix G, section 1.

TABLE 32

Cumulative Loss in Disposable Income and Cumulative Compensation to
Unemployed, from Seasonally Adjusted Quarterly Data, 1948-1950
(*dollars in millions*)

	Peak to Trough, 3rd 1948– 3rd 1949	*Peak to Initial Peak Level, 3rd 1948– 4th 1949*
Loss in disposable income[a] excluding compensation to unemployed	$6,453	$8,928
Compensation to unemployed	$749	$1,179
Compensation as percentage of disposable income loss	11.6%	13.2%

[a] Including realized net capital gains.
Source: Appendix G, section 1.

(unless the three monthly values are identical, which rarely happens). Hence the loss computed from quarterly data will be smaller than the loss computed from monthly data. By the same reasoning, the payroll loss computed from annual data will be smaller than the loss computed from quarterly data.

In the case of the offsets, the effect of the shift in the time unit is not so clear. A priori, one would expect compensation to the unemployed to be at a minimum in the peak payroll quarter and hence the difference between the monthly average compensation in the peak payroll quarter and compensation in the peak payroll month probably to be negligible. However, the monthly average for the quarter could be either larger or smaller than compensation in the peak payroll month and the differences need not be small. In this particular period (the fourth quarter of 1948 to the first quarter of 1950) the monthly average for the quarter of the payroll peak was larger than the offset in the peak payroll month and by a significant amount. This resulted in a smaller relative offset since the proportionate reduction in the offset exceeded that in the cumulative payroll loss.

Using annual data, we compute the loss in total payrolls between 1948 and 1949 at $982 million and the offset payments in 1949 at $1,097 million. That is, the offset exceeded the loss by 12 per cent. Thus the time unit is an important element in measuring the relative offset.

Finally, we note that compensation to the unemployed offset 12 per cent of the loss in disposable income (excluding compensation to the unemployed) that occurred during the contraction in disposable income from the third quarter of 1948 to the third quarter of 1949 (Table 32). If we cover the period from the initial peak until the same level is regained (the third quarter of 1948 to the fourth quarter of 1949), the offset amounts to 13 per cent of the loss in disposable income.

Because the business contractions of 1944-1946 and 1948-1949 were mild, these measures of relative offset have limited value. It would be more helpful to know the effectiveness of this type of offset when the loss of labor income is substantial. Some light is thrown on this question by data for certain states where, during the 1948-1949 contraction, the loss in labor income was relatively larger than in the country as a whole. The varying generosity of benefit payments among state laws, however, somewhat blurs this comparison.

For this analysis (Table 33), we have selected twelve of the twenty-three states in which payrolls, based on annual estimates, declined between 1948 and 1949, and prepared *quarterly* estimates of payrolls (wages and salaries) in the private sector and of offsets to loss in payrolls for 1948, 1949, and 1950.[11] The amount of payroll loss and of offsets during the recession and recovery were computed as described above.

There is some evidence of an inverse relation between the relative

[11] For sources of data and methods of estimation see Appendix G. For the analysis of the state data we are obliged to use data unadjusted for seasonal variations since the data are insufficient for reliable seasonal determination.

TABLE 33

Loss in Private Payrolls, Compensation to Unemployed,
and General Assistance, from Seasonally Unadjusted Quarterly Data, 1948-1950,
and Change in Number Exhausting Benefits, 1948-1949,
United States and Twelve States

(per cent)

	QUARTERS COVERED 1948 1950	LOSS AS % OF PEAK PAYROLLS[a]	COMPENSATION AS % OF LOSS	GENERAL ASSISTANCE AS % OF COMPENSATION	PERCENTAGE INCREASE IN NUMBER EXHAUSTING BENEFIT RIGHTS
South Carolina	4th – 2nd	6.0	13.6	2.2	174
California	3rd – 2nd	7.6	14.1	6.9	40
New York	4th – 3rd	9.2	9.4	13.4	66
Michigan	4th – 2nd	10.0	8.9	7.7	137
Kentucky	4th – 2nd	10.3	9.0	2.8	144
Pennsylvania	4th – 3rd	10.4	10.9	11.5	134
Rhode Island	4th – 3rd	10.5	15.8	18.3	122
Connecticut	4th – 3rd	10.9	9.2	5.7	241
Alabama	4th – 2nd	11.1	7.8	.9	106
Ohio	4th – 3rd	11.4	8.3	6.7	167
Illinois	4th – 3rd	13.1	5.7	9.6	88
West Virginia	4th – 4th	13.7	6.7	3.8	217
Twelve states		10.2	9.2	9.5	
United States	3rd – 2nd	4.3	20.3	9.7	

[a] This measure of relative loss in payrolls is the actual loss as a percentage of what would have been disbursed if payrolls in the peak quarter had been maintained in all quarters covered in the table.

Source: Percentage increase in number exhausting benefit rights based on annual data in *Handbook of Unemployment Insurance Financial Data, 1938-1951*, processed, Dept. of Labor, Bureau of Employment Security, revised November 1952, Table C-12. For other data see Appendix G, section 2.

payroll loss and the relative offset from compensation to the unemployed.[12] The relationship is most apparent at the extremes of the array. Thus the relative payroll loss is least in South Carolina and California, and the third and second largest relative offsets occur in these states. At the other extreme are Illinois and West Virginia, with the two largest relative payroll losses and the two smallest relative offsets. The least relationship is found in Rhode Island, with the seventh largest payroll loss and the highest offset. This is explained in part by the relatively high share of general assistance in total compensation of the unemployed. The right to general assist-

[12] The coefficient of rank correlation for these two variables in the twelve states is —.73.

ance, unlike the right to unemployment benefits, is not limited to a specified number of weeks in a given period. .

The inverse relationship between relative payroll loss and offset finds support in a comparison of the total loss and total offset of the twelve states and of the United States. In the twelve states the relative payroll loss is 10.2 per cent and the relative offset 9.2; the comparable percentages for the United States are 4.3 and 20.3. The relative payroll loss is less for the United States than for any of the selected states because the United States total includes states with payroll gains or negligible losses as well as the twelve selected states.

The explanation for the inverse relationship between relative payroll loss and offset is to be found in the following considerations. There appears to be a direct association between relative payroll loss and the percentage rise in the number of unemployed exhausting benefit rights before re-employment. This relationship among the twelve states is clouded by the inclusion of South Carolina and Illinois (Table 33). If these two states are excluded as being atypical, the coefficient of rank correlation is +.65. The continued unemployment of those exhausting benefit rights either is uncompensated or is compensated under a general assistance program at a lower rate than that of unemployment benefits. Finally, the inference seems warranted that because of the interdependence of the various segments of the economy the relative increase in the number laid off by employers not subject to unemployment compensation laws varies directly with the relative payroll loss.

These considerations, together with our evidence, suggest that in more severe business recessions the relative offset under present laws would be decidedly less than it was in the 1948-1949 recession.

Federal Personal Income Tax

The third program, the federal personal income tax, is not directed toward bolstering the income of any particular economic group; in the past decade at least it has affected virtually the entire population. The broadening of the tax base and the sharp elevation of effective tax rates which accompanied World War II and its aftermath have enhanced the power of the tax program to reduce fluctuations in personal income after taxes, i.e. disposable income. The proportional and progressive elements in the tax structure can cause this effect without any change in tax rates and exemption levels.

As long as the income tax is a percentage of personal income (i.e. proportional to income) and not an absolute amount, the amount of taxes paid by individuals will decline in periods of contraction in personal incomes. If the tax structure is progressive as well as proportional, the amount of personal taxes will decline further because the average effective tax rate falls during business contractions. During business expansions the tax program will produce contrary results.

This stabilizing effect might, of course, be negated if Congress lowered tax rates during business expansions or raised them during contractions. Congress in fact followed just such a course during some of the expansion years of the 1920's and during the Great Depression (Table 34). However, despite the rise in effective tax rates during the Great Depression, the average effective rate declined. On the other hand, a lowering of effective tax rates during a business contraction, which occurred in the 1920-1921 and 1923-1924 contractions, reinforces the stabilizing effect of a progressive income tax.

We shall now measure, for periods of contraction since 1920, the importance of (1) the total offset provided by the income tax system in relation to the loss in disposable income (personal income after taxes) and (2) the offset attributable to the progressive feature alone. These measures are carried out for four contraction periods, 1920-1921, 1929-1933, 1937-1938, and 1948-1949. (In the business contractions of 1923-1924, 1926-1927, and 1944-1946 there was no decline in annual disposable income.) For the first three contractions we are obliged to use annual data, but for the 1948-1949 contraction we use seasonally adjusted quarterly data.

To measure the total offset in relative terms, we express the cumulative decrease in personal income tax liabilities from the peak to the trough year (or quarter) as a percentage (Table 35, column 6) of the cumulative loss in disposable income in the same period. To estimate the loss in income for a given year (column 5), we calculate what the disposable income would have been if tax liabilities had remained at the peak figure (column 3), and then subtract the given year from the peak year.[13] In measuring the relative offset attributable to the progressivity feature, we find the average effective tax rate in the peak year (or quarter) and apply this rate to personal income in the given year. This gives us what tax liabilities would have been if the average tax rate had remained

[13] This loss is, of course, equal to the actual loss in personal income before taxes.

TABLE 34

Individual Income Tax Liabilities for Two Groups
of Taxpayers, 1913-1951

(*dollars*)

| | | INDIVIDUAL INCOME TAX LIABILITY FOR MARRIED PERSONS WITH TWO DEPENDENTS WITH A NET INCOME OF: | |
		$5,000	*$100,000*
P	1913	10	2,510
T	1914	10	2,510
	1915	10	2,510
	1916	20	3,920
	1917	64	16,164
P	1918	156	34,982
T	1919	104	31,158
P	1920	104	31,158
T	1921	68	31,126
	1922	68	30,076
P	1923	51	22,557
T	1924	26	22,535
	1925	8	16,029
P	1926	8	16,029
T	1927	8	16,029
	1928	8	15,739
P	1929	3	14,846
	1930	8	15,739
	1931	8	15,739
T	1932	68	30,036
	1933	68	30,036
	1934	48	30,162
	1935	48	30,162
	1936	48	31,997
P	1937	48	31,997
T	1938	48	31,997
	1939	48	31,997
	1940	75	42,948
	1941	271	52,160
	1942	592	63,479
	1943	730	67,803
P	1944	· 755	68,565
	1945	755	68,565
T	1946	589	62,301
	1947	589	62,301
P	1948	432	45,643
T	1949	432	45,643
	1950	452	47,208
	1951	520	51,912

P = peak; T = trough.

Source: Peaks and troughs are those in the National Bureau of Economic
Research business cycle chronology. Other data are from *Annual Report of the
Secretary of the Treasury on the State of the Finances for the Fiscal Year Ended
June 30, 1950*, Dept. of the Treasury, 1951, Table III, p. 247.

TABLE 35

Offsets to Loss in Disposable Income through Operation of Federal Personal
Income Tax in Selected Contraction Periods, 1920-1949

(dollars in billions)

	Personal Income[a] (1)	Federal Personal Income Tax Liabilities (2)	Disposable Income at Peak Taxes (1 − Peak in 2) (3)	Total Offset: Reduction in Taxes (Peak in 2 − 2) (4)	Loss in Disposable Income (Peak in 3 − 3) (5)	Total Offset as % of Income Loss (4 ÷ 5) (6)	Average Effective Tax Rate at Peak (2 ÷ 1) (7)	Tax Liabilities at Peak Rate (1 × 7) (8)	Offset from Reduction in Taxes Due to Progressivity of Tax System (8 − 2) (9)	Offset Due to Progressivity as % of Income Loss (9 ÷ 5) (10)	Change in Effective Tax Rates (11)
1920	$69.1	$1.1	$68.0								
1921	55.1	.7	54.0	$ .4	$ 14.0	2.9%	1.59%	$ .9	$ .2	1.4%	Lowered
1929	85.2	1.0	84.2				1.17				
1930	72.1	.5	71.1	.5	13.1	3.8		.8	.3	2.3	Raised
1931	59.4	.2	58.4	.8	25.8	3.1		.7	.5	1.9	No change
1932	43.9	.3	42.9	.7	41.3	1.7		.5	.2	.5	Raised
1933	42.8	.4	41.8	.6	42.4	1.4		.5	.1	.2	No change
1929-1933				2.6	122.6	2.1			1.1	.9	
1937	71.3	1.1	70.2				1.54				
1938	65.6	.8	64.5	.3	5.7	5.3		1.0	.2	3.5	No change
1948 4th Q	53.3	4.0[b]	49.3				7.50				
1949 1st Q	51.4	3.7	47.4	.3	1.9	15.8		3.9	.2	10.5	No change
1949 2nd Q	51.1	3.7	47.1	.3	2.2	13.6		3.8	.1	4.5	
1949 3rd Q	50.7	3.7	46.7	.3	2.6	11.5		3.8	.1	3.8	
1948-1949											
4th Q–3rd Q				.9	6.7	13.4			.4	6.0	

Notes to Table 35

a Including realized capital gains and losses.

b Beginning with 1949 the military pay of all members of the armed forces was subject to federal income tax. According to our estimates, if this tax provision had been in effect in 1948, about $.05 billion would have been added to the federal tax liabilities given above for the fourth quarter of 1948.

Q = quarter.

Column   Source

1   For annual data see Table 22. Quarterly data estimated by multiplying the ratio of seasonally adjusted quarterly personal income estimates to annual personal income (both from *National Income Supplement, 1951, Survey of Current Business*, Dept. of Commerce, Table 45, p. 209, and *Survey of Current Business*, July 1952, Table 45, p. 30) by the National Bureau of Economic Research annual estimates of personal income including net capital gains.

2   Annual data from the preliminary report of *Statistics of Income for 1949*, Part 1, Bureau of Internal Revenue, pp. 9 and 51-53. Quarterly data estimated by multiplying ratio mentioned above by annual federal income tax liabilities. This procedure makes no allowance for the possibility that the annual income-size structure implicit in quarterly totals probably varies from quarter to quarter during a cyclical contraction. We do not know how to adjust for this factor and merely note that the statistical procedure used serves to minimize the amount of the offset.

11   See Table 34.

at the peak level (column 8). Subtracting from this the actual tax liabilities gives us the amount of offset due to progressivity (column 9), which is then expressed as a percentage (column 10) of the loss in disposable income.

In the first three contractions the offset from the federal personal income tax did not exceed 5.3 per cent of the loss in disposable income (column 6)—a consequence of the narrow tax base and low effective rates of that period. Because of the broader tax base and higher rates that have characterized the postwar period, the relative offset was larger in the 1948-1949 contraction—13 per cent of the loss in disposable income—but still of a minor order of magnitude. The amount accounted for by the progressivity feature varied from about two-fifths to two-thirds of the entire tax offset (column 9 ÷ column 4). The latter fraction was registered in the 1937-1938 contraction; in the 1948-1949 contraction, progressive rates accounted for only 44 per cent of the tax offset,[14] or in absolute terms for $400 million.

This finding agrees with the inferences drawn by Melvin I. White from his analysis of illustrative figures. He concludes that "The automatic reduction in [tax] revenue that can be provided by a progressive rate schedule would be insufficient to cope with the deflationary pressures that accumulate in more than minor business contractions."[15]

We can indicate also the combined offset to the loss in disposable income during the 1948-1949 contraction provided by the "built-in" stabilizers—compensation to the unemployed and the tax program. Here income loss is defined as what the loss would have been if there had been no compensation to the unemployed and if income tax

[14] Differences in the relative importance of progressivity in 1937-1938 (67 per cent) and in 1948-1949 (44 per cent) are due to several factors: relative severity of the contractions, extent of shift in inequality of income during contractions, and the relative progressivity of the tax structures. The decline in personal income in the 1937-1938 contraction (8.0 per cent) was more than three times the decline in the 1948-1949 contraction (2.5 per cent). In the former contraction there was a shift toward greater equality, since the top 1 per cent received 13.27 per cent of total income in 1937 and 11.63 per cent in 1938 (Table 24). We do not have comparable figures for 1948 and 1949, but there is reason to doubt that a similar shift occurred, since salaries of corporate officers did not decline and dividend and interest payments continued to rise during the contraction in those years. Moreover, for incomes above $5,000 the 1937-1938 schedule of tax rates is more progressive than the 1948-1949 schedule (see R. A. Musgrave and Tun Thin, "Income Tax Progression, 1929-48," *Journal of Political Economy*, December 1948, Chart VI, p. 506).

[15] Melvin I. White, *Personal Income Tax Reduction in a Business Contraction*, Columbia University Press, 1951, p. 16.

liabilities had remained at peak levels. Based on quarterly data, the loss in disposable income during the 1948-1949 contraction would have been $7,449 million (Tables 32 and 35), and the combined offset was $1,649 million ($749 million from compensation to the unemployed and $900 million from the tax program)—that is, 22.1 per cent of the loss in disposable income was compensated. This is the direct offset; our calculation makes no allowance for the "multiplier" effect of the offsets, nor do we stop to consider whether the entire fiscal and monetary policy of the federal government on balance added to or subtracted from these direct offsets.

CHAPTER 9

SUMMARY OF FINDINGS

WE HAVE examined the shift in the relative importance of the major types of personal income over the forty-odd years 1909-1951. For selected years in which personal income was at a peak, we have expressed each type of income as a percentage of total personal income. Over these four decades labor income rose from about half of total income to about two-thirds. About half of this relative gain was made during and immediately after World War I. While labor income registered substantial relative gains during and after World War II, they were no more substantial than those made between 1929 and 1937. In both these periods the rise in transfer payments contributed significantly to the increasing share accruing to nonfarm labor. Our evidence suggests also that within the area of labor income clerical salaries made more rapid gains than executive salaries, particularly since the Great Depression, and that wages and salaries originating in government expanded faster than either total personal income or wages and salaries originating in private enterprise.

While labor income was gaining in importance, property income was declining, as, to a lesser degree, was net income of proprietors. The divergent movements in the shares of labor and property income were largely due to changes in the rate of return rather than in the volume of factor input.

Against this background of long-term shifts we have analyzed the cyclical movements in personal income. There is a one-to-one correspondence of personal income cycles and business cycles. At troughs the personal income cycle roughly corresponds with the business cycle, while at peaks it usually lags slightly. The turning points in personal income are very similar whether it is measured in current or in constant prices, except in periods of rapidly changing prices during war and its immediate aftermath.

Considering separately the major components of personal income, we have found that cycles in farm income over eighty years show a low conformity to business cycles, although this is less true after 1929. We should expect low conformity in this case, because farm income is influenced by the weather and by foreign demand for agricultural products. For the other major components—nonfarm labor income, net income of nonfarm proprietors, and property

110

income—the turns, as a rule, either coincide with those in general business or lag slightly; the few leads are short.

The largest fluctuations (cycle amplitudes) occur in net income of farm proprietors, and the second largest in net income of nonfarm proprietors. The third largest average amplitude, about three-fourths of the largest one, is in nonfarm wages and salaries. The smallest, in property income, is about half of the largest.

The major components of personal income—nonfarm labor income and property income—can be analyzed further in terms of their own components. Nonfarm labor income can be broken down according to source (type of industry, or government and private), wages can be separated from salaries, and the compensation of corporate officers (which indicates roughly the behavior of all executive and professional salaries) can be separated from other salaries. In the private economy, between 1929 and 1938, the turning points of wages and salaries in commodity-producing industries tend to coincide with those in general business, but in the distributive industries short lags are the rule, and service industries exhibit longer lags.

For information on salaries in manufacturing industries we were obliged to rely for the interwar decades on fragmentary statistics, some of which relate to employment rather than to salary payments. The available data indicate that turning points in salary payments lag behind those in wage payments, but these data do not suggest the typical length of the lag.

The turning points in labor income originating in government are different according to whether or not wages for work relief are included. Since unemployment rises during contractions in general business and falls during expansions, work-relief wages follow the same inverted cycle with a lag due to administrative delays. Inverted turns that lag, however, also appear as positive turns that lead. Hence in a period when work-relief wages are quantitatively important, as they were during most of the 1930's, wage and salary payments by government tend to lead turns in general business. If work-relief wages are excluded, the turns, if any, in the labor income of regular government employees lag markedly behind those in general business.

Fluctuations in labor income are much more marked in some types of industries than in others. The smallest amplitudes are found in service industries and the largest in commodity-producing industries. The latter group shows the greatest sensitivity to the business cycle in both amplitude and timing, and within this group the cyclical movements are dominated by labor income in the manufacturing industries.

Whether in expansion or in contraction, salary payments in manufacturing industries fluctuate less than wage payments. Moreover, among salaried personnel the compensation of corporate officers, and therefore of executives and professional personnel, typically fluctuates less than that of other salaried employees.

Did these prewar patterns in nonfarm labor income change in the war and postwar years? During the 1940's, specific cycles in labor income occur only in nonfarm commodity-producing industries and in government, and the timing of turning points follows in general the prewar pattern. In the case of salary disbursements, however, there is a significant departure: salary payments lead wage disbursements at the two troughs, those of 1945 and 1949, while at the 1945 and 1948 peaks salaries continue to lag, as before the war. The leading at the troughs is probably a temporary aberration in a period when salaries were catching up with the faster rate of increase in wages during the war.

During the war cycle, as before the war, salaries fluctuate less than wages, but this is not true in the expansion of the first postwar cycle. During the 1940's, fluctuations in executive and professional salaries are smaller than those in other salaries, repeating the prewar pattern.

When we turn from labor to property income, the data permit intensive analysis only of dividend and interest payments to individuals. Dividend payments turn later than corporate profits; it is clear that they also turn later than business activity. In recent decades this lag averages four to five months, and in the three decades preceding the outbreak of World War I the average lag is ten months. Similar measures for cycles in interest payments are not possible, since this type of property income has not traced a complete cycle from 1909 to 1950. Over these forty-odd years there are only two turning points, a peak in 1929 and a trough in 1943, while general business has twenty turns.

Because there were no specific cycles in interest, only fluctuations in dividends can be compared with those in other types of income. In the 1920-1921 contraction the fall in dividends is about 35 per cent of the fall in nonfarm labor income, but in the 1921-1929 expansion the former rises twice as much as the latter. Larger changes in dividends persist throughout the 1930's. Indeed, fluctuations larger than those in dividends are found only in the net income of proprietors, both farm and nonfarm, which includes the highly volatile element of business savings. During the expansion of World War II the rise in dividends, and in property income in general, is only about one-third of the rise in labor income and in the net income of proprietors. In the first cycle after World War II there is some indication of a reversion to the prewar relationship of amplitudes in dividends and labor income.

Capital gains and losses realized by individuals are closely related to property income. Their size is largely determined by changes in stock-market prices. The turns in the latter tend to lead turns in general business, and this presumably is also true of realized net capital gains or losses. But since we are obliged to use annual statistics this presumption cannot be tested. Annual estimates, however, are adequate for indicating the relative importance of capital gains and losses vis à vis the personal income total. These estimates are available for the thirty-four years 1917-1950. Net gains were realized in nineteen of these years and net losses in fifteen. In relative terms, the largest net gains and losses were realized in 1928 and 1932, respectively, and both equaled 6 per cent of personal income. In about 40 per cent of the years the net gain or loss amounted to less than 1 per cent of annual personal income.

Nonfarm personal income can also be broken down according to income-size groups. What has been the impact of business cycles on the share of total income going to the highest, middle, and lowest income groups? On the basis of Kuznets' estimates, we conclude that there is no clear-cut answer to this question. There is a tendency for the income shares of the highest income group (top 1 per cent) and middle income group (upper 2nd to 7th per cent) to decline during business expansions and to increase during business contractions. Conversely, the share of the lowest income group tends to conform with business cycle fluctuations. But for all groups, except the middle income group during business contractions, these tendencies are weak.

The long-term shifts, however, are unambiguous. The share of the highest income group, the top 1 per cent of the population, declined by nearly one-half from 1913 to 1948, from 16 to 9 per cent. For the middle income group, the upper 2nd to 7th per cent, a declining share has been evident only since the Great Depression. In 1932 this group's share was 16 per cent; by 1948 it had fallen to 13 per cent. These relative declines were offset by the relative gains of the lowest income group, the lower 93 per cent of the population. Its income share increased from 71 per cent in 1931 to 78 per cent in 1948. A large part of these relative gains can be attributed to relative gains in labor income, which in turn are explained in large part by the rise in average hourly earnings and in transfer payments.

In the previous chapter we have examined briefly several programs of the federal government commonly referred to as "built-in" stabilizers of personal income—agricultural price supports, compensation to the unemployed, and personal income taxes. In a quasi-automatic manner these programs provide offsets to cyclical losses in certain types of personal income or in the total of disposable income.

In the case of agricultural price supports, our data show only that this program has operated as a countercyclical force on the net income of farm operators during the period since World War II. We have not estimated the amount of this offset. For the other two programs measurement of direct effectiveness as offsets to income loss is possible. During the 1948-1949 business contraction, compensation to the unemployed offset about one-fifth of the loss in total payrolls and about one-eighth of the loss in disposable income, defined to exclude compensation to the unemployed. There is some evidence to suggest that under present provisions for the amount and duration of benefits the relative offset provided by compensation to the unemployed would be smaller in recessions more severe than that of 1948-1949.

The offset to the loss in disposable income in 1948-1949 provided by the personal income tax program was somewhat larger than that provided by compensation to the unemployed. Thus these two programs in combination offset about one-quarter of the loss in disposable income during the mild recession of 1948-1949.

APPENDIX A

ESTIMATES OF PERSONAL INCOME

1. Annual Estimates of Major Components of Personal Income in Current Prices, 1909-1951

TABLE A-1 presents the components of personal income by type of income. Table A-2 presents the percentage breakdown of components of personal income in Table A-1. Net realized capital gains and losses are not included in total personal income and are expressed merely as a percentage of personal income. Table A-3 presents the components of wage and salary receipts in the government and private sectors.

APPENDIX A

TABLE A-1

Personal Income in Current Prices by Type of Income, 1909-1951

(billions of dollars)

	TOTAL PERSONAL INCOME (2+10+13) (1)	Total (3+7+8) (2)	LABOR INCOME				Other Labor Income (7)	Transfer Payment (8)
			Wage and Salary Receipts[a]					
			Total (3)	Farm (4)	Manufac-turing (5)	All Other (3—4—5) (6)		
1909	29.4	14.9	14.6	.7	3.9	10.1	.2	
1910	31.0	16.0	15.8	.7	4.4	10.7	.3	
1911	31.1	16.3	16.0	.8	4.3	10.9	.3	
1912	33.2	17.3	17.0	.8	4.8	11.5	.3	
1913	34.8	18.5	18.2	.8	5.1	12.3	.3	
1914	34.2	18.2	17.9	.8	4.8	12.4	.3	
1915	36.5	19.1	18.7	.8	5.1	12.8	.3	
1916	43.2	22.0	21.6	.8	6.8	14.0	.4	
1917	52.2	25.3	24.9	1.0	8.5	15.3	.4	
1918	58.0	31.6	30.9	1.2	10.6	19.1	.7	
1919	66.2	34.6	33.8	1.5	11.9	20.5	.8	
1919	65.6	37.1	36.7	1.5	12.5	22.7	.4	
1920	69.2	43.9	43.3	1.8	14.6	26.9	.6	
1921	55.8	35.5	34.9	1.2	9.9	23.9	.6	
1922	60.0	37.0	36.4	1.1	10.5	24.8	.6	
1923	69.3	43.3	42.7	1.2	13.0	28.5	.6	
1924	70.1	43.3	42.7	1.2	12.4	29.1	.6	
1925	74.0	45.0	44.4	1.2	13.0	30.2	.6	
1926	76.7	48.0	47.4	1.3	13.5	32.6	.6	
1927	77.1	48.4	47.8	1.3	13.5	33.0	.6	
1928	78.9	49.4	48.7	1.3	13.9	33.6	.7	
1929	83.4	52.2	51.5	1.3	14.9	35.3	.7	
1929	82.3	51.5	50.0	1.3	16.1	32.7	.5	.9
1930	73.5	47.3	45.7	1.2	13.8	30.8	.5	1.0
1931	62.1	41.2	38.7	.9	10.8	27.1	.5	2.0
1932	46.6	32.0	30.1	.6	7.6	21.9	.4	1.4
1933	44.2	30.5	28.7	.6	7.8	20.3	.4	1.5
1934	50.7	35.3	33.4	.6	9.6	23.1	.4	1.6
1935	57.4	38.6	36.3	.7	10.8	24.8	.4	1.8
1936	65.8	45.0	41.6	.9	12.4	28.3	.5	2.9
1937	71.4	47.7	45.4	1.0	14.4	30.0	.5	1.9
1938	65.9	45.2	42.3	1.0	11.7	29.6	.5	2.4
1939	70.1	48.2	45.1	1.0	13.4	30.8	.5	2.5
1940	75.8	52.2	48.9	1.0	15.4	32.6	.6	2.7
1941	92.6	64.1	60.9	1.2	21.4	38.3	.6	2.6
1942	119.9	84.1	80.7	1.6	30.5	48.6	.7	2.7
1943	147.4	107.0	103.6	2.0	40.1	61.5	.9	2.5
1944	162.7	119.3	114.9	2.2	42.1	70.6	1.3	3.1
1945	168.4	122.5	115.3	2.3	37.5	75.5	1.5	5.6
1946	174.0	122.0	109.2	2.6	35.8	70.9	1.9	10.9
1947	187.0	133.4	119.9	2.8	41.7	75.3	2.4	11.1
1948	205.1	145.5	132.1	3.1	45.6	83.4	2.8	10.5
1949	201.1	145.8	131.2	2.9	43.1	85.2	3.1	11.6
1950	221.0	160.8	142.7	2.8	48.4	91.6	3.8	14.3
1951	248.4	182.2	166.5	2.9	57.2	106.4	4.2	11.5

TABLE A-1 (continued)
(*billions of dollars*)

| | COMPENSA-TION OF CORPORATE OFFICERS (9) | PROPRIETORS' NET INCOME | | | PROPERTY INCOME | | | | NET REALIZED CAPITAL GAINS AND LOSSES (17) |
		Total (10)	Farm (11)	Nonfarm (10—11) (12)	Total (14+15+16) (13)	Divi-dends (14)	Interest (15)	Net Rent (16)	
909	n.a.	8.5	3.6	4.9	6.0	1.5	1.2	3.3	n.a.
910	n.a.	8.5	3.8	4.7	6.5	1.8	1.3	3.5	n.a.
911	n.a.	8.1	3.3	4.8	6.7	1.8	1.3	3.6	n.a.
912	n.a.	8.9	3.8	5.2	7.0	1.9	1.4	3.7	n.a.
913	n.a.	8.9	3.5	5.3	7.4	2.1	1.4	3.9	n.a.
914	n.a.	8.5	3.5	5.1	7.5	2.0	1.5	4.0	n.a.
915	n.a.	9.7	3.9	5.9	7.7	2.0	1.6	4.2	n.a.
916	n.a.	11.8	4.9	7.0	9.3	3.3	1.6	4.4	n.a.
917	n.a.	16.8	7.1	9.7	10.2	3.7	1.8	4.7	.2
918	n.a.	15.9	8.8	7.1	10.4	3.5	2.0	5.0	—.1
919	2.0	20.4	9.3	11.1	11.2	3.2	2.6	5.4	.3
919	2.0	18.4	9.0	9.4	10.1	2.9	3.2	4.0	.3
920	2.4	14.1	6.9	7.3	11.2	3.2	3.7	4.3	b
921	2.3	8.9	3.9	5.1	11.3	3.0	3.9	4.5	—.6
922	2.4	11.1	4.2	6.9	11.9	3.0	4.0	4.9	.2
923	2.6	12.7	5.0	7.7	13.2	3.8	4.2	5.2	.2
924	2.6	13.0	5.4	7.6	13.8	3.8	4.4	5.6	1.0
925	n.a.	14.5	6.2	8.2	14.5	4.4	4.6	5.5	2.6
926	n.a.	14.1	5.7	8.4	14.6	4.7	4.7	5.1	2.2
927	n.a.	13.6	5.7	7.9	15.1	5.1	4.9	5.1	2.6
928	3.2	13.9	5.6	8.3	15.7	5.5	5.3	4.9	4.5
929	3.3	14.4	6.0	8.4	16.8	6.3	5.6	4.9	2.9
929	3.3	13.9	5.7	8.3	16.9	5.8	5.3	5.8	2.9
930	3.1	11.0	3.9	7.0	15.3	5.5	5.0	4.8	—1.4
931	2.7	8.2	2.9	5.3	12.7	4.1	5.0	3.6	—2.7
932	2.1	4.9	1.7	3.2	9.7	2.6	4.6	2.5	—2.7
933	2.0	5.2	2.3	2.9	8.5	2.1	4.4	2.0	—1.4
934	2.2	6.6	2.3	4.3	8.8	2.6	4.1	2.1	—.6
935	2.3	9.9	4.9	5.0	9.0	2.9	3.8	2.3	—.1
936	2.7	9.9	3.9	6.1	10.9	4.6	3.6	2.7	.6
937	2.8	12.2	5.6	6.6	11.4	4.7	3.6	3.1	—.1
938	2.6	10.8	4.4	6.3	9.9	3.2	3.5	3.3	—.3
939	2.7	11.3	4.5	6.8	10.6	3.8	3.4	3.5	—.3
1940	3.0	12.7	4.9	7.7	11.0	4.0	3.3	3.6	—.4
1941	3.5	16.5	6.9	9.6	12.0	4.5	3.2	4.3	—.9
1942	3.7	23.0	10.5	12.6	12.8	4.3	3.1	5.4	—.4
1943	3.7	26.7	11.8	15.0	13.7	4.5	3.1	6.1	1.1
1944	3.8	29.0	11.8	17.2	14.4	4.7	3.2	6.5	1.6
1945	4.1	31.2	12.5	18.7	14.7	4.7	3.7	6.3	4.3
1946	5.1	35.4	14.8	20.6	16.6	5.8	4.2	6.6	6.6
1947	6.0	35.4	15.6	19.8	18.2	6.6	4.6	7.1	4.4
1948	6.7	39.8	17.7	22.1	19.8	7.2	5.1	7.5	4.4
1949	6.7	34.4	12.8	21.6	20.8	7.5	5.6	7.7	3.1
1950	n.a.	37.0	13.3	23.7	23.2	9.0	6.1	8.2	5.8
1951	n.a.	41.8	15.6	26.2	24.4	9.0	6.5	8.9	n.a.

APPENDIX A

Notes to Table A-1

a Includes compensation of corporate officers.
b Loss of less than $.05 billion (—$16 million).
n.a. = not available.
Note: Details may not add to totals because of rounding.

Column	Source
1	Total personal income: sum of columns 2, 10, and 13.
2	Total labor income: sum of columns 3, 7, and 8.
3	Wages and salaries, total: *1909-1919*—(1) Simon Kuznets' worksheets, in which data from Willford Isbell King's *The National Income and Its Purchasing Power* (National Bureau of Economic Research, 1930) are adjusted to conform to Kuznets' estimates, and (2) Kuznets, *National Product in Wartime*, NBER, 1945, Appendix Table iii 9, p. 141; *1919-1929*—Kuznets, *National Income and Its Composition, 1919-1938*, NBER, 1941, Table 62, pp. 332-333; *1929-1951*—*Survey of Current Business*, Dept. of Commerce, July 1952, Table 3, pp. 14-15.
4	Wages and salaries, farm: *1909-1919*—Kuznets' worksheets and his *National Product in Wartime*, Appendix Table iii 9, p. 139; *1919-1929*—Kuznets, *National Income and Its Composition, 1919-1938*, Table 50, pp. 314-315; *1929-1951*—farm wage and salary disbursements from the *National Income Supplement, 1951* (*Survey of Current Business*, Table 14, pp. 160-161) and the *Survey of Current Business* (July 1952, Table 14, p. 18) are used, since no breakdown of receipts by industrial source is available. Wage and salary disbursements (i.e. wages and salaries before employee contributions for social insurance) equal receipts in the farm sector for 1929-1950, since farm workers were not covered by the old age and survivors' insurance program. Beginning with 1951, farm workers have been covered; a rough estimate was made of their contribution to the program for 1951 and was subtracted from disbursements.
5	Wages and salaries, manufacturing: *1909-1951*—the same source as that for column 4; for 1929-1951 the ratio of manufacturing to nonagricultural wage and salary disbursements was applied to nonagricultural wage and salary receipts (column 3 minus column 4).
6	Wages and salaries, all other: column 3 minus columns 4 and 5.
7 and 8	Other labor income and transfer payments: *1909-1919*—Kuznets' worksheets and his *National Product in Wartime*, Appendix Table iii 9, p. 141; *1919-1929*—employee compensation minus total wages and salaries from his *National Income and Its Composition, 1919-1938*, Table 50, pp. 314-315, and Table 62, pp. 332-333. The data for 1909-1929, which include pensions, compensation for injuries, and direct relief, are fragmentary and actually cover the government and the transportation and other public utilities sectors.
	Other labor income: *1929-1951*—*Survey of Current Business*, July 1952, Table 3, pp. 14-15.
	Transfer payments: *1929-1951*—Total transfer payments (*loc. cit.*) minus business transfer payments (*National Income Supplement, 1951*, Table 36, p. 201, and *Survey of Current Business*, July 1952, Table 36, p. 27).
9	Compensation of corporate officers: *1919-1924 and 1928-1929*—Kuznets, *National Income and Its Composition, 1919-1938*, Table i 1, p. 853; *1925-1927*—no data available; *1930-1949*—*National Income Supplement, 1951*, Table 12, p. 157, and *Survey of Current Business*,

Column	Source

July 1952, Table 12, p. 17. The primary source of these data is *Statistics of Income*, Bureau of Internal Revenue.

10 Net income of proprietors, total: *1909-1919*—the sum of entrepreneurial withdrawals and savings and imputed rent on owner-occupied farm homes from Kuznets' worksheets and his *National Product in Wartime*, Appendix Table III 9, pp. 139-141; *1919-1929*—the sum of entrepreneurial withdrawals and savings, which include imputed rent on owner-occupied farm dwellings, from his *National Income and Its Composition, 1919-1938*, Table 52, pp. 316-317, and Table 48, pp. 312-313; the data on entrepreneurial net income (except for farm net income) for 1909-1929 are not adjusted for inventory revaluation; *1929-1951*—data adjusted for inventory revaluation are from *Survey of Current Business*, July 1952, Table 1, pp. 12-13.

11 Net income of proprietors, farm: *1909-1951*—data are adjusted for inventory revaluation and are from same source as column 10; for 1909-1919, the sum of farm entrepreneurial withdrawals and savings and imputed rent on owner-occupied farm dwellings; for 1919-1929, the sum of farm entrepreneurial withdrawals and savings, which include imputed rent on owner-occupied farm dwellings.

12 Net income of proprietors, nonfarm: column 10 minus column 11.

13 Property income, total: sum of columns 14, 15, and 16.

14 Dividends: *1909-1919*—Kuznets, *National Income and Its Composition, 1919-1929*, Table 93, p. 473; *1919-1929—ibid.*, Table 70, pp. 348-349; *1929-1951*—*Survey of Current Business*, July 1952, Table 3, pp. 14-15.

15 Interest: *1909-1919*—Kuznets, *National Income and Its Composition, 1919-1929*, Table 93, p. 473; *1919-1929—ibid.*, Table 55, pp. 318-319; *1929-1951*—total (monetary and imputed) interest (*Survey of Current Business*, July 1952, Table 3, pp. 14-15) minus imputed interest (*National Income Supplement, 1951*, Table 37, p. 202, and *Survey of Current Business*, July 1952, Table 37, p. 27).

16 Net rent: *1909-1919*—Kuznets, *National Income and Its Composition, 1919-1929*, Table 93, p. 473; *1919-1929—ibid.*, Table 57, pp. 322-323; *1929-1951*—*Survey of Current Business*, July 1952, Table 1, pp. 12-13.

17 Net realized capital gains and losses: *1917-1946*—Lawrence H. Seltzer, *The Nature and Tax Treatment of Capital Gains and Losses*, NBER, 1951, p. 367; *1947-1950*—preliminary estimates by the NBER.

TABLE A-2

Percentage Distribution of Personal Income in Current Prices by Type of Income, 1909-1951

	TOTAL PERSONAL INCOME (2+10+13) (1)	Total (3+7+8) (2)	LABOR INCOME					
			Wage and Salary Receipts[a]				Other Labor Income (7)	Transfer Payments (8)
			Total (3)	Farm (4)	Manufac- turing (5)	All Other (3—4—5) (6)		
1909	100.0	50.7	49.7	2.4	13.3	34.4	.7	
1910	100.0	51.6	51.0	2.3	14.2	34.5	1.0	
1911	100.0	52.4	51.4	2.6	13.8	35.0	1.0	
1912	100.0	52.1	51.2	2.4	14.5	34.6	.9	
1913	100.0	53.2	52.3	2.3	14.7	35.3	.9	
1914	100.0	53.2	52.3	2.3	14.0	36.3	.9	
1915	100.0	52.3	51.2	2.2	14.0	35.1	.8	
1916	100.0	51.0	50.1	1.9	15.8	32.5	.9	
1917	100.0	48.4	47.6	1.9	16.3	29.3	.8	
1918	100.0	54.6	53.4	2.1	18.3	32.9	1.2	
1919	100.0	52.3	51.1	2.3	18.0	31.0	1.2	
1919	100.0	56.6	55.9	2.3	19.1	34.6	.6	
1920	100.0	63.4	62.6	2.6	21.1	38.9	.9	
1921	100.0	63.7	62.7	2.2	17.8	42.9	1.1	
1922	100.0	61.7	60.7	1.8	17.5	41.3	1.0	
1923	100.0	62.6	61.7	1.7	18.8	41.1	.9	
1924	100.0	61.8	60.9	1.7	17.7	41.5	.9	
1925	100.0	60.8	60.0	1.6	17.6	40.8	.8	
1926	100.0	62.6	61.8	1.7	17.6	42.5	.8	
1927	100.0	62.8	62.0	1.7	17.5	42.8	.8	
1928	100.0	62.5	61.6	1.6	17.6	42.6	.9	
1929	100.0	62.6	61.8	1.6	17.9	42.3	.8	
1929	100.0	62.6	60.8	1.6	19.6	39.7	.6	1.1
1930	100.0	64.3	62.1	1.6	18.8	41.8	.7	1.4
1931	100.0	66.3	62.3	1.4	17.4	43.6	.8	3.2
1932	100.0	68.7	64.6	1.3	16.3	47.0	.9	3.0
1933	100.0	69.0	64.9	1.4	17.6	45.9	.9	3.4
1934	100.0	69.6	65.9	1.2	18.9	45.6	.8	3.2
1935	100.0	67.1	63.1	1.2	18.8	43.1	.7	3.1
1936	100.0	68.4	63.2	1.4	18.8	43.0	.8	4.4
1937	100.0	66.9	63.7	1.4	20.2	42.1	.7	2.7
1938	100.0	68.6	64.2	1.5	17.8	44.9	.8	3.6
1939	100.0	68.8	64.3	1.4	19.1	43.9	.7	3.6
1940	100.0	68.8	64.4	1.3	20.3	43.0	.8	3.6
1941	100.0	69.2	65.8	1.3	23.1	41.4	.6	2.8
1942	100.0	70.1	67.3	1.3	25.4	40.5	.6	2.3
1943	100.0	72.6	70.3	1.4	27.2	41.7	.6	1.7
1944	100.0	73.3	70.6	1.4	25.9	43.4	.8	1.9
1945	100.0	72.7	68.5	1.4	22.3	44.8	.9	3.3
1946	100.0	70.1	62.8	1.5	20.6	40.7	1.1	6.3
1947	100.0	71.3	64.1	1.5	22.3	40.3	1.3	5.9
1948	100.0	70.9	64.4	1.5	22.2	40.7	1.3	5.1
1949	100.0	72.5	65.3	1.4	21.4	42.4	1.5	5.8
1950	100.0	72.8	64.6	1.3	21.9	41.4	1.7	6.5
1951	100.0	73.3	67.0	1.2	23.0	42.8	1.7	4.6

	COMPENSA-TION OF CORPORATE OFFICERS (9)	PROPRIETORS' NET INCOME			PROPERTY INCOME				NET REALIZED CAPITAL GAINS AND LOSSES (17)
		Total (10)	Farm (11)	Nonfarm (10—11) (12)	Total (14+15+16) (13)	Divi-dends (14)	Interest (15)	Net Rent (16)	
1909	n.a.	28.9	12.2	16.7	20.4	5.1	4.1	11.2	n.a.
1910	n.a.	27.4	12.3	15.2	21.0	5.8	4.2	11.3	n.a.
1911	n.a.	26.0	10.6	15.4	21.5	5.8	4.2	11.6	n.a.
1912	n.a.	26.8	11.4	15.7	21.1	5.7	4.2	11.1	n.a.
1913	n.a.	25.6	10.1	15.2	21.3	6.0	4.0	11.2	n.a.
1914	n.a.	24.9	10.2	14.9	21.9	5.8	4.4	11.7	n.a.
1915	n.a.	26.6	10.7	16.2	21.1	5.5	4.4	11.5	n.a.
1916	n.a.	27.4	11.4	16.2	21.5	7.6	3.7	10.2	n.a.
1917	n.a.	32.1	13.6	18.5	19.5	7.1	3.4	9.0	.4
1918	n.a.	27.4	15.2	12.2	17.9	6.0	3.4	8.6	—.2
1919	3.0	30.8	14.0	16.8	16.9	4.8	3.9	8.2	.5
1919	3.0	28.0	13.7	14.3	15.4	4.4	4.9	6.1	.5
1920	3.5	20.4	10.0	10.5	16.2	4.6	5.3	6.2	b
1921	4.1	16.0	7.0	9.2	20.3	5.4	7.0	8.1	—1.1
1922	4.0	18.5	7.0	11.5	19.8	5.0	6.7	8.2	.3
1923	3.8	18.4	7.2	11.1	19.0	5.5	6.1	7.5	.3
1924	3.7	18.5	7.7	10.8	19.7	5.4	6.3	8.0	1.4
1925	n.a.	19.6	8.4	11.1	19.6	5.9	6.2	7.4	3.5
1926	n.a.	18.4	7.4	11.0	19.0	6.1	6.1	6.6	2.9
1927	n.a.	17.6	7.4	10.2	19.6	6.6	6.4	6.6	3.4
1928	4.1	17.6	7.1	10.5	19.9	7.0	6.7	6.2	5.7
1929	4.0	17.3	7.2	10.1	20.1	7.6	6.7	5.9	3.5
1929	4.0	16.9	6.9	10.1	20.5	7.0	6.4	7.0	3.5
1930	4.2	14.9	5.3	9.5	20.8	7.5	6.8	6.5	—1.9
1931	4.3	13.2	4.7	8.5	20.5	6.6	8.1	5.8	—4.3
1932	4.5	10.5	3.6	6.9	20.8	5.6	9.9	5.4	—5.8
1933	4.5	11.8	5.2	6.6	19.2	4.8	10.0	4.5	—3.2
1934	4.3	13.0	4.5	8.5	17.4	5.1	8.1	4.1	—1.2
1935	4.0	17.2	8.5	8.7	15.7	5.0	6.6	4.0	—.2
1936	4.1	15.0	5.9	9.3	16.6	7.0	5.5	4.1	.9
1937	3.9	17.1	7.9	9.3	16.0	6.6	5.0	4.3	—.1
1938	3.9	16.4	6.7	9.6	15.0	4.9	5.3	5.0	—.5
1939	3.9	16.1	6.4	9.7	15.1	5.4	4.9	5.0	—.4
1940	4.0	16.7	6.5	10.1	14.5	5.3	4.3	4.7	—.5
1941	3.8	17.8	7.5	10.4	13.0	4.9	3.5	4.6	—1.0
1942	3.1	19.2	8.8	10.5	10.7	3.6	2.6	4.5	—.3
1943	4.2	18.1	8.0	10.2	9.3	3.1	2.1	4.1	.7
1944	2.3	17.8	7.3	10.6	8.9	2.9	2.0	4.0	1.0
1945	2.4	18.5	7.4	11.1	8.7	2.8	2.2	3.7	2.6
1946	2.9	20.3	8.5	11.8	9.5	3.3	2.4	3.8	3.8
1947	3.2	18.9	8.3	10.6	9.7	3.5	2.5	3.8	2.4
1948	3.3	19.4	8.6	10.8	9.7	3.5	2.5	3.7	2.1
1949	3.3	17.1	6.4	10.7	10.3	3.7	2.8	3.8	1.5
1950	n.a.	16.7	6.0	10.7	10.5	4.1	2.8	3.7	2.6
1951	n.a.	16.8	6.3	10.5	9.8	3.6	2.6	3.6	n.a.

a Includes compensation of corporate officers.

b Loss of less than $.05 billion or less than .05 per cent of personal income.

n.a. = not available.

Note: Details may not add to totals because of rounding.

Source: Based on Table A-1.

TABLE A-3

Wage and Salary Receipts, Government and Private Sectors, 1909-1951

(billions of dollars)

| | TOTAL WAGE AND SALARY RECEIPTS (2+6) (1) | GOVERNMENT | | | | PRIVATE | | |
		Total (3+4+5) (2)	*Civilian* (3)	*Military* (4)	*Work Relief*[a] (5)	*Total* (7+8) (6)	*Farm* (7)	*Nonfarm* (8)
1909	14.6	1.2	1.1	.1		13.4	.7	12.7
1910	15.8	1.3	1.2	.1		14.5	.7	13.8
1911	16.0	1.4	1.3	.1		14.6	.8	13.8
1912	17.0	1.5	1.3	.1		15.5	.8	14.7
1913	18.2	1.6	1.4	.1		16.6	.8	15.8
1914	17.9	1.7	1.5	.1		16.2	.8	15.4
1915	18.7	1.7	1.6	.1		17.0	.8	16.2
1916	21.6	1.8	1.7	.1		19.8	.8	19.0
1917	24.9	2.5	1.8	.7		22.4	1.0	21.4
1918	30.9	5.3	2.2	3.0		25.6	1.2	24.4
1919	33.8	4.5	2.6	1.9		29.3	1.5	27.8
1919	36.7	3.6	2.3	1.3		33.1	1.5	31.6
1920	43.3	3.4	2.7	.7		39.9	1.8	38.1
1921	34.9	3.4	2.9	.5		31.5	1.2	30.3
1922	36.4	3.4	3.1	.3		33.0	1.1	31.9
1923	42.7	3.5	3.2	.3		39.2	1.2	38.0
1924	42.7	3.7	3.4	.3		39.0	1.2	37.8
1925	44.4	3.9	3.6	.3		40.5	1.2	39.3
1926	47.4	4.1	3.8	.3		43.3	1.3	42.0
1927	47.8	4.4	4.1	.3		43.4	1.3	42.1
1928	48.7	4.6	4.3	.3		44.1	1.3	42.8
1929	51.5	4.8	4.5	.3		46.7	1.3	45.4
1929	50.0	4.8	4.6	.2		45.2	1.3	43.9
1930	45.7	5.0	4.8	.2	b	40.7	1.2	39.5
1931	38.7	5.1	4.8	.2	b	33.6	.9	32.7
1932	30.1	4.8	4.5	.2	.1	25.3	.6	24.7
1933	28.7	5.0	4.1	.2	.7	23.7	.6	23.1
1934	33.4	5.9	4.3	.2	1.4	27.5	.6	26.9
1935	36.3	6.4	4.7	.2	1.4	29.9	.7	29.2
1936	41.6	7.7	5.2	.3	2.2	33.9	.9	33.0
1937	45.4	7.3	5.3	.3	1.7	38.1	1.0	37.1
1938	42.3	8.1	5.6	.3	2.1	34.2	1.0	33.2
1939	45.1	8.0	5.8	.3	1.9	37.1	1.0	36.1
1940	48.9	8.2	6.1	.5	1.6	40.7	1.0	39.7
1941	60.9	9.9	6.9	1.8	1.2	51.0	1.2	49.8
1942	80.7	15.6	8.9	6.1	.6	65.1	1.6	63.5
1943	103.6	25.8	11.9	13.8	.1	77.8	2.0	75.8
1944	114.9	32.1	12.4	19.7		82.8	2.2	80.6

TABLE A-3 (continued)
(billions of dollars)

| | TOTAL WAGE AND SALARY RECEIPTS (2+6) (1) | GOVERNMENT | | | | PRIVATE | | |
		Total (3+4+5) (2)	Civilian (3)	Military (4)	Work Relief[a] (5)	Total (7+8) (6)	Farm (7)	Nonfarm (8)
1945	115.3	34.1	12.5	21.6		81.2	2.3	78.9
1946	109.2	19.6	12.2	7.3		89.6	2.6	87.0
1947	119.9	16.3	12.7	3.6		103.6	2.8	100.8
1948	132.1	17.7	14.2	3.6		114.4	3.1	111.3
1949	131.2	19.3	15.4	3.8		111.9	2.9	109.0
1950	142.7	20.9	16.4	4.5		121.8	2.8	119.0
1951	166.5	27.2	19.1	8.1		139.3	2.9	136.4

[a] None before 1930 or after 1943.
[b] Less than $.05 billion.
Note: Details may not add to totals because of rounding.

Column	Source
1	Total wages and salaries: see Table A-1, note on column 3.
2	Government, total: *1909-1919*—Willford Isbell King, *The National Income and Its Purchasing Power*, National Bureau of Economic Research, 1930, Table 128, p. 364; *1919-1929*—Simon Kuznets, *National Income and Its Composition, 1919-1938*, NBER, 1941, Table G 2, p. 812; *1929-1951*—sum of columns 3, 4, and 5.
3	Government, civilian: *1909-1929*—same source as that for this period in column 2; *1929-1951*—government civilian wage and salary disbursements minus civilian employee contributions to government retirement systems; disbursement and contribution data are from *National Income Supplement, 1951* (*Survey of Current Business*, Dept. of Commerce, Table 14, pp. 160-161, and Table 35, p. 201, respectively) and *Survey of Current Business* (July 1952, Table 14, p. 18, and Table 35, p. 26, respectively).
4	Military: *1909-1929*—same source as that for this period in column 2; *1929-1951*—military wage and salary disbursements minus contributions by military personnel for government life insurance, from same source as that for this period in column 3.
5	Work relief: *1929-1951*—*National Income Supplement, 1951*, Table 14, pp. 160-161, and *Survey of Current Business*, July 1952, Table 14, p. 18.
6	Private, total: column 1 minus column 2.
7	Farm: see Table A-1, note on column 4.
8	Nonfarm: column 6 minus column 7.

2. Annual Estimates of Total Personal Income in 1935-1939 Dollars, 1909-1951

a. 1929-1951

Annual Department of Commerce estimates of personal income for 1929-1951 were reduced to dollars of constant purchasing power by deflating its three components: (1) personal consumption expenditures, (2) personal savings, and (3) personal tax and nontax payments. The price indexes used as deflators were those derived by the Department of Commerce by dividing three of the four components of gross national product—(1) personal consumption expenditures, (2) gross private domestic investment, and (3) government purchases of goods and services in current dollars—by the components in constant (1939) dollars. Each component of personal income was then divided by its appropriate implicit price index shifted to a 1935-1939 = 100 base. The sum of the three deflated components yields personal income as defined by the Department of Commerce in 1935-1939 dollars. The composite implicit price index derived by dividing the personal income estimates of the Department of Commerce in current prices by those in constant (1935-1939) prices was used to deflate our annual personal income estimates in Table A-1. Annual data for 1929-1951 for the implicit price indexes on the base 1939 = 100 are from the *National Income Supplement, 1951* (*Survey of Current Business*, Dept. of Commerce, Table B, p. 146) and subsequent issues of the *Survey of Current Business*.

b. 1909-1929

Annual estimates of personal income for 1909-1929 were reduced to constant (1935-1939) dollars by deflating separately personal income originating in agricultural and personal income originating in nonagricultural sources. The deflation was accomplished by dividing nonagricultural income by the Bureau of Labor Statistics Consumers Price Index for moderate income families in large cities, and agricultural income by the Bureau of Agricultural Economics index of prices paid by farmers for commodities used for family living. Since the BLS index is available on the base 1935-1939 = 100, the BAE index, which is published on the base 1910-1914 = 100, was converted to a 1935-1939 = 100 base. The two deflated components were then added to secure personal income in 1935-1939 dollars.

This procedure involves some assumptions that can be defended only on the ground that the paucity of data does not permit assumptions of greater validity. One of the assumptions of our procedure, for example, is that the relative price movements of goods and services purchased by personal savings and taxes are very similar to the weighted average of the relative movements of prices of consumers' goods purchased by farmers and by moderate income families in large cities. It also assumes that relative price movements of all purchases except those of farmers, regardless of level of income and size of locality, are similar to those covered by the BLS Consumers Price Index.

To compare the results of the procedure used for 1909-1929 with those of the more elaborate procedure used for 1929-1951 (section 2 a above), we extended the 1909-1929 series deflated by the BAE and BLS indexes to 1950. Personal income figures, whether deflated by the BLS and BAE indexes or by the more extensive group of indexes, are almost identical from 1929 to 1943; from 1944 to 1946 a gap exists which is narrowed from 1947 on. Since the movements of the two series between 1929 and the entrance of the United States into World War II are so close, we believe that the method used for the years before 1929 gives us a reliable picture of the course of personal income in constant dollars, except possibly for the years 1917-1918 of World War I.

For 1909-1929 the method of estimating personal income in current dollars is described in section 1. Agricultural income is from Kuznets' *National Income and Its Composition, 1919-1938* (National Bureau of Economic Research, 1941, Table 91, p. 470, and Table 43, pp. 310-311). Nonagricultural income is derived by subtracting agricultural income from personal income.

To deflate the annual components, we used the BLS annual index, which goes back to 1910, and the BAE index, which begins with 1913. Two series on prices paid by urban manual and clerical workers and farmers for consumers' goods published in Willford Isbell King's *The National Income and Its Purchasing Power* (NBER, 1930, p. 63) were used to extrapolate these indexes to 1909. The BLS index for 1913-1946 is from the *Handbook of Labor Statistics, 1947 Edition* (BLS Bulletin 916, p. 107) and for 1947-1950 from the *Monthly Labor Review* (BLS). The BAE index for 1910-1949 is from *Agricultural Prices* (Supplement 1, BAE, January 1950); for 1950 the BAE index is computed using monthly data in subsequent issues of *Agricultural Prices*. Table A-4 presents the annual estimates of personal income in 1935-1939 dollars for 1909-1951.

TABLE A-4

Personal Income in Constant (1935-1939) Prices, 1909-1951
(*billions of dollars*)

	Personal Income		Personal Income
1909	42.9	1929	66.0
1910	44.1	1930	61.8
1911	44.4	1931	58.1
1912	46.8	1932	49.2
1913	48.3	1933	48.8
1914	46.7	1934	53.0
1915	49.3	1935	58.6
1916	54.1	1936	66.7
1917	55.0	1937	69.2
1918	51.8	1938	65.7
1919	51.3	1939	70.3
1919	50.9	1940	75.2
		1941	86.0
1920	46.8	1942	99.3
1921	43.5	1943	116.4
1922	50.0	1944	122.0
1923	56.7	1945	120.3
1924	57.2	1946	113.8
1925	58.8	1947	110.7
1926	60.6	1948	114.6
1927	62.1	1949	113.8
1928	64.2	1950	121.8
1929	68.0	1951	127.1

Source: See text, Appendix A, sections 2 a and 2 b.

3. Monthly Estimates of Total Personal Income in 1935-1939 Dollars, 1929-1950

a. 1929-1942

Since no monthly data for the components of personal income according to its disposition or for the implicit deflators of the components of gross national product are available, monthly personal income could not be deflated using the method described in section 2 a above. However, seasonally corrected monthly data at annual rates on nonagricultural and personal income published by the Department of Commerce are available from 1929. Agricultural income is derived by subtracting the former income from the latter. Nonagricultural income and agricultural income were deflated to constant (1935-1939) dollars by dividing them by, respectively, the BLS Consumers Price Index and BAE index of prices paid by farmers for commodities used for family living. Since the BLS index is available on the base 1935-1939 = 100, the BAE index, available on a 1910-1914 base, was converted to a 1935-1939 base. The BAE index is a quarterly index before 1937 and thereafter is available monthly. A straight-line interpolation of the quarterly data was made to secure a monthly series for the 1929-1936 period. All data utilized are seasonally adjusted; however, in the BAE index seasonal movement is negligible and no correction is necessary. The two deflated components were added to secure personal income in 1935-1939 dollars.

b. 1943-1950

Because of the gap in 1943-1950 between the annual Department of Commerce personal income series deflated by the BLS and BAE indexes and the series deflated by the more extensive Department of Commerce implicit price indexes (section 2 b), we decided to make a monthly interpolation of the latter series, using monthly data computed in the manner described in section 3 a as our interpolating series for 1943-1950. The interpolation was made by using an adaptation of a method developed by V Lewis Bassie which least affects the relative monthly movement within each year and the December-January movement between consecutive years (see Frederick M. Cone, *Monthly Income Payments in the United States, 1929-40*, Dept. of Commerce, Economic Series No. 6, 1940, pp. 27-28).

Monthly data used in section 3 on personal and nonagricultural income are from *National Income Supplement, 1947* (*Survey of Current Business*, July 1947) for 1929-1942; the *Survey of Current Business* (July 1949) for 1943-1948; and subsequent issues of the *Survey of Current Business* thereafter. The monthly BLS Consumers Price Index is from an unpublished table furnished by the Bureau of Foreign and Domestic Commerce, which placed the irregularly published BLS index on a monthly basis for 1913-1938; monthly data from 1939 on are available in the *Monthly Labor Review* and BLS mimeographed releases. The BAE index of prices paid by farmers for commodities used for family living is from *Agricultural Prices* (Supplement 1, January 1950, and subsequent monthly issues).

The annual Department of Commerce personal income totals deflated by the Department of Commerce implicit price indexes which were used as benchmarks are described in section 2 a.

APPENDIX B

ESTIMATES OF FACTOR INPUTS AND RETURNS, 1900-1950 (CHART 3)

IN ALL but one of the series which appear in Chart 3 and Table B-1, the data were converted to an index on the base 1925 = 100. Wherever data in a given series were obtained from different sources and were not strictly comparable, the segments were spliced before conversion to the 1925 = 100 base. Since no data were available for 1925 for total nonfarm reproducible tangible assets (other than those of households, government, and nonprofit institutions) in 1929 prices (Table B-1, Part C), the series was placed on a 1929 = 100 base.

TABLE B-1

Indexes of Factor Inputs and Factor Returns by Type of Income, 1900-1950
A. Labor: Farm and Nonfarm

(1925 = 100)

	Hired Farm Workers[a] (1)	Composite Farm Wage Rate[b] (2)	Full-Time Equivalent Nonfarm Employees[c] (3)	Annual Full-Time Equivalent Earnings per Nonfarm Employee[d] (4)
1900	n.a.	n.a.	n.a.	38.8
1901	n.a.	n.a.	n.a.	39.9
1902	n.a.	n.a.	n.a.	40.6
1903	n.a.	n.a.	n.a.	42.1
1904	n.a.	n.a.	n.a.	42.0
1905	n.a.	n.a.	n.a.	42.8
1906	n.a.	n.a.	n.a.	43.8
1907	n.a.	n.a.	n.a.	45.4
1908	n.a.	n.a.	n.a.	43.4
1909	n.a.	n.a.	78.5	45.4
1910	99.7	52	82.0	47.2
1911	99.4	54	83.5	46.7
1912	100.1	56	85.8	48.7
1913	100.6	57	88.3	50.6
1914	101.1	56	91.4	48.3
1915	101.6	56	91.8	50.3
1916	102.7	61	93.6	57.0
1917	101.6	77	92.6	65.9
1918	98.4	97	99.8	76.3
1919	96.4	113	95.3	86.9
1920	99.9	132	96.4	99.9
1921	100.5	85	84.3	92.9
1922	101.0	84	89.3	91.7
1923	100.2	97	98.7	97.4
1924	99.5	99	97.9	98.1
1925	100.0	100	100.0	100.0
1926	104.3	101	104.5	102.0
1927	102.4	101	105.0	102.6
1928	102.3	101	105.7	103.9
1929	103.2	102	111.2	105.9
1930	98.1	96	104.6	103.1
1931	93.5	73	94.4	97.2
1932	87.6	55	83.2	86.3
1933	86.1	49	84.9	80.7
1934	83.9	55	96.0	83.3
1935	87.4	60	100.6	87.0
1936	93.9	64	111.1	91.4
1937	97.0	73	115.5	97.4
1938	97.1	70	110.0	96.5
1939	97.3	70	115.1	98.8

129

TABLE B-1 (continued)

A. Labor: Farm and Nonfarm (continued)
(1925 = 100)

	Hired Farm Workers[a] (1)	Composite Farm Wage Rate[b] (2)	Full-Time Equivalent Nonfarm Employees[c] (3)	Annual Full-Time Equivalent Earnings per Nonfarm Employee[d] (4)
1940	97.2	72	121.9	101.4
1941	95.8	87	137.8	111.9
1942	95.9	114	155.2	130.8
1943	90.9	150	176.8	151.4
1944	83.5	179	182.1	163.1
1945	78.5	200	176.3	169.4
1946	80.6	218	154.2	176.6
1947	83.4	232	154.0	193.9
1948	86.1	243	156.7	209.9
1949	84.2	234	152.6	214.8

[a] Base = 2,887,000 persons.
[b] Index on 1910-1914 base converted to 1925 = 100.
[c] Base = 29,047,000 persons.
[d] Base = $1,450.
n.a. = not available.

Column	Source
1	Average number of hired farm workers: *Agricultural Statistics, 1950,* Dept. of Agriculture, Table 638, p. 584.
2	Composite farm wage rate: *ibid.,* Tables 640 and 641, p. 586. Index on a 1910-1914 base.
3	Average number of full-time equivalent nonfarm employees: *1909-1919*—nonfarm wages and salaries (see notes on columns 3 and 4, Table A-1) divided by average annual nonfarm full-time equivalent earnings (Stanley Lebergott, "Earnings of Nonfarm Employees in the U.S., 1890-1946," *Journal of the American Statistical Association,* March 1948, Table 2, pp. 76-77); *1919-1929*—Simon Kuznets, *National Income and Its Composition, 1919-1938,* National Bureau of Economic Research, 1941, Table 51, pp. 314-315; *1929-1949*—*National Income Supplement, 1951, Survey of Current Business,* Dept. of Commerce, Table 24, pp. 180-181, and *Survey of Current Business,* July 1952, Table 24, p. 22. The Department of Commerce series for 1929-1949 was extrapolated backward by the Kuznets series for 1919-1929 and by the 1909-1919 segment, with splicing ratios based on 1929 and 1919, respectively. The data were then converted to indexes on the base 1925 = 100.
4	Average annual full-time equivalent earnings of nonfarm employees: *1900-1946*—Lebergott, *op. cit.,* Table 2, pp. 76-77; *1946-1949*—nonfarm wages and salaries (*National Income Supplement, 1951,* Table 14, pp. 160-161, and *Survey of Current Business,* July 1952, Table 14, p. 18) divided by the number of full-time equivalent nonfarm employees (Table 24, pp. 180-181, and Table 24, p. 22, respectively, in the same sources). Lebergott's series for 1900-1946 was extrapolated forward by the Department of Commerce series with a splicing ratio based on 1946. The data were then converted to indexes on the base 1925 = 100.

TABLE B-1 (continued)

B. Proprietors: Farm and Nonfarm
(1925 = 100)

	Family Workers in Agriculture[a] (1)	Farm Proprietors' Net Income[b] (2)	Nonfarm Proprietors[c] (3)	Nonfarm Proprietors' Net Income[d] (4)
1909	n.a.	55.2	89.1	50.7
1910	108.0	58.1	89.6	48.6
1911	106.9	50.4	89.8	49.5
1912	106.6	58.0	90.0	53.3
1913	106.4	54.8	90.3	54.5
1914	105.9	54.0	90.8	51.8
1915	105.5	59.6	91.1	60.1
1916	105.5	75.3	91.3	71.5
1917	103.2	109.8	90.8	99.2
1918	99.2	136.2	85.8	73.2
1919	97.0	144.1	89.0	113.7
1920	98.8	110.0	89.4	88.0
1921	99.2	62.2	88.4	61.5
1922	99.4	67.6	91.2	83.2
1923	99.0	80.1	93.7	93.7
1924	98.9	86.5	96.9	92.0
1925	100.0	100.0	100.0	100.0
1926	99.1	92.3	101.8	101.6
1927	96.6	91.6	103.8	96.2
1928	97.2	89.9	105.3	100.5
1929	96.8	96.0	108.0	101.7
1930	97.1	66.6	109.1	86.6
1931	99.8	49.1	107.7	65.4
1932	102.0	29.1	105.7	39.5
1933	103.3	38.7	104.2	36.0
1934	103.3	39.4	105.0	52.6
1935	106.4	82.5	106.0	61.4
1936	104.6	65.5	108.3	74.8
1937	103.2	95.2	110.2	81.6
1938	103.2	74.9	111.1	78.1
1939	103.9	76.3	112.4	83.4
1940	103.3	83.7	113.9	95.0
1941	100.9	117.6	111.9	117.8
1942	101.3	177.4	109.1	154.8
1943	101.5	199.4	99.9	184.2
1944	100.7	200.6	100.8	211.2
1945	99.6	212.3	109.1	230.4
1946	102.2	250.6	124.2	253.4
1947	102.1	264.1	133.8	243.5
1948	100.2	299.3	138.1	271.9
1949	97.1	216.5	138.0	266.3
1950		226.2	140.0	291.4

APPENDIX B

Notes to Table B-1 (B)

a Base = 8,579,000 persons.
b Base = $5,902,000.
c Base = 4,417,000 persons.
d Base = $8,123,000.
n.a. = not available.

Column	Source
1	Average number of family workers in agriculture: *Agricultural Statistics, 1950*, Table 638, p. 584.
2	Net income of farm proprietors: see Table A-1, note on column 11. The Department of Commerce series for 1929-1950 was extrapolated backward by the 1919-1929 and 1909-1919 segments, with splicing ratios based on 1929 and 1919, respectively. The data were then converted to indexes on the base 1925 = 100.
3	Average number of nonfarm proprietors: *1909-1919*—Willford Isbell King, *The National Income and Its Purchasing Power*, NBER, 1930, Table VI, p. 62; *1919-1929*—Kuznets, *op. cit.*, Table 53, pp. 316-317; *1929-1950*—*National Income Supplement, 1951*, Table 27, pp. 186-187, and *Survey of Current Business*, July 1952, Table 27, p. 23. Series spliced in manner similar to that described in note on column 2 of the present table.
4	Net income of nonfarm proprietors: see Table A-1, note on column 12. Series spliced in manner similar to that described in note on column 2 of the present table.

TABLE B-1 (continued)

C. Capital: Input and Rate of Return

	Ratio of Net Dividend Disbursements to Corporate Net Worth[a] (1925 = 100) (1)	Total Nonfarm Reproducible Tangible Assets (Other than Those of Households, Government, and Nonprofit Institutions) in 1929 Prices[b] (1929 = 100) (2)
1900	n.a.	37.6
1904	n.a.	44.2
1908	n.a.	53.1
1909	69.7	n.a.
1910	73.9	n.a.
1911	72.3	n.a.
1912	75.4	59.5
1913	79.6	n.a.
1916	n.a.	66.4
1918	113.4	n.a.
1919	91.6	n.a.
1920	89.6	78.3
1921	76.5	n.a.
1922	80.1	79.5
1923	99.2	n.a.
1924	88.2	85.1

TABLE B-1 (continued)

1925	100.0	n.a.
1926	103.6	n.a.
1927	98.9	n.a.
1928	101.1	96.1
1929	104.8	100.0
1930	91.0	n.a.
1931	72.5	n.a.
1932	49.0	93.4
1933	41.7	n.a.
1934	48.2	n.a.
1935	52.7	n.a.
1936	90.2	87.9
1937	89.1	n.a.
1938	62.2	n.a.
1939	75.6	88.2
1940	79.8	91.2
1941	86.8	n.a.
1942	87.7	n.a.
1943	88.8	n.a.
1944	89.4	95.3
1945	87.1	n.a.
1946	103.4	102.7
1947	107.6	n.a.
1948	110.1	116.8
1949	103.4	n.a.
1950	116.2	n.a.

[a] Base = 3.57 per cent.
[b] Base = $128.6 billion.
n.a. = not available.

Column	Source
1	Ratio of net dividend disbursements to corporate net worth: (a) net dividend disbursements (see Table A-1, note on column 14) divided by (b) corporate net worth (*1909-1913 and 1918-1937*—Martin Taitel, *Profits, Productive Activities and New Investment*, Temporary National Economic Committee, Monograph 12, 1941, p. 18; *1914-1917*—no data available; *1938-1947*—since data on net worth are available only for corporations with balance sheets in *Statistics of Income* [Bureau of Internal Revenue], the procedure used by Taitel for 1931-1937 was adopted to adjust the balance sheet data to the level of all corporations and to place the estimates at the beginning of the year; *1948-1950*—extrapolations were made by the use of data for about 3,300 leading corporations from the *Monthly Letter* of the National City Bank of New York [April issues, 1949-1951]).
2	Total nonfarm reproducible tangible assets (other than those of households, government, and nonprofit institutions) in 1929 prices: *1900-1948, selected years*—the sum of the following reproducible tangible assets: (a) nonfarm nonresidential structures, including mining and excluding institutional and governmental structures, (b) producers' durable equipment, and (c) nonfarm private inventories (Raymond W. Goldsmith, "A Perpetual Inventory of National Wealth," *Studies in Income and Wealth, Volume Fourteen*, NBER, 1951, Table 1, pp. 18-19).

TABLE B-1 (continued)
D. Capital: Rate of Return
($1925 = 100$)

	RENT INDEX IN BLS CONSUMERS PRICE INDEX[a]	AVERAGE YIELD OF HIGH-GRADE CORPORATE BONDS[b]	AVERAGE YIELD OF LONG-TERM UNITED STATES GOVERNMENT BONDS[c] *Partially Tax-Exempt*[d]	*Taxable*[e]
	(1)	(2)	(3)	(4)
1900		91.1	56.5	
1901		88.8	51.0	
1902		88.0	51.3	
1903		91.7	51.6	
1904		91.1	54.1	
1905		86.8	51.8	
1906		88.8	52.8	
1907		95.7	56.5	
1908		96.6	63.2	
1909		91.5	66.8	
1910		93.3	71.8	
1911		92.9	69.9	
1912		93.3	72.8	
1913	60.6	97.0	72.0	
1914	60.6	96.3	74.4	
1915	61.0	98.0	74.6	
1916	61.8	95.9	71.2	
1917	61.2	101.2	84.5	
1918	62.4	111.0	116.6	
1919	67.5	111.8	122.5	
1920	79.3	125.4	137.8	
1921	91.1	122.3	131.9	
1922	93.8	104.9	111.4	
1923	96.2	105.9	113.0	
1924	99.6	102.8	105.2	
1925	100.0	100.0	100.0	
1926	99.0	96.8	95.3	
1927	97.4	94.3	86.5	
1928	95.1	93.9	86.3	
1929	92.9	98.6	93.3	
1930	90.3	95.5	85.2	
1931	85.6	92.3	86.5	
1932	76.8	107.1	95.3	
1933	66.2	95.1	85.8	
1934	62.0	84.0	80.8	
1935	61.9	73.2	72.3	
1936	63.3	67.7	68.7	
1937	66.3	66.9	69.4	
1938	68.4	64.9	66.3	
1939	68.5	61.3	61.1	
1940	68.7	59.2	57.3	

TABLE B-1 (continued)

D. Capital: Rate of Return (continued)
(1925 = 100)

| | RENT INDEX IN BLS CONSUMERS PRICE INDEX[a] | AVERAGE YIELD OF HIGH-GRADE CORPORATE BONDS[b] | AVERAGE YIELD OF LONG-TERM UNITED STATES GOVERNMENT BONDS[c] | |
| | | | *Partially Tax-Exempt*[d] | *Taxable*[e] |
	(1)	(2)	(3)	(4)
1941	69.9	57.6	50.5	
1942	71.5	57.8	54.1	63.7
1943	71.4	56.8	51.3	64.0
1944	71.7	56.4	49.7	64.2
1945	71.9	52.9	43.0	61.4
1946	72.3	50.9		56.7
1947	74.6	52.3		58.3
1948	79.6	56.8		63.2
1949	83.0	53.8		59.8
1950	86.1	52.5		

[a] Index on 1935-1939 base converted to 1925 = 100; index begins in 1913.
[b] Base = 4.93 per cent.
[c] Base = 3.86 per cent; see note on column 4 below.
[d] Series ends in 1945.
[e] Series begins in 1942.

Column	Source
1	Rent index in Bureau of Labor Statistics Consumers Price Index: rent index on 1935-1939 = 100 base from *Handbook of Labor Statistics*, BLS, Bulletin 1016, 1950, p. 100, and *Monthly Labor Review*, BLS, October 1952, p. 153.
2	Average yield of high-grade corporate bonds: *Security Price Index Record*, Standard and Poor's Corp., 1952, p. 153.
3	Average yield of long-term United States government bonds, partially tax-exempt: *1900-1918*—from table submitted by the Department of Research and Statistics, Savings Banks Trust Co., New York City; *1919-1945—Historical Statistics of the United States, 1789-1945*, Dept. of Commerce, 1949, p. 280.
4	Average yield of long-term United States government bonds, taxable: *1942-1945—Statistical Abstract of the United States, 1948*, Dept. of Commerce, Table 496, note 1, p. 465; *1946-1949—Statistical Abstract of the United States, 1950*, Table 482, p. 421. Although fully taxable United States government bonds were initially issued in 1941, the yields of these bonds are related to the base-year yield of partially tax-exempt bonds in order to indicate the level of the two types of bond yields during the overlapping years 1942-1945.

WAGE EARNERS AND SALARIED PERSONNEL
IN MANUFACTURING, 1919-1939

1. Employment of Wage Earners and Salaried Personnel
in Ohio Manufacturing Industries, 1919-1939

STATISTICAL information on the monthly employment of (1) wage earners, (2) bookkeepers, stenographers, and office clerks, and (3) salespeople (not traveling) is supplied by Ohio establishments under the jurisdiction of the state workmen's compensation insurance law. From 1919 to 1923, establishments employing five or more persons were required to report; after 1923, establishments employing three or more were required to report.

Since the number of manufacturing establishments reporting is not the same from year to year, we considered the monthly data within each year to be a separate segment. Throughout the twelve months of each year, however, the establishments are identical. Firms required to report which failed to do so were mostly those employing a relatively small number of persons. Firms employing less than the minimum in one year will report the next year if they employ more than the minimum, and vice versa. Some small firms employing less than the minimum in one year may merge or be absorbed by a large firm the next year.

The wage-earner employment segments were brought into alignment by a method developed by V Lewis Bassie which least affects the relative monthly movement within each year and the December-January movement between consecutive years (see Frederick M. Cone, *Monthly Income Payments in the United States, 1929-40,* Dept. of Commerce, Economic Series No. 6, 1940, pp. 27-28). We first distributed the difference between the "true" movement from December of the preceding year to January of a given year and the December-January movement of the Ohio wage-earner series by applying an annual correction factor to the original monthly data in the given year. We then applied monthly correction factors based on a third-degree curve to the two years to smooth the December-January discontinuity. For 1919-1923 the annual correction factor was computed by dividing (1) the ratio of the Bureau of Labor Statistics index of factory employment, United States manufactures, for January of a given year to the December index of the preceding year by (2) the ratio of the number of wage earners employed in

Ohio manufactures in January of the given year to the number of wage earners employed in December of the preceding year. For 1924-1939 the factor was computed by using (1) December and January data of the index of factory employment, Ohio manufactures, in the numerator and (2) the number of Ohio wage earners in the denominator. The index of factory employment, Ohio manufactures, was constructed by the Bureau of Business Research of Ohio State University. This series, which starts in 1923, is from the *Survey of Current Business* (Dept. of Commerce, March 1942, p. 17).

The monthly data on salaried personnel in manufacturing were aligned by applying the monthly ratios of number of salaried employees to wage earners, based on the original data, to the aligned original wage-earner series.

The wage-earner series was adjusted for seasonal variations by the National Bureau of Economic Research. No adjustment of the salaried employee series was necessary since it showed virtually no seasonal movement. The two series appear in Table C-1.

Ohio employment data are from *Fluctuation in Employment in Ohio, 1914 to 1929* (BLS, Bulletin 553, 1932); *Rates of Wages, Fluctuations of Employment, Wage and Salary Payments in Ohio, 1930 to 1937 Inclusive, Exclusive of Coal Mines and Quarries* (Division of Labor Statistics, Dept. of Industrial Relations of Ohio, Report 29); and unpublished tables furnished by the Department of Industrial Relations of Ohio for 1938-1939.

2. Employment and Payrolls of Wage Earners, 1920-1939, and Salaried Personnel, 1922-1936, in Wisconsin Manufacturing Industries

The indexes of employment and payrolls of wage earners in Wisconsin for July 1920 to December 1929 on the base 1925-1927 = 100 are from *Wisconsin Labor Market* (Industrial Commission of Wisconsin, July 1931, January 1932, and August 1937); data for the second segment, January 1929 to February 1939, are from the December 1938 and succeeding issues of the *Wisconsin Labor Market*. The indexes in the second segment have been adjusted by the Industrial Commission of Wisconsin to the levels of successive United States censuses of manufactures, while in the first segment, census of manufactures data were used only for weighting indexes of component industrial groups.

Indexes of employment and payrolls of salaried personnel in

TABLE C-1
Wage Earners and Salaried Personnel, Ohio Manufacturing Industries, 1919-1939
(thousands of persons)

A. Wage Earners

	Jan.	Feb.	Mar.	Apr.	May	June	July	Aug.	Sept.	Oct.	Nov.	Dec.
1919	678.0	643.6	627.4	621.0	619.0	643.3	690.6	716.5	715.9	686.1	736.2	774.7
1920	773.2	747.5	758.1	746.6	727.9	751.8	760.6	728.5	706.3	677.7	631.0	574.4
1921	502.0	482.1	465.5	463.1	460.0	455.7	436.9	443.3	440.7	450.0	467.1	463.0
1922	465.3	475.0	490.1	505.2	526.4	557.6	570.3	580.8	574.0	581.7	603.6	633.0
1923	637.9	642.5	658.4	655.5	662.8	672.2	660.0	666.0	645.1	645.6	654.7	649.0
1924	652.3	650.5	646.3	633.9	600.0	562.5	562.3	573.5	586.1	595.5	598.9	617.8
1925	637.1	629.2	629.9	631.9	636.6	638.8	650.2	656.8	666.7	677.0	687.2	685.9
1926	675.0	665.0	659.8	662.4	658.4	663.7	672.2	681.4	690.1	688.6	679.9	667.8
1927	653.4	661.3	663.5	660.0	657.5	658.8	651.5	648.6	644.1	635.7	628.0	625.4
1928	634.6	645.8	647.7	645.4	653.9	662.6	673.6	686.2	690.5	693.3	698.5	699.4
1929	717.8	722.2	720.4	725.6	733.3	734.7	746.7	738.4	728.6	717.7	677.3	651.5
1930	648.9	634.6	621.6	628.7	621.9	604.0	585.0	570.9	559.1	547.5	534.0	525.7
1931	512.4	505.6	504.5	506.1	503.0	493.4	486.8	472.1	465.1	450.5	450.4	441.1
1932	437.9	434.0	419.8	405.3	397.3	394.3	387.6	372.4	382.4	387.5	391.3	389.8
1933	383.8	388.7	354.5	375.7	403.9	452.0	491.7	522.2	525.3	514.5	487.5	490.8
1934	498.1	522.6	548.1	553.2	576.3	582.7	536.8	526.4	508.1	507.1	503.5	532.5
1935	566.9	588.4	590.2	586.8	579.7	583.8	585.2	586.6	596.6	605.5	602.3	607.4
1936	612.1	606.1	601.6	622.7	624.6	635.0	656.7	657.1	662.8	673.3	668.4	694.1
1937	692.0	712.1	710.9	708.8	725.5	702.9	741.2	734.1	730.1	711.0	657.7	630.6
1938	576.2	576.3	560.2	548.7	536.9	536.1	543.8	554.9	569.1	572.9	584.5	601.7
1939	596.8	599.5	596.0	594.0	585.9	600.9	608.7	615.6	639.4	666.3	670.3	685.1

TABLE C-1 (continued)

B. Salaried Personnel

(thousands of persons)

	Jan.	Feb.	Mar.	Apr.	May	June	July	Aug.	Sept.	Oct.	Nov.	Dec.
1919	68.9	69.1	69.8	70.5	70.9	72.0	74.1	76.1	76.1	77.1	78.7	79.8
1920	76.9	79.3	80.7	81.7	82.0	82.6	82.5	80.8	78.4	75.9	73.4	71.3
1921	70.8	69.0	67.7	66.3	65.2	63.6	61.8	61.2	60.3	59.6	59.4	59.1
1922	61.2	61.2	61.3	61.8	62.5	63.8	64.3	64.7	65.0	65.1	65.4	65.8
1923	69.1	69.9	70.9	71.5	72.1	72.8	73.1	73.0	72.8	72.5	72.3	72.6
1924	72.6	72.9	73.1	73.5	73.0	72.6	73.0	73.0	72.9	72.7	73.0	73.0
1925	74.1	74.6	75.0	75.2	75.5	75.9	76.7	76.9	77.0	77.1	77.4	77.1
1926	77.8	78.2	78.8	79.0	79.4	79.5	79.8	80.1	80.0	80.1	80.4	79.8
1927	79.5	80.0	80.3	80.6	80.6	80.8	80.7	80.3	80.5	79.8	79.3	79.1
1928	79.0	79.1	79.5	79.8	79.8	80.3	80.8	81.2	81.4	81.4	81.1	81.4
1929	85.8	86.7	87.5	87.8	88.3	89.1	90.0	90.4	90.0	89.5	88.9	87.7
1930	85.6	85.3	85.3	85.0	84.7	84.0	82.9	81.8	80.4	80.0	78.6	77.9
1931	73.7	73.4	73.2	72.7	72.1	71.4	70.2	69.3	68.2	66.7	65.7	64.8
1932	65.9	65.4	64.9	63.8	62.5	61.2	60.0	59.0	59.0	58.7	58.3	57.9
1933	57.7	57.3	55.8	55.4	56.1	57.2	58.5	60.3	60.9	61.8	61.4	61.3
1934	63.1	63.8	64.5	65.5	66.3	66.7	66.9	67.1	66.8	66.7	66.6	67.2
1935	69.3	69.9	70.5	71.0	71.6	72.0	72.3	72.8	72.9	73.0	73.1	73.3
1936	75.2	75.5	76.1	76.8	77.6	78.6	79.8	80.6	80.9	81.3	81.9	82.9
1937	84.5	85.4	86.4	88.0	88.9	89.5	91.3	91.9	92.1	91.9	90.8	90.2
1938	85.2	84.4	83.9	83.3	83.1	83.0	83.2	83.3	83.2	83.3	83.9	84.4
1939	83.4	83.6	83.8	83.9	84.2	84.9	85.7	86.2	86.7	87.2	87.9	88.1

Source: See Appendix C, section 1.

139

Wisconsin manufactures for 1922 to January 1927 were constructed by using data on the percentage change in employment and payrolls from January 1922 to a given month, and for February 1927 to 1936 by using the percentage change from the preceding to a given month. Where data were missing—i.e. for August-October 1929 (employment and payrolls), January-February 1932 (employment), and January-March 1932 (payrolls)—it was assumed that the percentage change was zero. The index was computed on the base January 1922 = 100. The data on percentage change, taken from monthly issues of *Wisconsin Labor Market*, cover nonmanual workers in manufacturing and in a very small number of mines and quarries for 1922-1931; from 1932 to January 1936, after which no data are available, clerical employees in manufacturing are represented.

The employment and payrolls series for wage earners were adjusted by the National Bureau of Economic Research for seasonal variations. No seasonal adjustment was made of the two salaried personnel series (except for employment in 1922-1929), since their seasonal variation was negligible. Table C-2 presents the employment and payroll data for wage earners and salaried personnel.

TABLE C-2

Indexes of Employment and Payrolls of Wage Earners, 1920-1939,
and of Salaried Personnel, 1922-1936, Wisconsin Manufacturing Industries

A. Wage Earners

(1925-1927 = 100)

	Jan.	Feb.	Mar.	Apr.	May	June	July	Aug.	Sept.	Oct.	Nov.	Dec.
1920												
Employment	n.a.	n.a.	n.a.	n.a.	n.a.	n.a.	115.9	115.6	113.9	108.7	101.9	94.9
Payrolls	n.a.	n.a.	n.a.	n.a.	n.a.	n.a.	130.3	132.6	129.5	120.8	110.1	98.6
1921												
Employment	84.3	84.0	80.9	76.8	76.3	73.7	72.0	74.9	77.2	78.3	78.5	79.4
Payrolls	84.7	76.5	74.0	70.7	67.3	62.6	61.4	64.9	64.5	63.8	63.4	65.4
1922												
Employment	79.4	78.9	81.5	83.5	87.4	91.2	91.8	91.9	91.8	93.3	97.0	98.6
Payrolls	63.8	63.8	64.9	67.9	72.4	77.0	78.6	77.9	80.1	81.3	88.1	90.4
1923												
Employment	101.1	101.9	101.7	103.1	102.3	103.6	103.5	103.3	101.8	100.6	101.8	100.7
Payrolls	92.8	90.4	90.3	94.6	97.2	98.7	98.1	97.6	97.3	96.7	99.1	96.4
1924												
Employment	100.7	102.0	103.0	101.1	96.9	92.8	93.1	93.0	93.9	95.6	97.4	98.1
Payrolls	96.6	99.0	99.6	96.8	93.0	85.5	86.6	87.1	88.6	91.5	94.2	97.0
1925												
Employment	99.5	99.3	98.8	99.4	101.3	102.0	103.6	101.5	102.5	102.6	102.6	104.1
Payrolls	100.1	98.0	96.3	98.3	101.3	100.3	104.8	102.8	102.3	104.0	103.1	105.8
1926												
Employment	104.1	103.8	102.6	102.0	101.7	101.0	101.5	102.9	102.5	100.7	99.8	98.0
Payrolls	107.2	105.4	104.4	104.5	102.8	101.7	102.0	101.2	102.2	102.9	96.7	95.0
1927												
Employment	97.5	98.3	98.0	96.9	96.2	96.6	96.4	99.2	97.8	97.3	93.8	94.0
Payrolls	98.2	98.5	96.9	97.1	93.7	96.9	96.7	100.2	97.8	94.8	93.0	93.5
1928												
Employment	94.0	93.9	93.8	93.5	94.6	95.4	96.1	98.4	98.8	99.3	98.7	98.4
Payrolls	90.9	93.2	99.2	92.2	94.2	99.3	97.3	102.0	102.4	103.8	103.4	98.4
1929												
Employment	98.1	99.1	99.7	101.1	102.0	101.1	99.6	102.3	101.0	102.0	99.6	95.1
Payrolls	98.3	103.5	103.0	105.3	103.8	101.5	98.9	103.3	98.9	102.0	99.6	90.2

TABLE C-2 (continued)

A. Wage Earners (continued)
(1925-1927 = 100)

	Jan.	Feb.	Mar.	Apr.	May	June	July	Aug.	Sept.	Oct.	Nov.	Dec.
1929												
Employment	104.1	105.3	106.0	107.6	108.6	107.5	105.8	108.6	107.1	107.9	105.2	100.2
Payrolls	106.7	112.8	112.5	115.1	113.5	110.9	107.9	112.6	107.5	110.6	107.7	97.1
1930												
Employment	102.2	100.6	97.6	96.5	96.0	91.2	87.9	85.3	84.3	82.3	80.2	80.2
Payrolls	99.9	99.5	96.9	93.6	92.0	85.6	80.0	75.3	74.1	72.1	67.6	67.3
1931												
Employment	80.4	79.3	77.0	76.7	77.2	75.0	73.8	72.3	72.7	68.5	66.7	66.4
Payrolls	65.5	67.5	66.3	65.1	65.1	62.1	59.0	56.5	53.6	49.2	48.4	48.8
1932												
Employment	65.3	66.3	64.5	62.6	60.7	58.7	55.6	55.3	56.9	56.2	56.4	56.0
Payrolls	45.9	47.0	44.9	40.9	38.6	35.5	32.1	33.0	34.8	35.8	36.1	34.3
1933												
Employment	55.1	55.3	53.2	55.2	57.9	63.1	65.5	69.2	72.4	72.9	72.3	71.9
Payrolls	33.0	32.6	29.5	32.7	37.1	42.8	45.2	48.7	49.6	49.3	48.4	48.1
1934												
Employment	72.2	72.3	72.0	72.4	77.2	76.8	74.5	74.1	74.1	73.7	74.0	76.3
Payrolls	50.4	51.2	52.3	52.6	57.5	57.7	56.1	54.4	52.3	53.3	54.8	58.9
1935												
Employment	78.1	79.3	78.4	78.1	79.3	79.7	80.8	82.0	82.7	82.6	82.8	83.4
Payrolls	60.9	62.3	60.7	60.6	61.5	62.7	68.1	66.1	70.3	67.5	69.2	73.3
1936												
Employment	83.3	83.0	82.1	82.8	85.0	85.7	85.0	84.7	89.3	91.5	92.9	95.3
Payrolls	74.6	69.5	70.6	70.2	73.1	74.9	73.5	76.2	77.4	83.7	88.3	93.0
1937												
Employment	99.1	99.6	100.2	101.8	101.7	101.0	104.1	102.2	105.2	101.5	98.0	94.0
Payrolls	97.6	99.4	99.3	102.0	103.7	104.0	108.3	107.4	106.1	104.9	101.4	94.1
1938												
Employment	88.5	86.7	83.7	82.7	81.8	82.0	86.4	84.2	82.8	81.3	82.4	84.8
Payrolls	87.9	84.3	79.5	76.8	76.2	76.0	80.6	79.3	77.5	78.2	82.1	87.4
1939												
Employment	84.0	84.6	n.a.	n.a.	n.a.	n.a.	n.a.	n.a.	n.a.	n.a.	n.a.	n.a.
Payrolls	86.4	88.0	n.a.	n.a.	n.a.	n.a.	n.a.	n.a.	n.a.	n.a.	n.a.	n.a.

TABLE C-2 (continued)

B. Salaried Personnel

(January 1922 = 100)

	Jan.	Feb.	Mar.	Apr.	May	June	July	Aug.	Sept.	Oct.	Nov.	Dec.
1922												
Employment	100.0	101.4	102.6	102.4	103.0	104.7	105.4	108.4	105.7	105.5	102.6	105.3
Payrolls	100.0	100.3	101.4	97.3	100.4	102.3	103.2	105.0	100.3	101.1	100.1	103.1
1923												
Employment	106.0	106.0	106.0	105.8	106.8	108.1	108.1	110.4	109.3	110.1	110.5	111.3
Payrolls	101.7	102.5	101.9	102.1	103.7	106.4	106.6	109.0	108.5	109.3	109.9	110.1
1924												
Employment	110.5	110.8	110.7	109.6	108.6	109.2	107.9	109.7	109.7	108.0	110.6	110.8
Payrolls	109.5	112.0	112.8	113.0	114.1	115.0	115.5	114.1	113.9	117.4	117.5	117.4
1925												
Employment	111.7	111.5	111.6	112.5	111.1	113.6	113.4	112.7	114.0	114.9	114.7	113.2
Payrolls	121.2	120.5	121.0	124.1	120.6	126.0	124.1	122.1	122.6	123.7	124.4	124.2
1926												
Employment	114.5	116.3	116.5	116.6	116.3	116.3	117.4	119.4	119.8	120.5	120.5	120.4
Payrolls	124.2	127.3	127.7	126.6	126.9	128.3	129.4	130.2	128.9	130.2	130.3	129.9
1927												
Employment	120.9	121.0	121.7	122.2	122.8	121.7	121.9	122.8	123.5	123.8	124.9	124.1
Payrolls	132.4	134.0	135.6	135.9	138.1	137.0	136.9	139.0	137.6	136.5	137.7	139.8
1928												
Employment	122.3	120.9	119.9	120.9	120.4	118.9	119.7	122.1	124.1	124.3	124.3	123.9
Payrolls	137.0	135.8	139.9	139.6	139.2	137.4	140.0	142.2	139.9	142.8	140.8	142.1
1929												
Employment	124.9	124.6	124.3	124.9	126.4	124.6	124.8	124.8	124.8	124.8	125.0	125.7
Payrolls	145.2	145.5	145.4	146.6	149.4	148.8	149.2	149.2	149.2	149.2	149.2	147.4

TABLE C-2 (continued)

B. Salaried Personnel (continued)

(January 1922 = 100)

	Jan.	Feb.	Mar.	Apr.	May	June	July	Aug.	Sept.	Oct.	Nov.	Dec.
1930												
Employment	126.2	127.0	127.7	126.3	125.9	125.2	124.4	124.3	121.2	119.2	118.3	115.8
Payrolls	149.2	150.1	151.7	150.1	128.3	131.6	125.9	123.5	122.2	121.6	119.4	116.8
1931												
Employment	113.8	114.9	114.4	113.6	112.6	111.2	110.6	109.1	108.1	107.7	105.1	104.2
Payrolls	114.9	122.5	120.9	111.3	111.2	108.6	108.8	106.7	105.3	102.8	104.9	100.4
1932												
Employment	104.2	104.2	102.7	99.6	96.8	93.5	91.2	90.1	90.2	90.7	90.6	89.1
Payrolls	100.4	100.4	100.4	97.3	97.7	85.9	80.7	78.6	79.2	80.3	79.7	77.1
1933												
Employment	86.7	86.2	85.4	85.6	86.1	88.6	91.5	95.1	97.1	98.8	98.3	98.6
Payrolls	76.7	73.9	72.8	71.9	72.4	74.2	76.2	79.8	81.8	87.3	84.3	85.3
1934												
Employment	97.0	95.8	96.8	97.2	98.7	100.2	98.1	97.5	97.3	96.7	97.8	98.7
Payrolls	85.8	82.5	83.6	87.4	85.0	85.9	84.1	80.1	80.0	80.1	81.2	81.9
1935												
Employment	99.0	100.0	100.8	101.8	102.2	102.8	103.5	105.1	105.5	104.8	105.0	105.3
Payrolls	82.8	84.3	85.2	85.5	86.2	86.7	86.8	87.7	94.0	89.1	88.9	94.7
1936												
Employment	106.3	n.a.	n.a.	n.a.	n.a.	n.a.	n.a.	n.a.	n.a.	n.a.	n.a.	n.a.
Payrolls	102.2	n.a.	n.a.	n.a.	n.a.	n.a.	n.a.	n.a.	n.a.	n.a.	n.a.	n.a.

n.a. = not available.
Source: See Appendix C, section 2.

DIVIDEND DISBURSEMENTS, 1884-1919, AND TOTAL
DIVIDEND PAYMENTS TO INDIVIDUALS, 1919-1950

THE series on dividend payments to individuals for 1919 to 1941 was computed by adjusting the level of a monthly sample series published by the *New York Journal of Commerce* to annual bench-mark data. For 1919-1921 the annual data used are from an article by J. F. Ebersole, S. B. Burr, and G. M. Peterson, "Income Forecasting by the Use of Statistics of Income Data" (*Review of Economic Statistics*, November 1929), and for 1922 to 1941 from appropriate years of *Statistics of Income* (Bureau of Internal Revenue).

We used an adaptation of the method developed by V Lewis Bassie which least affects the relative monthly movement within each year and the December-January movement between consecutive years (see Frederick M. Cone, *Monthly Income Payments in the United States, 1929-40*, Dept. of Commerce, Economic Series No. 6, 1940, pp. 27-28).

The annual data used as control totals were computed by subtracting dividends received by corporations from dividends paid out by corporations. The result is a close approximation of dividend payments to individuals, although we have not been able to exclude from it receipts of (1) individuals residing abroad, (2) foreign corporations, and (3) eleemosynary and other nonprofit institutions.

The monthly series includes manufacturing, retailing, mining, shipping, railroad, and traction companies. In 1925 the sample is placed on a more inclusive basis. From May 1934 onward the data exclude semiprivate and closed corporations and include financial corporations. Neither the 1919-1924 nor the 1925-1941 segment is a continuous sample; the number of corporations included changes from year to year. For 1939-1950 the National Income Division of the Department of Commerce has compiled a monthly series on dividends received by individuals. Its procedure is very similar to ours; it adjusts its own sample of monthly dividend payments using annual control totals (dividends paid by corporations less dividends received) from *Statistics of Income*. The sample is a large one and is stratified by industry groups. The Bassie method is used in making the interpolation. This series has not been published but has been made available to us by the Department of Commerce. Table D-1 presents total dividend payments to individuals for 1919-1950. Data

TABLE D-1

Total Dividend Payments to Individuals, 1919-1941 and 1939-1950
(*millions of dollars*)

	Jan.	Feb.	Mar.	Apr.	May	June	July	Aug.	Sept.	Oct.	Nov.	Dec.
1919	218.6	213.0	220.6	213.9	214.7	202.2	211.5	213.8	218.4	223.1	225.3	223.0
1920	231.9	235.5	235.7	239.0	254.1	244.0	248.0	245.3	249.0	244.4	243.5	236.5
1921	230.6	230.1	220.5	221.3	216.2	215.4	222.2	219.9	210.2	218.7	204.6	209.8
1922	212.7	218.4	209.8	212.3	204.4	211.0	215.1	221.8	223.6	232.8	228.9	243.9
1923	244.6	260.0	257.0	260.3	279.2	278.7	269.3	294.4	300.0	283.3	295.5	301.2
1924	283.9	281.7	283.2	277.6	265.9	273.3	281.8	300.9	279.2	301.4	289.9	299.2
1925	309.3	312.3	331.4	314.5	347.4	355.8	340.2	338.5	377.6	327.3	380.9	307.4
1926	346.3	363.8	354.6	366.5	401.5	388.7	370.8	376.5	386.0	377.2	389.4	338.1
1927	390.7	384.4	392.0	407.8	371.8	392.5	393.2	404.3	384.7	411.0	411.5	421.3
1928	391.5	423.6	405.2	425.3	413.4	399.7	473.8	450.2	434.7	463.9	438.1	455.9
1929	496.0	477.8	473.9	452.4	505.2	479.6	503.0	500.1	520.4	514.6	503.9	511.0
1930	539.5	486.5	510.4	478.3	478.2	496.7	454.1	442.1	438.2	405.1	405.9	408.1
1931	391.9	502.3	387.9	369.1	325.1	346.3	310.6	323.1	306.8	292.1	291.7	283.6
1932	255.1	224.3	240.1	245.9	236.1	240.1	199.0	200.4	196.2	194.4	177.9	172.9
1933	183.6	172.4	166.1	152.2	192.1	166.5	177.4	190.4	155.6	190.4	170.6	173.7
1934	213.8	261.9	190.4	149.7	245.8	224.9	237.8	228.7	220.5	247.8	229.2	221.3
1935	249.6	197.7	223.6	271.4	228.0	188.2	253.3	255.3	236.9	257.3	292.4	259.8
1936	275.1	315.1	323.9	329.6	369.4	349.1	336.2	414.8	405.1	375.7	463.4	613.0
1937	336.4	334.1	376.2	387.1	364.6	501.0	389.3	366.5	456.9	374.2	312.0	453.6
1938	367.5	301.1	298.2	301.3	248.1	245.5	284.4	248.0	234.4	280.8	261.1	212.8
1939	299.2	319.8	310.1	308.4	333.6	289.4	317.2	348.4	331.6	313.7	374.1	334.4
1940	328.3	324.8	331.5	341.3	284.0	360.1	332.1	315.9	387.7	341.0	296.5	342.4
1941	298.2	310.5	408.0	340.9	335.4	417.2	359.0	368.1	435.7	364.2	384.3	380.5

TABLE D-1 (continued)

(*millions of dollars*)

	Jan.	Feb.	Mar.	Apr.	May	June	July	Aug.	Sept.	Oct.	Nov.	Dec.
1939	362	335	274	314	321	268	317	310	299	317	335	342
1940	359	349	305	338	336	335	332	342	355	351	335	331
1941	346	341	369	351	364	380	365	362	387	381	376	389
1942	376	359	371	381	357	351	369	358	342	354	368	342
1943	369	396	363	376	390	368	381	383	377	387	395	363
1944	361	369	385	389	373	398	397	370	407	384	384	405
1945	370	371	388	376	354	422	388	375	388	408	395	398
1946	454	426	424	464	468	447	490	526	491	489	563	545
1947	529	546	513	530	568	527	556	605	552	589	566	549
1948	611	596	604	612	551	586	624	669	638	651	672	643
1949	610	614	692	643	595	650	633	600	674	632	630	685
1950	636	643	752	655	671	639						

Source: See Appendix D.

for earlier years are not presented because they do not give us a reliable picture of the amplitude of their specific cycles.

A test was made in which the turning points in the specific cycles of the interpolation series were compared with those of the series adjusted to annual control totals for 1919-1941. There were seven turning points in each series, all comparable. Of the seven, there were four coincidences, and no difference greater than three months. We therefore decided that the *Journal of Commerce* data available for years before 1919, unadjusted to annual control totals, would be reliable in determining cyclical turning points in dividend disbursements; however, *the sample series cannot be used in measuring cyclical amplitude.*

DATE OF TURNING POINTS IN:

LEVEL	Journal of Commerce Series	Journal of Commerce Series Adjusted to Annual Control Totals
T	Sept. 1919	June 1919
P	July 1920	May 1920
T	May 1922	May 1922
P	Dec. 1929	Jan. 1930
T	Apr. 1933	Apr. 1933
P	June 1937	June 1937
T	Dec. 1938	Dec. 1938

P = peak; T = trough.

The *Journal of Commerce* series extends back to 1906. For the years 1904 and 1905, no record of monthly dividend payments was published. For the years 1884-1903, monthly data are available in the *Daily Stockholder*. It should be noted again that in compiling these series the payments of a constant sample of corporations were not added, but only those of corporations whose reports happened to be seen by the *Journal of Commerce* and *Daily Stockholder* compilers. For 1884-1908, banks and trust companies are included in the data; from 1909 to April 1934 they are excluded.

The entire series from 1884 to 1950 has been corrected for seasonal variation by the National Bureau of Economic Research, using a moving seasonal index.

APPENDIX E

INTEREST ON GOVERNMENT SECURITIES
RECEIVED BY INDIVIDUALS, 1913-1949

THERE are no data available on government interest received by individuals. The Department of Commerce series on net interest paid by the federal and state and local governments for 1929-1949 (available annually since 1929 and quarterly since 1939 in published form, and monthly since 1929 in unpublished form) is equivalent to the amount paid to the private sector (i.e. households and nonhouseholds). Since payments made to corporations and other nonhouseholds were not excluded by the Department, we made our own estimates of government interest paid to individuals. To eliminate government interest received by nonindividuals, including the government, we adjusted the available annual data on *gross* government interest payments for 1913-1949. This was accomplished by using midyear data on individual and total holdings of government debt. Table E-1 presents estimates of federal, state and local, and total government interest paid to individuals.

149

TABLE E-1

Federal, State and Local, and Total Government Interest
Received by Individuals, 1913-1949
(*millions of dollars*)

	Federal Interest (1)	*State and Local Interest* (2)	*Total Government Interest* (1 + 2) (3)
1913	0	100	100
1914	0	110	110
1915	0	123	123
1916	0	135	135
1917	16	143	159
1918	134	151	285
1919	376	{ 251 129	{ 627 505
1920	532	151	683
1921	547	182	729
1922	511	207	718
1923	476	234	710
1924	415	260	675
1925	373	301	674
1926	350	324	674
1927	313	344	657
1928	249	366	615
1929	{ 228 250	{ 407 393	{ 635 643
1930	217	424	641
1931	214	438	652
1932	230	483	713
1933	248	459	707
1934	242	421	663
1935	217	384	601
1936	245	375	620
1937	295	355	650
1938	257	344	601
1939	256	320	576
1940	{ 282 275	307	{ 589 582
1941	287	277	564
1942	413	269	682
1943	558	260	818
1944	750	253	1,003
1945	1,001	248	1,249
1946	1,236	234	1,470
1947	1,360	225	1,585
1948	1,419	239	1,658
1949	1,531	285	1,816

APPENDIX E

Notes to Table E-1

| Column | Source |

1   Federal interest received by individuals: *1913-1929*—gross federal
interest payments on the public debt during fiscal years are available
in *Annual Report of the Secretary of the Treasury on the State of the
Finances for the Fiscal Year Ended June 30, 1949*, Dept. of the
Treasury, 1950, pp. 359 and 361. Pairs of fiscal year data were averaged
and centered at midyear. *1929-1949*—annual data on gross federal
interest paid are taken from *National Income Supplement, 1947,
Survey of Current Business*, Dept. of Commerce, p. 23, and *Survey of
Current Business*, July 1950, p. 13. Annual ratios of individual holdings
to total holdings of federal securities were applied to gross federal
interest paid to secure federal interest received by individuals in 1913-
1949. Data on holdings of federal and state and local securities are
from George E. Lent, *The Ownership of Tax-Exempt Securities, 1913-
1953*, National Bureau of Economic Research, Occasional Paper 47,
1955. The data in Lent's study cover wholly and partially tax-exempt
holdings. Since interest on federal bonds issued after 1940 became
wholly taxable by the federal government, data on holdings of federal
securities for 1940-1949 are from *Treasury Bulletin*, Dept. of the
Treasury, October 1950, p. 32. Since the *Treasury Bulletin* data on
holdings were used for 1940-1949, there are two segments for 1929-
1949: 1929-1940 and 1940-1949.

2   State and local interest received by individuals: *1913-1919*—gross interest paid by the federal government was subtracted from estimates of
gross interest paid by all governments (Willford Isbell King, *The
National Income and Its Purchasing Power*, NBER, 1930, p. 370) to
secure gross state and local interest paid; *1919-1929*—data on gross
state and local interest paid annually from Simon Kuznets' worksheets;
1929-1949—gross interest data from *National Income Supplement,
1947*, p. 23, and *Survey of Current Business*, July 1950, p. 13.
Annual ratios of individual holdings to total holdings of state and
local debt were applied to gross state and local interest paid to
secure state and local interest received by individuals in 1913-1949.
Data on holdings of state and local securities are from Lent, *op. cit.*

3   Total government interest received by individuals: column 1 plus
column 2.

APPENDIX F

ESTIMATES OF UNDERREPORTING OF DIVIDENDS
AND INTEREST BY INCOME GROUPS, 1939-1948

SINCE the share of the lowest income group (lower 93 per cent in Kuznets' classification) in total dividends and interest payments is the difference between the country-wide total and the amount received by the top 7 per cent, any increase in underreporting by the top 7 per cent would increase the share of the lower 93 per cent, as would any addition to the share of dividends going to nonprofit institutions (which are included in the lower 93 per cent). Both factors, it seems, were operating during the 1940's. That underreporting in general increased during the war years, despite the tremendous broadening of the tax base from 18 to 43 million taxable returns, is clearly established by the figures in Table F-1. It must be more than coincidental that the first large relative decline in reported dividends occurs between 1941 and 1942, when there was a sharp upward revision in tax rates (Table 34).

This deficiency in reported dividends can be traced to three sources: (1) temporary exemption from filing income tax returns given to members of the armed forces serving abroad or on sea duty,[1] (2) underreporting by individuals filing returns, and (3) dividends received by nonprofit institutions not obliged to file tax returns. Any relative increase in nonreporting and underreporting—categories 1 and 2—by individuals in the top 7 per cent would exaggerate the share received by the lower 93 per cent. Some of the dividend recipients among the armed forces, temporarily exempt from filing, probably had incomes that placed them in the top 7 per cent. Their quantitative importance, however, cannot be estimated.

Substantial underreporting by the top 7 per cent, particularly by those toward the bottom of that bracket, is suggested by the Bureau of Internal Revenue's sample audit of 1948 tax returns. Preliminary estimates by Daniel Holland based on unpublished tabulations of the Bureau of Internal Revenue indicate that about 69 per cent of the amount of the dividends detected by the authorities as unreported can be attributed to taxpayers with incomes over $7,000,

---

[1] "Beginning 1941, members of the Armed Forces serving abroad or on sea duty may postpone the filing of returns and payment of tax until the 15th day of the sixth month following the month in which they return to the United States (but not beyond June 15, 1948)." *Statistics of Income for 1945*, Bureau of Internal Revenue, Part I, p. 352.

TABLE F-1

Number of Taxable Income Tax Returns,
and Dividends and Interest Reported as Percentage
of Dividends and Interest Received, 1939-1948

	Taxable Returns (thousands)	Dividends Reported as % of Total Dividends Received (per cent)	Interest Reported as % of Total Interest Received (per cent)
1939	3,959	79.1	23.0
1940	7,505	85.7	26.6
1941	17,587	88.7	32.3
1942	27,718	82.2	33.8
1943	40,319	78.7	32.5
1944	42,447	n.a.	n.a.
1945	42,764	n.a.	n.a.
1946	38,037	78.5	27.1
1947	41,689	80.7	24.6
1948	36,513	81.7	23.4

n.a. = not available.

Column	Source
1	Taxable individual and fiduciary income tax returns: *Statistics of Income for 1945*, Bureau of Internal Revenue, Part I, p. 219, and preliminary releases of *Statistics of Income* after 1945.
2	Dividends and interest reported on taxable individual and fiduciary income tax returns as percentages of total dividends and total interest received: unpublished memorandum of Daniel Holland, National Bureau of Economic Research.

who received 77 per cent of all dividends eventually reported on individual tax returns.

If nonprofit institutions had increased their share of dividends, this also would exaggerate the share received by the lower 93 per cent. To judge by the crude estimates now available, private nonprofit organizations did not increase their share of stocks, hence of dividends, during the war but did during the postwar years.[2]

[2] Raymond Goldsmith estimates the market value of equities outstanding, excluding intercorporate holdings, at $82.3, 127.7, and 131.6 billion in 1939, 1945, and 1949, respectively. The book value of equities owned by nonprofit institutions is placed by the same estimator at $1.7, 2.7, and 3.6 billion for the same selected years. On a percentage basis the institutional holdings represent 2.1, 2.1, and 2.7 per cent of all equities for 1939, 1945, and 1949, respectively. These estimates have been prepared for the Capital Requirements Study of the National Bureau of Economic Research. Estimates of all equities are from Raymond W. Goldsmith, *The Share of Financial Intermediaries in National Wealth and National Assets, 1900-1949*, National Bureau of Economic Research, Occasional Paper 42, 1954, Table 16, p. 69; estimates of equity holdings by private nonprofit institutions are from Raymond W. Goldsmith, "Estimate

In the case of interest receipts there were no significant shifts in the shares received by the three income-size groups between 1937 and 1943, despite a substantial increase in the proportion of interest reported by taxpayers. However, some time between 1943 and 1946 a shift occurred in favor of the lower 93 per cent, and between 1946 and 1948 their share continued to increase, which was not the case with dividends. This increasing share of interest received by the lowest income group is correlated with the relative decline in the interest reported on individual tax returns. Underreporting increased continuously from 1943 to 1948.

Both phenomena probably can be traced to the same factor: the accrued interest on Series A to F savings bonds issued by the federal government enters the country-wide total of personal interest receipts, but it is a widespread practice for individuals to report this type of interest receipt, if at all, on a cash basis. Accordingly, most of the accrued interest earned by the holders of these savings bonds in the top 7 per cent is counted as interest received by the lower 93 per cent.

The maximum size of this distortion in 1948 can be estimated. The Federal Reserve Board in its postwar Surveys of Consumer Finances has shown that the 10 per cent of the nation's spending units with the highest incomes owned 43 per cent of all personal holdings of liquid assets in 1948. These Surveys also show that the distribution of all liquid assets and that of Series A to F savings bonds are very similar by income-size classes, at least in 1950, when the two distributions can be reliably compared (see Table F-2). We assume, therefore, that the upper 10 per cent owned also 43 per cent of all savings bonds in 1948. On this assumption and on the assumption that the top 10 per cent did not report any interest on savings bonds, we estimate that about $405 million in federal government interest, or 8 per cent of total monetary interest, actually accrued to the top 10 per cent in 1948 but was counted as having been received by the lower 90 per cent (see Table F-2). Again, we point out that it must be more than accidental that the gain in the interest share received by the lower 93 per cent between 1943 and 1948 was about 6.5 percentage points. Another factor that might help to account for this shift in dividends and interest is that the relative decline in property incomes placed those who received their income mainly from prop-

of the Aggregate Value and the Distribution of the Nonoperating Assets of Private Nonprofit Institutions, Selected Years, 1900-1949," mimeographed, NBER, Work Memorandum 36, 1952, Table 1, p. 2.

TABLE F-2

Derivation of 1948 Accrued Interest on United States Savings Bonds, Series A to F, Received by 10 Per Cent of the Population with Highest Annual Incomes in 1947

(dollars in millions)

1. Value of A to D savings bonds outstanding[a]	$2,250
2. Value of E savings bonds outstanding[a]	$32,188
3. Value of A to E savings bonds outstanding[a] $(1+2)$	$34,438
4. Computed annual interest rate, A to E bonds	2.9%
5. Accrued interest on A to E savings bonds (3×4)	$999
6. Value of F savings bonds outstanding[a]	$3,505
7. Computed annual interest rate, F bonds	2.53%
8. Accrued interest on F savings bonds (6×7)	$89
9. Total accrued interest on A to F savings bonds $(5+8)$	$1,088
10. All (A to G) savings bonds outstanding[b]	$55,197
11. Total savings bonds owned by individuals[b]	$47,800
12. Per cent of all savings bonds owned by individuals $(11 \div 10)$	86.6%
13. Accrued interest received by individuals (9×12)	$942
14. Per cent of individually owned savings bonds held by upper 10 per cent of population	43%
15. Accrued interest received by upper 10 per cent (13×14)	$405
16. Total monetary interest received by individuals	$5,092
17. Accrued interest received by upper 10 per cent as percentage of total monetary interest $(15 \div 16)$	8.0%

[a] Interest-bearing debt; end-of-year figure.
[b] Interest-bearing and matured debt; end-of-year figure.

Line	Source
1	*Treasury Bulletin*, Dept. of the Treasury, February 1952, Table 3, p. 37.
2	*Treasury Bulletin*, June 1952, Table 3, p. 28.
4	*Ibid.*, Table 6, note 4, p. 18.
6	*Ibid.*, Table 3, p. 29.
7	Same as source for line 4.
10	*Ibid.*, Table 2, p. 27.
11	*Ibid.*, Table 3, p. 33.
14	The figure, 43 per cent, is the percentage of all liquid assets owned by the upper 10 per cent of the population ("1951 Survey of Consumer Finances," *Federal Reserve Bulletin*, June 1951, Table 10, p. 636). The distributions of all liquid assets and of A to F savings bonds by income-size classes seem to be very similar, at least in 1950, the only year the two distributions can be reliably compared:

INCOME CLASS	1950 PERCENTAGE SHARE OF:	
	All Liquid Assets	*A to F Bond Holdings*
Under $1,000	6	5
$1,000–1,999	9	8
2,000–2,999	15	13
3,000–3,999	15	15
4,000–4,999	11	12
5,000–7,499	18	17
7,500 and over	26	30

Notes to Table F-2 (continued)

In this table the distribution of liquid assets is from the "1951 Survey of Consumer Finances," as cited, Table 24, p. 643; distribution of A to F bond holdings is from letter from the Survey Research Center, University of Michigan.

16 *National Income Supplement, 1951, Survey of Current Business*, Dept. of Commerce, Table 37, p. 202.

erty lower in the income scale. Its quantitative importance, however, cannot be measured.[3]

These deficiencies in the property-income data[4] oblige us to be cautious in interpreting any change in the shares of property income received by the highest, middle, and lowest income groups during the war and postwar years.

[3] See Simon Kuznets, *Shares of Upper Income Groups in Income and Savings*, National Bureau of Economic Research, 1953, pp. 64-73, and Geoffrey H. Moore, "Secular Changes in the Distribution of Income," Papers and Proceedings, *American Economic Review*, May 1952, p. 536.

[4] In this context also we consider the changes in the share of rent received by the three income-size groups not worth analyzing because of the weaknesses of the country-wide estimates of rent.

APPENDIX G

UNEMPLOYMENT COMPENSATION AND LOSSES IN INCOME

1. Payrolls, Disposable Income, and Payments to Unemployed, United States, 1945-1950

a. PAYROLLS

Seasonally adjusted private payrolls used in Table 30 above were derived by subtracting government from total wage and salary disbursements. Government and total payroll data, seasonally adjusted, are from the *National Income Supplement, 1951* (*Survey of Current Business*, Dept. of Commerce, Table 48, p. 215) and the *Survey of Current Business* (July 1952, Table 48, p. 31).

b. DISPOSABLE INCOME

Disposable income on a quarterly basis was computed by subtracting state and local personal tax payments and federal personal income tax liabilities from personal income and adding realized net capital gains or losses. Seasonally adjusted quarterly personal income and state and local tax data are from the *National Income Supplement, 1951* (Table 45, p. 209) and the *Survey of Current Business* (July 1952, Table 45, p. 30). Quarterly estimates of federal personal income tax liabilities were made by multiplying annual data from the preliminary report of *Statistics of Income for 1949* (Bureau of Internal Revenue, Part 1, pp. 9 and 51-53) by the ratio of seasonally adjusted quarterly personal income to annual personal income. Quarterly estimates of net capital gains or losses were computed by applying the same ratio to annual data from Table A-1 above.

c. PAYMENTS TO UNEMPLOYED

Table G-1 presents payments to the unemployed used in estimating offsets in Tables 30 to 32. These payments are computed by adding (1) state and (2) railroad unemployment insurance benefits and (3) general assistance, seasonally adjusted by the National Bureau of Economic Research. Data for the three series are from monthly issues of the *Social Security Bulletin* (Social Security Administration, Federal Security Agency).

Quarterly data for all series used in Tables 31 and 32 except disposable personal income are three-month totals of the monthly data.

TABLE G-1

Total Payments to Unemployed, Seasonally Adjusted, 1945-1950
(*millions of dollars*)

	1945	1946	1947	1948	1949	1950
January	14.4	119.9	79.0	66.7	107.5	191.2
February	13.0	120.8	76.8	73.0	129.4	189.5
March	13.9	116.8	75.2	81.8	153.5	193.4
April	12.9	114.5	83.2	87.9	156.5	161.9
May	13.8	110.3	84.0	80.8	164.0	157.9
June	16.9	102.4	86.3	87.0	175.9	141.9
July	21.5	101.9	93.6	86.4	179.7	127.7
August	25.3	93.3	84.7	84.4	208.2	118.1
September	58.0	90.0	88.2	90.4	219.5	101.9
October	114.8	97.0	84.7	88.5	213.3	94.4
November	117.3	83.8	69.5	97.7	240.0	99.9
December	115.6	85.9	78.3	113.5	237.9	98.3

Source: See Appendix G, section 1 c.

2. Quarterly Estimates of Payrolls in Private Sector and Payments to Unemployed, Twelve States, 1948-1950

The sources and methods of estimation of the payroll and compensation data presented in Table G-2, and used in columns 1 to 3 of Table 33 above, for each of twelve states selected from the twenty-three which incurred a loss in annual wages and salaries in 1948-1949 (see *Survey of Current Business*, Dept. of Commerce, August 1952, Table 6, p. 18) are described below. Since the data are insufficient for reliable seasonal determination, we are obliged to use data unadjusted for seasonal variations.

a. PAYROLLS

Payrolls in the private sector are secured by adding (1) private nonfarm payrolls and (2) farm wages (both unadjusted).

1. Annual private nonfarm payrolls were converted to a quarterly basis by using a quarterly percentage breakdown of payrolls covered by state unemployment insurance for each year. Data are from unpublished tables of the National Income Division of the Department of Commerce.

2. Annual farm wages were converted to a quarterly basis by using the product of quarterly estimates of the number of hired farm workers employed and the hourly composite farm wage rate. Annual farm wages are from an unpublished table of the National

Income Division. Monthly data on the number of hired farm workers in each state are from *Farm Labor* (Bureau of Agricultural Economics, January 13, 1949) and *Crops and Markets* (BAE, 1950 and 1951). Three-month averages of the employment data were computed to place the data on a quarterly basis. Hourly composite farm wage rates for the beginning of the months of January, April, July, and October for geographical regions are from *Farm Labor*, January 12, 1951, and January 14, 1952. The wage rate data for the New England region, for example, were used for Connecticut and Rhode Island. Quarterly wage rate estimates were made by averaging data for pairs of given months.

b. PAYMENTS TO UNEMPLOYED

Payments to the unemployed are the sum of (1) state and (2) railroad unemployment compensation benefits and (3) general assistance (all unadjusted).

1. State unemployment insurance benefits: quarterly data from unpublished tables of the National Income Division.

2. Railroad unemployment insurance benefits: semi-annual benefit data were converted to a quarterly basis by using a quarterly percentage breakdown of the number of railroad unemployment insurance beneficiaries during the half year. Data on the amount of benefits and the number of beneficiaries are from unpublished tables of the Railroad Retirement Board.

3. General assistance: same source as that for 1.

TABLE G-2

Payrolls in Private Sector and Payments to Unemployed, Seasonally Unadjusted, Twelve States, 1948-1950

(*millions of dollars*)

	QUARTER, 1948				QUARTER, 1949				QUARTER, 1950			
	1st	*2nd*	*3rd*	*4th*	*1st*	*2nd*	*3rd*	*4th*	*1st*	*2nd*	*3rd*	*4th*
Alabama												
Payrolls	299.6	314.4	317.6	340.3	301.7	300.2	300.3	302.7	292.0	317.7	340.5	372.3
Payments to unemployed	2.3	2.3	2.6	2.5	3.9	5.5	7.0	6.1	5.4	4.7	3.4	2.1
California												
Payrolls	2,183.3	2,286.2	2,498.8	2,445.4	2,145.0	2,267.1	2,401.8	2,376.5	2,160.7	2,367.2	2,654.7	2,748.8
Payments to unemployed	38.3	47.2	40.2	41.2	76.7	76.7	65.2	63.3	84.5	60.5	35.1	29.3
Connecticut												
Payrolls	531.4	543.7	545.9	597.8	520.3	507.3	502.6	551.1	511.4	551.4	583.9	684.4
Payments to unemployed	3.4	3.7	4.6	4.6	8.3	14.7	16.6	10.8	11.1	7.6	4.7	2.8
Illinois												
Payrolls	2,191.3	2,188.3	2,259.4	2,603.8	2,185.2	2,195.9	2,214.6	2,332.8	2,166.1	2,304.7	2,437.7	2,725.0
Payments to unemployed	15.8	19.7	18.4	14.8	24.9	34.6	40.6	35.6	40.3	36.3	27.2	18.7
Kentucky												
Payrolls	297.3	313.8	332.7	351.7	301.9	317.6	309.6	325.0	298.1	339.8	359.3	389.4
Payments to unemployed	1.4	1.5	1.4	1.8	4.0	4.7	6.0	5.5	5.7	4.5	3.1	2.4
Michigan												
Payrolls	1,452.7	1,472.7	1,572.7	1,702.8	1,494.4	1,477.5	1,589.2	1,515.0	1,469.0	1,653.7	1,864.0	2,000.2
Payments to unemployed	14.6	15.1	10.3	10.7	22.2	25.6	22.3	32.1	33.5	19.4	7.8	8.4
New York												
Payrolls	3,987.4	4,003.5	4,130.8	4,557.8	3,988.3	3,997.3	4,080.2	4,352.9	4,022.8	4,156.9	4,379.0	4,940.2
Payments to unemployed	52.4	56.8	63.1	65.8	95.1	97.0	120.9	120.9	120.9	94.0	86.2	73.1

TABLE G-2 (continued)
(*millions of dollars*)

	QUARTER, 1948				QUARTER, 1949				QUARTER, 1950			
	1st	*2nd*	*3rd*	*4th*	*1st*	*2nd*	*3rd*	*4th*	*1st*	*2nd*	*3rd*	*4th*
Ohio												
Payrolls	1,802.6	1,871.3	1,959.5	2,136.5	1,829.3	1,828.3	1,845.1	1,889.0	1,778.3	1,954.2	2,121.0	2,369.3
Payments to unemployed	9.3	9.2	7.6	7.9	16.2	22.4	27.1	39.3	46.4	30.0	15.0	9.7
Pennsylvania												
Payrolls	2,306.1	2,367.7	2,441.5	2,654.9	2,362.1	2,373.1	2,297.6	2,319.5	2,239.8	2,470.1	2,587.5	2,853.7
Payments to unemployed	18.0	17.0	14.6	15.0	29.6	36.7	53.7	65.1	61.9	42.0	26.5	18.8
Rhode Island												
Payrolls	180.8	182.8	179.3	196.0	167.7	164.1	165.5	188.4	172.2	179.4	190.5	226.0
Payments to unemployed	2.8	4.5	4.3	4.4	6.7	12.6	9.7	6.0	6.0	7.9	4.5	2.7
South Carolina												
Payrolls	210.1	223.4	225.9	234.1	214.5	209.5	212.0	231.3	219.7	232.9	242.2	270.0
Payments to unemployed	1.1	1.1	1.3	1.5	2.5	3.9	4.3	3.3	3.4	3.0	2.5	1.7
West Virginia												
Payrolls	332.3	341.1	377.7	385.9	344.8	355.2	299.9	287.6	281.1	365.4	354.6	376.0
Payments to unemployed	2.1	1.6	1.2	1.5	3.4	4.1	6.7	7.7	7.0	5.0	4.1	2.5

Source: See Appendix G, section 2.

INDEX

Baker, John C., 51
Barger, Harold, *xxv*, 63
Bassie, V Lewis, 127, 136, 145
Bean, L. H., 28
Burkhead, Jesse, *xvin*
Burns, Arthur F., *ix*, 25n
Burr, S. B., 145
Business activity,
    dates of turns in, *xxiv, xxv*
    and personal income, *ix-x*

Capital gains and losses,
    data and sources, 117, 119
    defined, 6, 72
    and personal income, *xv-xvi*, 6-7, 73-74
    and property income, *xvi*, 9, 12
    and stock-market prices, 73, 75, 76, 113
    timing, *xi*, 73, 75, 76, 113
Capital input and returns,
    data and sources, 132-135
    secular change in, 15, 16
Carson, Daniel, 28n
Compensation of corporate officers
(*or* Executive salaries),
    in all corporations,
        as percentage of total income, 9, 10, 11, 21
        data and sources, 117, 118
    in manufacturing,
        compared with other salaried personnel, 50, 51, 52, 53, 58, 59, 77, 110, 112
Cone, Frederick M., 127, 136, 145
Conformity indexes, defined, 23, 25
Creamer, Daniel, 21n, 35n, 41n, 44n
Cycle relatives, defined, 21-22

Direct-relief payments, *see* General assistance
Disposable personal income,
    defined, 6n, 78n
    government offsets to losses in, 97, 100, 101, 103, 104, 106-109, 114, 157, 158
    shares of income-size groups in, 78, 80
Dividends,
    amplitude, 68-69, 77, 112
    and corporate net profits, 61-65, 69, 112

    data and sources, 117, 119, 145-148
    as percentage of total income, *xv, xvi, xvii, xxix*, 9, 12, 121
    as percentage of total income, by income-size groups, *xx, xxii*, 79, 80
    shares of income-size groups in, 84, 85, 86, 87, 88
    timing, *xi, xii*, 61-67, 69, 79, 112
    underreporting by income groups, 87-88, 152-153
Dobrovolsky, Sergei P., 61n, 68n

Ebersole, J. F., 145
Executive salaries, *see* Compensation of corporate officers

Fabricant, Solomon, 46n
Factory employment, *see* Wage earners in manufacturing
Factory payrolls, *see* Wages in manufacturing
Farm income, total,
    as percentage of total income, by income-size groups, *xix*
    timing, *xi*, 23, 25, 29
Farm proprietors' gross income,
    conformity to business cycles, 26, 28
    timing, 26, 27, 28
Farm proprietors' net income,
    amplitude, 30, 31, 32, 33, 68-69, 111, 112-113
    conformity to business cycles, 23, 25-26, 28-29
    data and sources, 117, 119, 131, 132
    government offsets to losses in, 90-97, 114
    as percentage of total income, *xvi, xvii, xviii, xxviii, xxix*, 8, 9, 11, 121
    as percentage of total income, by income-size groups, *xixn*
    timing, *xii, xiii*, 23, 24, 25, 27, 94-95, 110
Federal agricultural programs, 90-96
Federal cash benefits to farmers, 90-91
Federal farm price-support program, 90-96, 114
Federal personal income tax program, 90, 103-109

General assistance (*or* Direct-relief

163

payments), 8, 10, 31, 97, 99, 102, 103, 157, 159
Goldsmith, Raymond W., 133, 153n

Hart, A. G., 90n
Holland, Daniel, 152, 153
Hourly earnings in manufacturing, amplitude, 48, 49, 56
  secular change, 57, 114
  timing, xv, 38, 40, 41
Hours of work per week in manufacturing, amplitude, 48, 49, 56
  secular change, 57
  timing, xv, 39, 40, 41
Hultgren, Thor, 61n

Income-size groups, characteristics, dominant types of income, 78-79, 81
  income range and average per capita income, 78n
  shares in total income, 82
Interest on government debt, compared with holdings and interest rates, 70-72
  data and sources, 149-151
  timing, 69-72
Interest on private debt, 73
Interest, total, data and sources, 5, 117, 119
  as percentage of total income, xvi, xvii, xxviii, xxix, 9, 12, 121
  as percentage of total income, by income-size groups, xx, 79, 80
  shares of income-size groups in, 84, 85, 86, 87, 88
  underreporting by income groups of, 87-88, 152, 153, 154-156

King, Willford Isbell, 74, 82, 118, 119, 123, 125, 132, 151
Klein, Lawrence, 76n
Kuznets, Simon, xvi, xix, xx, xxin, xxii, 53, 74, 77-78, 80, 81, 82, 84n, 85, 86n, 87, 88, 113, 118, 119, 123, 125, 130, 132, 151, 156

Labor income, total, data and sources, 116, 118
  defined, 7
  as percentage of total income, xv, xvi, xvii, xviii, xix, 7, 8, 9, 10, 11, 12, 110, 120
  as percentage of total income, by

income-size groups, xx, see also Nonfarm labor income, total
Labor input and returns, data and sources, 129-130
  farm, 13, 14, 16
  nonfarm, 13, 14, 15, 16
  manufacturing, 37-41, 47-50, 56-57, 114
Lebergott, Stanley, 130
Lent, George E., 69n, 151

Mack, Ruth P., xn
Man-hours, total, in manufacturing, amplitude, 48, 49, 56
  secular change, 56, 57
  timing, xv, 39, 40, 41
Mehren, George, 93n
Merriam, Ida, 99n
Mitchell, Wesley C., ix, xxiv, 25n, 26n
Modigliani, Franco, 35n
Moore, Geoffrey H., 64n, 79n, 156n
Musgrave, R. A., 108n

Nonfarm labor income, total, amplitude, 30, 47, 56, 68, 69, 77, 112, 113
  defined, 34
  as percentage of total income, 110
  as percentage of total income, by income-size groups, 78, 79, 80-89
  shares of income-size groups in, 84, 85, 87, 89
  timing, 24, 25, 29, 36, 37, 52-53, 110-111, 112
Nonfarm personal income, shares of income-size groups in, 78-85, 88-89, 113-114
Nonfarm proprietors' net income, amplitude, 30, 31, 32, 33, 68-69, 77, 111, 112-113
  data and sources, 117, 119, 131, 132
  as percentage of total income, xvi, xvii, xviii-xix, xxix, 9, 11, 121
  as percentage of total income, by income-size groups, xixn, 78, 79, 80
  shares of income-size groups in, 84, 85, 86, 87
  timing, xii, xiii, 24, 25, 29, 110-111

Personal income, total, amplitude, 3, 21, 22, 30, 31, 32, 33, 47, 56
  compared with real per capita personal income, 3-4, 20

compared with real personal income, 18-20

data and sources, 115, 116, 118-119

defined, 6-7

government offset to losses in, *xxxi, see also* Disposable personal income, Farm proprietors' net income, *and* Wages and salaries, total

rates of change during business cycles, *xxiii-xxviii*

shares of income-size groups in, *xxi-xxii*, 78-85, 88-89, 113-114, *see also* Nonfarm personal income

timing, *x, xii, xiii*, 3, 4, 5, 17-20, 24, 25, 110

Peterson, G. M., 145

Property income, total,
amplitude, 30, 31, 32, 33, 60, 68-69, 111

data and sources, 117, 119

defined, 7, 60

as percentage of total income, *xv, xvi, xvii, xviii, xxviii, xxix*, 8, 9, 11, 12, 110, 121

as percentage of total income, by income-size groups, 78, 79, 80

shares of income-size groups in, 84, 85

timing, *xiii*, 24, 25, 29, 60, 72, 110-111

Proprietors' inputs and returns,
data and sources, 131-132

farm, 13, 14

nonfarm, 13, 14

Proprietors' net income, total,
amplitude, 68-69, 112-113

data and sources, 117, 119

defined, 11, 12n

as percentage of total income, *xv, xvi, xvii*, 8, 9, 11, 12, 110, 121

as percentage of total income, by income-size groups, *xx, see also* Nonfarm proprietors' net income

Real per capita personal income,
amplitude, 3

timing, 3, 4, 17

Real personal income,
amplitude, 21-22

data and sources, 125-127

timing, 18, 19, 20, 110

Rent,
data and sources, 117, 119

as percentage of total income, *xvi, xvii, xxviii, xxix*, 9, 12, 121

as percentage of total income, by income-size groups, *xx*, 79, 80

shares of income-size groups in, 85, 86n

timing, *xi*, 72

Salaries in manufacturing,
amplitude, 50, 51, 52, 53, 57, 77, 112

data and sources (Wisconsin), 137, 140, 143-144

as percentage of total manufacturing labor income, 41

timing, 44, 45, 50, 53, 54, 55, 58n, 112

Salaries in nonfarm commodity-producing industries,
as percentage of total income, *xvi, xvii, xviii*

Salaried personnel in manufacturing,
amplitude, 49, 50, 57

data and sources,
Ohio, 136-137, 139
Wisconsin, 137, 140, 143-144

timing, 41, 42, 43, 44, 45, 53, 54, 55

Seltzer, Lawrence H., 6n, 73, 74, 75, 119

Strauss, F., 28

Taitel, Martin, 133

Transfer payments and other labor income,
amplitude, 31, 32, 33

data and sources, 116, 118

defined, 6

as percentage of total income, *xv, xvi, xvii, xviii, xxviii, xxix*, 9, 10, 11, 77, 110, 114, 120

timing, 31, 77

Tun, Thin, 108n

Unemployment benefits, 96, 97, 99, 100, 101, 102, 103, 114, 157, 159

Unemployment compensation and related payments,
data and sources, 157-161

as offset to losses in income, 90, 96-103, 114

Wage earners in manufacturing (*or* Factory employment)
amplitude, 49, 50, 56, 57

data and sources,
Ohio, 136-137, 138

Wisconsin, 137, 140, 141-142
secular change, 57
timing, *xv*, 39, 40, 41, 42, 43, 44, 45, 53, 54, 55
Wages,
in manufacturing (*or* Factory payrolls),
amplitude, 48, 49, 50, 51, 52, 53, 56, 57, 77, 112
data and sources (Wisconsin), 137, 140, 141, 142
secular change, 56, 57
timing, *x*, 37, 38, 40, 41, 44, 45, 47, 52, 53, 54, 55, 111, 112
in nonfarm commodity-producing industries, *xvi, xvii, xviii*
Wages and salaries,
in agriculture,
amplitude, 30, 31, 32, 33
data and sources, 116, 118, 122, 123
as percentage of total income, *xvi, xvii, xviii*, 9, 10, 120
timing, *xii, xiii*, 23, 24, 25
civilian government,
data and sources, 122, 123
percentage of total income, 9, 11
timing, 53, 54-55
in distributive industries,
amplitude, 47, 55, 56, 111
as percentage of total income, *xvi, xvii, xviii*
timing, *xii, xiii*, 35, 36, 37, 52, 111
in government,
amplitude, 56
data and sources, 122, 123
percentage of total income, *xvi, xvii, xviii*, 8, 9, 10, 11, 110
timing, *xi, xii, xiii, xxix*, 36, 37, 46, 111, 112

in manufacturing,
amplitude, 112
data and sources, 116, 118
relative importance, 37, 120
timing, 37, 111
military,
data and sources, 122, 123
percentage of total income, 9, 10
timing, 36, 37, 53
nonfarm,
amplitude, 31, 32, 33, 111
in nonfarm commodity-producing industries,
amplitude, 47, 55, 56, 111
as percentage of total income, *xvi, xvii, xviii*
timing, *xi, xii, xiii*, 34, 35, 36, 37, 52, 111, 112
in private sector,
data and sources, 122, 123, 157-161
government offsets to losses in, 96-99, 101-103
as percentage of total income, *xxix*, 8, 9, 10, 11, 110
in service industries,
amplitude, 47, 55, 56, 111
as percentage of total income, *xvi, xvii, xviii*
timing, *xii, xiii*, 35, 36, 37, 52, 111
total,
data and sources, 116, 118
government offsets to losses in, 99-101, 114, 157-158
as percentage of total income, *xvi, xvii, xviii*, 7, 8, 9, 10, 11, 120
White, Melvin I., 108
Work-relief wages,
data and sources, 122, 123
as percentage of total income, 9, 10
timing, 36, 37, 46, 111

Date Due

May 26			
MAR 1 8			
AP 4 68			
AP 3 '68			
Demco 293-5			